THE SOLITARY VICE

THE SOLITARY VICE

against reading

MIKITA BROTTMAN

COUNTERPOINT

BERKELEY

"A Study of Reading Habits," from Collected Poems by Philip Larkin. Copyright © 1988, 2003 by the Estate of Philip Larkin. Reprinted by permission of Farrar, Straus and Giroux, LLC, and Faber and Faber, Ltd. (U.K.). "At Last the Secret is Out," copyright 1940 & renewed 1968 by W.H. Auden, from Collected Poems by W. H. Auden. Used by permission of Random House, Inc. Dorothy Parker, "Autobiography," © NAACP. The author wishes to thank the National Association for the Advancement of Colored People for this use of Dorothy Parker's work.

Illustrations and photographs: Orpheus Collar, p1; Mark C. Elliot, p4; Ana Benaroya, p14; Mark Grambau, p21; Henry C. Kiefer; p24, p40; Geoffrey Biggs, p31; Norman Nodel, p33; Marina Kharkover, p35; Ahu Sulker, p41; Michael Gent, p46; Nicolas Djandji, p75; David Meinrath, p78; Louis Zansky, p80; Alex Blum, p87, p89; Alyse Poole, p92; Ryan Emge, p97; Alessa Kreger, p122; Jeremy Enecio, p125, p127; Jingyao Guo, p142; Eddie Campbell, p157; Megan Russell, p168; Eamon Donelly, p182.

Library of Congress Cataloging-in-Publication Data

Brottman, Mikita
  The solitary vice : against reading / Mikita Brottman.
     p. cm.
  "A PopMatters Book."
  Includes bibliographical references.
  ISBN-13: 978-1-59376-187-5
  ISBN-10: 1-59376-187-2
  1. Books and reading—Psychological aspects. I. Title.
  Z1003.B883 2008
  028'.9—dc22
                           2007035135

Book design by David Barnett
Printed in the United States of America

COUNTERPOINT
2117 Fourth Street
Suite D
Berkeley, CA 94710
www.counterpointpress.com
Distributed by Publishers Group West

10 9 8 7 6 5 4 3 2 1

contents

a study of reading habits

When getting my nose in a book
Cured most things short of school,
It was worth ruining my eyes
To know I could still keep cool,
And deal out the old right hook
To dirty dogs twice my size.

Later, with inch-thick specs,
Evil was just my lark:
Me and my coat and fangs
Had ripping times in the dark.
The women I clubbed with sex!
I broke them up like meringues.

Don't read much now: the dude
Who lets the girl down before
The hero arrives, the chap
Who's yellow and keeps the store
Seem far too familiar. Get stewed:
Books are a load of crap.

philip larkin (1964)

OUR BRAINS ARE TRAINED, OUR BOOKS ARE BIG,

AND YET WE ALWAYS FAIL,

TO ANSWER WHY THE GUINEA-PIG

IS BORN WITHOUT A TAIL.

—*HILAIRE BELLOC, "MORE BEASTS FOR WORSE CHILDREN" (1897)*

"The Solitary Vice," if you're unfamiliar with the phrase, is perhaps the best-known Victorian euphemism for masturbation, an activity that, at the time, was widely believed to cause not only physical breakdown and moral collapse in this lifetime, but eternal damnation in the next.

This book is about a different solitary vice—the act of reading.

Though it may not be apparent at first, the two activities—masturbating and reading—have a lot in common. Both are usually carried out alone and in private, often in bed at night, before you fall asleep. Both are best enjoyed at leisure, since they tend to absorb your entire attention. Neither can be rushed, and both involve acts of fantasy and the imagination. Both can be so exciting that some people get addicted to them, and, like all addictions, they can be difficult to kick. Both may become lifelong practices, picked up in early childhood and continuing well into old age. Both are habits some people discover by themselves and others are introduced to, usually at school. Both are encouraged by solitude, especially if you're sent to bed too early.

Prior to the twentieth century, masturbation was widely considered to have such dire effects that it was seen as a terribly dangerous habit, which, if not broken, could lead to all kinds of suffering in later life. These days, many people regard "self-love" as the best way of learning about your own body and your own sexual responses, and strongly encourage it as a way of reducing physical and emotional tension—a message emphasized in books like Edward L. Rowan's *The Joy of Self-Pleasuring: Why Feel Guilty About Feeling Good?*, Walter O. Bocking and Eli Coleman's *Masturbation as a Means of Achieving Sexual Health*, and Betty Dodson's *Sex for One: The Joy of Self-Loving.* In fact, sexologists Masters and Johnson suggest we're not "loving ourselves" enough, letting our vestigial guilt and fear prevent us from getting to know our own bodies in a way that's essential to our sexual well-being.

And what about reading?

THIS IS A MESSAGE FROM THE NATIONAL COALITION AGAINST READING

It's not as different as you might think. Believe it or not, people once considered reading to be a dangerous vice, although it's now—according to one slogan—"what makes America great." Other book-promoting campaigns try to persuade us that reading is sexy ("Get Caught Reading!"), radical ("Reading Changes Lives"), hip ("Get Real @ Your Library"), sporty ("Champions Read"), virile and productive ("Read and Grow"), and, of course, "fun-damental."

So in-your-face, so taken for granted is this faith in the healing power of literature, it's hard to believe such assumptions have emerged only in the last fifty years, postdating the development of all the other kinds of entertainment that now compete for our time and make reading look quaint and old-fashioned in comparison—cable TV, the Internet, hand-held electronic devices, cell phones, and video games. And yet, as historians of mass literacy have shown, our indiscriminate faith in the act of reading would, not so long ago, have seemed gloriously insane. While illiteracy is just as dangerous as sexual ignorance, in both cases there's a case to be made for moderation.

There is no shortage of people who still argue against masturbation, but who, these days, has anything to say against reading? On the contrary, there seems to be a new reading rally every month, from Pizza Hut's "Book It!" campaign and the "America Reads Challenge" to the "Building a Nation of Readers" crusade from the Library of Congress, the READ*WRITE*NOW program from the American Initiative on Reading and Writing, and the USA Football "Tackle Reading" drive. A few years ago, in an apparent attempt to bolster its declining literacy rate, Baltimore—where I live—was promoted as "The City that Reads." The originator of the slogan, Mayor Kurt Schmoke, seems to have intended it to work like a magic spell—say it over and over again, and it might just come true. But the spell wasn't strong enough, and during Schmoke's term in office the literacy rate in Baltimore continued to decline.

Don't get me wrong—I love Baltimore, and I understand the imperative to fight illiteracy. It's the absurdity of these slogans that bothers me, the way they take for granted the "fact" that reading is, by its very nature, "good for you." It may not be the most exciting way to spend your free time, the campaigns seem to imply, but it's fortifying, full of nutrients, and will be beneficial in the long run, like spinach. Of course, the ability to read is vital for anyone who wants to live a fully functional life, but I'm not surprised the slogan did little to resolve the city's literacy troubles. While the ability to read may be valuable, is reading in itself really *always* a good thing? From the people I see on the subway and buses, the preferred reading of the good burghers of Baltimore seems to be lottery tickets, which don't appear to have much of an improving effect (unless you've won the jackpot, of course). Anyway, who says prolific readers are necessarily civic-minded people? Hitler was a great reader, after all, and so was the Unabomber.

Baltimore is just one among many cities that's pushing literature. Over the summer of 2004, the *New York Times*, apparently to great success, serialized four novels, including *The Great Gatsby* and *Breakfast at Tiffany's*, as part of a promotion campaign called the "Great Summer Read." Less predictably, on September 17, 2004, the *New York Post*, a popular tabloid, announced to its readers a "book giveaway" in which they could collect a series of fourteen titles, designated "Family Classics." "We believe we have come up with a collection that will truly be beloved by the entire family," said Col Allen, editor-in-chief of the *Post*. The "giveaway"

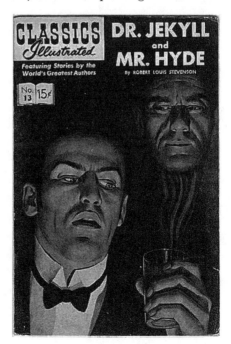

began by offering a free copy of *Huckleberry Finn*, the first in the series—after which you were required to pay $5.99 (plus tax) for the remaining books, starting with *Moby-Dick*, which you could get by sending off a coupon from the newspaper. ("Unlike Ahab, the *Post* will make your hunt of the great white whale easy.")

As these and other campaigns testify, there's no getting away from the fact that literature today is all the rage, championed by One-City-One-Book programs, reading groups, literary gatherings, and poetry slams. With book lovers like Laura Bush and Oprah Winfrey cheering them on, readers today have a new profile. To be a reader is to be a thoughtful, sensitive, child-friendly, civic-minded human being. To be a reader, in fact, is to be the best you can be.

Take a closer look at the *New York Post* promotion, however, and you'll notice that virtually all the "classics" in the series are short, such as *Frankenstein*, *Alice in Wonderland*, and *The Jungle Book*. It shouldn't come as a surprise that all these books can be bought online for a dollar or less (and how many long-time readers don't own copies already?).

This suggests the offer isn't aimed at habitual book buyers, but at those who consider bound editions to be a type of sophisticated home décor, in the style of the collectible china plates and porcelain dolls advertised regularly in the same newspaper. Or perhaps the offer was aimed at the parents of school-age children, since many of the volumes seem to be written, at least ostensibly, for younger readers, including *The Time Machine*, *The Wonderful Wizard of Oz*, and *Robinson Crusoe*. Maybe the idea was to get your kids to read the books you "loved so much," with the added bonus of having the whole set be complete with Dickens's *A Christmas Carol* on December 20, just in time to be gift-wrapped for the holidays.

Either way, both the *Times* and the *Post* were eager to jump on the reading bandwagon, to join the voices on radio and television imploring us to "Read a Book, Save a Life" and the posters in streets and subways reminding us that "Books Make You a Better Person," something which would seem difficult to substantiate. This slogan was ridiculed in a perceptive article by Cristina Nehring entitled "Books Make You a Boring Person," published in the *New York Times Book Review* on June 27, 2004. "Long considered immune to criticism by virtue of being outnumbered by channel surfers, Internet addicts, video maniacs, and other armchair introverts, bookworms have developed a semi-mystical complacency about the moral and mental benefits of reading," writes Nehring. "Books keep kids off drugs. They keep gang members out of prison. They keep terrorists, for all we know, at the gates."

Nehring's piece is satirical, but I think she's mocking a real tendency. All this self-congratulation about how much better books can make you has made the very idea of "reading" a good in itself, along with recycling, meditation, and cutting back on carbs. In other words, the abstract notion of "reading," regardless of the material being read, is privileged over whatever complex interchange actually takes place during the reading process.

So? What's wrong with reading? you might ask.

Nothing, of course. But once you assign an intellectual value to the act, you not only overlook the nature of the text itself, you also make universal and one-dimensional what is essentially a private process of engagement. After all, we read for lots of reasons, not all of them obvious, or easy to distinguish. Yes, we read for pleasure and knowledge, but we also read out of habit, compulsion, necessity, laziness, and—perhaps more often than we think—for no reason at all. Perhaps the fear of books expressed by earlier generations was no less a superstition than our faith in them today—a faith that draws its power from a toxic brew of magical thinking, narcissism, and nostalgia.

The recent flurry of reading campaigns can be attributed to various points of origin, the most significant of which are: (a) the Laura Bush Foundation's organized promotion of libraries, especially children's libraries; (b) the widely-trumpeted results of a 2002 NEA survey reporting that reading in America is "in dramatic decline"; and (c) anxieties about the impact of the Internet. These three points, rooted in commonly held cultural assumptions about the way things work, connect to make a story so "obvious" it simply "goes without saying," it's "common sense": the Internet is responsible for the national drop in literacy rates among the young, an issue which the Laura Bush Foundation is trying to tackle.

People have always been worried about the capacity of new technology—whether radio, television, or video games—for impeding literacy, and the Internet is no different except in one respect. While television and radio have been shown to have a real connection with declining literacy rates, the Internet, instead of drowning book culture, has actually helped increase the base of readers by completely democratizing the market in used books. Although Amazon and eBay are often accused of putting small and independent bookstores out of business, the opposite is actually true, if you include used booksellers. Amazon and eBay allow anyone with an Internet connection to buy and sell used books at a fraction of their cost price, and this instantaneous access to readers all over the world has saved countless book dealers from bankruptcy. With a few clicks of the mouse, you can order a decent copy of almost any book in print (and many out of print) to be delivered to your home, generally for less than $10, and many books that would be otherwise unavailable can now be published cheaply on demand, in short runs from text stored in a database.

The common assumption that literacy is on the decline just doesn't stand up to close scrutiny. The truth is, there are currently more books being published in the U.S. than at any other period in history. In 2002, for example—the year of the NEA "Reading at Risk" survey—the total output of new titles and editions came to roughly 150,000, which means there were around 500 books published everyday of the year, including weekends and holidays—far more than any one person could ever manage to read in a single lifetime. About half of these books are novels, of which author and critic John Sutherland, in his book *How to Read a Novel* (2006), has calculated that more than 2,000 are published every week, or 10,000 a year. "Given a forty-hour reading week, a forty-six-week working year, and three hours per novel, you would need 163 lifetimes to read them all," Sutherland concludes. With these figures in mind, it strikes me that the importance of reading (not to mention writing) has been enormously overstated, and what we should really be paying attention to, in a marketplace stuffed and glutted with books, isn't the death of reading, but the death of discrimination. It's easy enough to get into the habit of reading; what's much more difficult is learning to become a conscientious, discerning reader.

In fact, the very idea that books should give pleasure of any kind is one that has raised concerns among many great thinkers, from Montaigne in the sixteenth century to Samuel Johnson in the eighteenth and Hazlitt and Emerson in the nineteenth—all eras in which reading (like masturbation) was frowned upon by the church, which considered it to be a secular distraction. At certain times, among the less puritanical, reading, like other worldly pleasures, was tolerated in moderation, as long as the reading material had a "moral aesthetic"—that is, as long as its primary purpose was to teach, direct, criticize, and inspire the reader.

Actually, through much of our history, rather than "making you a better person," reading was considered as a priori "bad for you." And it's not hard to see why. The earliest secular manuscripts, produced long before the advent of general literacy (and often the work of alchemists and magicians), must have seemed suspiciously cryptic to ordinary, law-abiding nonreaders, who, imagining these bibliomancers sitting silently with their volumes of spells, symbols, and formulae, probably wondered what on earth they were doing that needed to be hidden from the world of decent, honest folk with no use for codes or cipher.

Books, it was once believed, had hidden powers; they could cast a spell on you. One of the earliest forms of book was the *grimoire*—a magical spell-book felt to be so powerful that if you read it aloud (and reading aloud was the only kind of reading there was), you'd get tangled up in the words, like a fly in a spider's web. To reverse the spell, you'd have to read the words backwards, to the place you started from. Books, it was felt, were repositories of magic symbols that, when recited in a certain way, could release hidden forces or summon the dead. Beliefs about the written word are some of the oldest and most common superstitions, as current today as ever; only today they've been turned inside out. Today, instead of hexing or cursing you, wrapping you up, intoxicating you, absorbing you so completely that you'll never have your own experiences or formulate your own ideas, books have the power to save lives, to make you a better, more interesting person, to lift you out of poverty, to bring you joy, success, and a prosperous future.

paradise lost

You'd think, then, that the wise would always have endorsed reading. Not so. Plato banned poets from his ideal Republic after being infected by the fears of Socrates, who, in his dialogues, made the case that books are an impediment to real learning. He saw them as artificial aids to memory and knowledge, like Post-its or CliffsNotes—useful for remembering things, maybe, but nothing the true scholar would have any use for. Books, felt Socrates, can only remind people of things they already know; real knowledge is gained from experience, not from dead letters. Plato passed these ideas on to his own disciples, like Theophrastus, who noted that books are particularly dangerous for the gentler sex. Women, he claimed, should be taught only whatever is necessary to run a household, because anything more brings with it the danger of turning them into quarreling, lazy gossips, or, even worse, can make them serious, philosophical, and dissatisfied, not the easygoing, home-loving creatures nature meant them to be.

In the Middle Ages, the threat of books took a different form. According to common medieval doctrine, students were supposed to learn ideas by heart, not necessarily to understand them; understanding was for the privileged few, and had little to do with knowledge. Even sacred books were not above this general rule; in fact, the first holy books were considered by medieval scholars to be fakes, since the very idea of translating sacred doctrine into common human language was a sacrilege. Historian Robert I. Moore, in his book *The Birth of Popular Heresy*, explains that the Church rejected the Scriptures in Orléans in 1022 as "fabrications which men have written on the skins of animals," arguing that the true words of God could only come directly from the Holy Spirit, and couldn't be mediated in the corrupt, worldly form of human writing.

I was once a great lover of eighteenth-century Gothic novels like *The Monk*, *The Castle of Otranto*, and *The Mysteries of Udolpho*. I thought them the height of literary sophistication, unaware that, when they first came out, novels like these were denounced for encouraging unrestrained self-absorption. This was considered a particular sin among Regency high-brows, whose special disdain for the Gothic mode is nicely mocked in a book I'd yet to discover, Jane Austen's *Northanger Abbey* (and even Jane Austen's novels were originally published "By a Lady," to reassure parents they wouldn't contain anything that might shock or harm young girls):

> 'I am no novel-reader—I seldom look into novels—Do not imagine that I often read novels—It is really very well for a novel.'—Such is the common cant.—'And what are you reading, Miss—?' 'Oh! It is only a novel!' replies the young lady, while she lays down her book with affected indifference, or momentary shame.

In the nineteenth century in particular, novel reading was considered an especially inappropriate pastime for well-bred young girls. Novelist Harriet Martineau wrote in her *Autobiographical Memoir*, published after her death in 1876, that when she was young, "it was not thought proper for a young lady to study very conspicuously; she was expected to sit down in the parlor with her sewing." Romantic novels in particular, it was believed, gave young women the impression that falling in love was a wonderfully passionate affair, and that marriage would be full of excitement and emotion, not practical things like finances, housekeeping, and child-rearing. In other words, it was feared that young ladies who read romantic novels would be deeply disillusioned by the bitter realities of marriage. On top of that, too much reading was considered an impediment to living a full life; people believed that reading novels would fill your head with dreams, leaving you unprepared for the disappointing bleakness of the real world. Writing novels was considered equally unrespectable; eighteenth- and nineteenth-century novelists (including Daniel Defoe, Jane Austen, George Eliot, and the Brontë sisters) often concealed their identity behind a pseudonym unless they'd already made a name for themselves in another literary form.

The Victorians relegated the aesthetic side of life—including sensory and imaginative experience—to a separate and distinct place, to be expressed and indulged at certain appropriate moments perhaps, but not to be considered coequal with the practical concerns of day-to-day living. Their guiding philosophy was utilitarianism, which opposed literature on pragmatic grounds, since literature was based on fantasy, not reality. The utilitarian assumption was that, as civilization advanced, the popularity of literature would necessarily decline, since those with a sound mind and a sense of mental tranquility would find enough inspiration in external things—ideas, values, collections, acts of discrimination, and appreciation: the real daily business of life. Jeremy Bentham denounced all poetry as "misrepresentation," and a columnist in the *Benthamite Westminster Review* claimed in 1825 that "literature is a seducer; we had almost said a harlot." When, for the first time in history, almost the entire population could read (to some degree at least), books began to be attacked for taking up time that would better be spent working. Novels in particular were considered "vampiric" and "addictive."

Adding his voice to the debate in 1891, William Morris, founder of the Arts and Crafts movement and famous for his wallpaper and furniture designs, published a novel entitled *News from Nowhere*, set in an "unbooked" world meant as a critique of capitalist society. In this utopian tract, Morris harks back to a preindustrial past, a world of unique craftsmanship and traditional forms, full of fantasy and enchantment. Labor, he felt, should provide us with the gratification we now expect from art, especially reading, which Morris regarded as a celebration of "bourgeois individualism." In Morris's utopia, people would bond together to make beautiful, useful things, which would satisfy their creative instincts in a communal way, leaving no place for the private fantasies offered by literature.

11

Morris was afraid of the atomizing potential of mass literacy, with all its individual aesthetic choices and possibilities. Letting ordinary people read and write whatever they liked, he felt, would lead to a complete breakdown of integrated, communal life. After all, the process of reading involves the private experience of one individual personally engaging with the mind of another, an exchange so intimate and restricted that, once caught up in a novel, the reader might become detached from other people.

One of the most controversial things about reading—and, even today, one of the things that distinguishes it from television, movies, and video games—is its use of words without images, allowing you, the reader, to exercise your imagination, to transcend ordinary possibilities, to be "carried away" somewhere remote from your own place and time, to escape from your own personality. When reading, or listening to a story, you can escape for a while from your daily responsibilities, tune out your everyday practical duties. This is the kind of thing that once made reading seem radical, even revolutionary. In his book *A History of Reading*, Alberto Manguel describes how cigar factories in Cuba used to hire someone to read historical compendiums or didactic novels to the laborers as they worked, not only to educate and inform them, but also to make their factory work a little less tedious. At least they did so until the political governor of Cuba issued an edict banning these public readings for being subversive and "distracting" the workers with "discussions foreign to the work in which they are engaged."

The success of a capitalist economy depends, in part, on mass literacy, and the social prerequisites for mass literacy were in place in England before almost anywhere else in the world. One of the first side effects of Victorian capitalism was a new market for books and newspapers catering to working class readers, many of whom were so barely literate they could handle only the most undemanding material. A new branch of publishing was established to print cheap paperbacks—the Penny Dreadfuls and Shilling Thrillers that were especially popular in the age of railways, when travelers wanted something cheap and compact to read during long train journeys. Victorian intellectuals were horrified. This was just what they'd feared—the rise of Grub Street hacks and panderers, turning literature from a refined art form to a paid-by-the-word commodity. The new market for melodramas, bodice rippers, ghost stories, and other commodity fictions aimed at newly literate readers made it impossible, felt the intellectuals, for "real" writers to find an audience (a situation that forms the plot of George Gissing's bleak and depressing industrial-era novel, *New Grub Street*). For the educated classes, the threat of revolution gave way to the dread that mass taste would soon come to dominate the publishing industry, and traditional culture would be abandoned to the lowest common denominator—a prospect that was increasingly likely, according to the numbers. John Stuart Mill, writing in the late 1850s, began to consider the bleak specter of a society that had given way to the tyranny of the majority, not only in its reading patterns, but in its moral values, its fine arts, and its intellectual life—since, in the free operation of the cultural market, it was felt that mediocrity and vulgarity would always drive out "superior goods." The reading habit was catching on, and those in charge wanted to keep it under control. In the new Victorian lending libraries, for example, fiction was banned and the selection of books was limited to those containing "instructive value."

However ridiculous and elitist these anxieties seem to us today, it's important to remember they continued well into the twentieth century, both in Europe and the U.S. The earliest critics of postwar popular fiction, for example, expected its popularity to be accompanied by the spread of moral laxity, idleness, and cultural degeneration. In the U.S., slaves had traditionally been discouraged from reading (on the grounds that it could lead only to "useless knowledge") because the idea of a literate black population was considered dangerous—so dangerous, in fact, that in some states strict laws prevented blacks from being taught to read, and there were severe punishments for a slave caught with any book other than the Bible.

Throughout most of the twentieth century, everyone who had anything to say on the subject seemed to agree that mass literacy was a regrettable part of the price that had to be paid for the benefits of a democratic system, both because of the necessarily poor quality of popular fiction, and because subjection to its influence would inevitably have a harmful moral influence on the reader, an opinion that was held by such otherwise progressive thinkers as George Orwell and D. H. Lawrence. Although by the 1970s and '80s, it was no longer common to think of popular fiction as a cheap, trivial version of "high" literature, nor to equate "high" literature with lofty, humane thoughts and benevolent government, conservative detractors of mass fiction continued to make a case for its morally detrimental effects, arguing that it pandered to the reader's desire for escape, sensation, and infantile fantasy. Consumer capitalism, it was felt, had become so pervasive it even had the power to weaken and cheapen the stories we tell, draining them of the richness and variety they possessed among earlier cultures.

"the opposite of reading a book is mental atrophy."

the way we live now

In the last twenty years, we've gone from a deeply entrenched fear of reading to its promotion as a universal panacea. At this stage in history, at least in the West, books are commonplace, comfortable, and utterly familiar. Many of us grew up surrounded by them, at school if not at home. Books are something we all recognize and understand.

Whoever predicted the death of the book couldn't have been more wrong; there are more books around today than ever before—so many, in fact, that a whole genre of books about reading has emerged just to help us make sense of them all. This genre has, in the last few years, expanded so rapidly that a new example seems to appear every week. There are so many that it would take a whole book to discuss them all—a book about books about books. To avoid tumbling into this frightful abyss, I'll limit myself to mentioning only the most popular titles published during the year of writing, 2006.

There has always been a market for annotated anthologies about books, collections of reading lists, and reading guides; this year's compilations included: *1001 Books You Must Read Before You Die*, edited by Peter Boxall, a hefty compendium of enthusiastic recommendations; *The Book of Lost Books* by Stuart Kelly, a whimsical look at the missing pieces of literary history; and Roxanne Coady and Joy Johannson's *The Book that Changed My Life*, a survey of books that had an impact on the lives of famous writers (proceeds go to Coady's nonprofit Read to Grow foundation).

Some interesting examples of the genre were published this year by authors best known for their fiction, including Jane Smiley's *Thirteen Ways of Looking at the Novel*. Stymied by the frustrations of her latest work, in this book Smiley recounts her decision to shut down her laptop, put her feet up, and reread one hundred of her favorite novels, keeping us informed of her thoughts as she does so. Equally smart is *Reading Like a Writer* by Francine Prose, a detail-oriented meditation on the subtle craft of good writing. A couple of heavyweight academics also gave us their thoughts on the subject. John Sutherland, chair of the 2005 Booker Prize jury, published *How to Read a Novel*, and Edward Mendelson of Columbia University reminded us of *The Things That Matter*, in an attempt to relate "seven classic novels" (all, incidentally, by women) to "the stages of life."

Then there were the books about books by professional book critics like Michael Dirda of the *Washington Post Book World*, who, in the last five years, has published five collections of his earnest and popular column, "Readings" (this year's collection was entitled *Book by Book: Notes on Reading and Life*). Nick Hornby has a monthly column in *The Believer* magazine called "Stuff I've Been Reading," in which he lists books he bought and planned to read alongside those he actually read; a compilation of all his columns so far was published this year by McSweeney's, under the title *The Complete Polysyllabic Spree*. Maureen Corrigan, book critic for National Public Radio, published a book called *Leave Me Alone, I'm Reading*, a memoir that discusses the way books have shaped her life, from her Irish Catholic upbringing to the books she now reads to her recently adopted daughter.

Corrigan's book is an autobiography of reading—let's call it a "bibliofessional," a hybrid form combining two of today's most popular literary genres: the book about books, and the personal memoir. Other examples of the form published this year include *An Alphabetical Life* by Wendy Werris, a part-funny, part-sad account of the author's long career in the book trade, and *The Yellow Lighted Bookshop* by author and former bookseller Lewis Buzbee, an interweaving of bookselling history with private memories of a reading life.

On the subject of bookselling, there was *Reluctant Capitalists*, sociologist Laura J. Miller's study of the used book trade, and *Book Talks*, a collection of essays on book collecting edited by Robert Jackson and Carol Zeman Rothkopf. But now we're getting tangential, and I haven't even mentioned all the new readers' blogs that sprouted up this year, though none, so far, is any substantial threat to BookSlut, Maud Newton, Beatrice, Galleycat, or any of the other leading book blogs—except, perhaps, Babes with Books, a blog for the incurable book fetishists in our midst, devoted entirely to pictures of hot girls reading books. See, it's true—reading IS sexy.

Most people continue to read books in their traditional form, whether or not they also spend time online. But while the Internet is smoothly merging into everyday life, a lot of people are still wary of it, and of all the other new things that aren't books—things that beep, ping, flash, and glow; LifeDrives, Sidekicks, smart phones, BlackBerrys, Treos, iPhones, and similar handheld devices. To many people, electronic gadgets are the opposite of books, and are killing them. These people are afraid that "the death of the book" will have a terrible effect on our continuity with the past, and on how we see ourselves, our world, and our culture, possibly even paving the way toward a bookless dystopia where the illiterate masses depend on their leaders to do their reading for them (which, by the way, is pretty much the way things have always been).

The fear comes down to something like this: Since "serious reading" was the most common way of learning in the past, it's generally considered to be the only reliable way to provide continuity over the generations, and continuity is how we accumulate knowledge, how we learn complex ideas about human nature and the ways of the world. This fear—that modes of communication are shifting from reading text to other kinds of visual processes—has mutated into the idea that "reading is good for you"—a superstition perhaps even less rational than the old fear that books are dangerous, since, if the results of the 2002 NEA survey are anything to go by, over 50 percent of Americans are reading—and reading LITERA-TURE—on a semi-regular basis, which suggests the printed book is in no grave danger of obsolescence.

In a 2004 *New York Times* editorial column responding to this survey, Andrew Solomon, the author of a book on depression, makes the case that, as he sees it, depression is on the rise partly due to "the loneliness that comes of spending the day with a TV or a computer or video screen." According to Solomon, reading is an entry into dialogue; books can be friends who talk to you; yet many people today, he feels, are indifferent to them, since we tend to devalue literature as a means to illumination. "That rates of depression are going up as the rates of reading are going down is no happenstance," argues Solomon. He also suggests there might be a connection between those who don't read and those who develop Alzheimer's, since, as Solomon puts it, "if you read nothing, your mind withers, and your ideals lose their vitality and sway."

This argument—a common one—is based on the assumption that the opposite of reading is mental atrophy, and it's only readers of LITERATURE who are constantly in the process of gathering fresh experience and new knowledge.

It overlooks the very obvious fact that digital media also require reading—a kind of reading that's no less "active" than any other form, and often more so. To make the case that "visuals" have triumphed over "text," you have to ignore the fact that text is also a visual medium.

Once you include digital text, it becomes obvious that people are spending more time reading than ever before, only it tends to be the kind of reading that's done sitting in front of a computer screen, perhaps in the middle of a busy office, rather than curled up quietly with a book in the lap. If, as a lot of people claim, books are less common than they used to be (though I haven't noticed it, have you?), it's probably because sites like Amazon and eBay have made them so cheap to come by that they're virtually disposable, hardly worth the space they take up in your apartment (especially if you live in Manhattan or San Francisco). Even people who used to turn to their books all the time—fact-checkers, editors, archivists, and researchers—now use mainly electronic resources. When a date needs looking up or a fact confirming, it's so much faster and easier to click on the e-version of the *OED*, the *Encyclopedia Britannica*, or the *Physician's Desk Reference* than to actually get up and look for the appropriate volume on your shelves.

Some have also made the case that watching television or playing video games can help the brain develop in ways more fitting to today's society than the literacy skills associated with reading. For example, author Steven Johnson, in his book *Everything Bad Is Good for You*, makes the case that the complexity of today's video games and television dramas are actually giving you a "cognitive workout," helping to improve your problem-solving abilities, which—rather than literacy skills—are the key to individual success in today's dynamic, fast-paced society. Advanced literacy, in comparison, seems almost a hindrance, which I suspect is one of the reasons why the many reading campaigns appear to be having little effect. If reading were as vital as its exponents like to claim, why would we need all this organized pressure to encourage us to do it? The fact is, reading plays a very small role in the capitalist model; you could almost say that reading is antithetical to consumer capitalism, in that it doesn't produce anything, it doesn't make any money, and it doesn't make you look any younger, feel any better, or go any faster. Those promoting the campaigns that reading is "good for you" and "fun-damental" need, if they're going to have any success, to substantiate the idea of a "good" and a "great" that aren't bound up with what most people consider the most important achievements in life—earning money, being attractive, healthy, and popular, and having a happy and loving family—since none of these achievements require us to read, at least not in a serious or thoughtful way.

Dare I even suggest, dear reader, that the opposite might be true: that, basic literacy aside, the more time you spend reading, the less likely it is you'll achieve any of these things?

What if reading didn't make you feel better?

What if it were more likely to INDUCE depression than relieve it?

As you'll soon discover, I'm not REALLY going to give you "a case against reading" (that was just to lure you in). Books, I have to say, have given me more consistent, undiluted pleasure than almost anything else in my life, and I'm sure anyone who's bought this book, or been given it as a gift, is already a thoughtful, well-informed reader. I simply want to suggest that there's nothing inherently worthy or decent in the act of reading itself. I'm just wondering whether reading might not, in fact, be all it's cracked up to be.

Unconvinced? If you've been reading all your life, ask yourself the following questions:

Did it take you to the top of the class?

Has it made you happy?

Has it made you a "better person"?

Has it taken you to "wonderful places"?

Has it taken you anywhere at all?

In this book, I'm going to advise that, if you must read, or go on reading, you should do so with thought, care, and discrimination. Don't give in to your prejudices; don't read books just because you feel you "ought to," because they'll be "good for you"; do it because you just can't help yourself.

Read carefully, and you'll come to see the difference.

MINIVER SIGHED FOR WHAT WAS NOT,

AND DREAMED, AND RESTED FROM HIS LABORS;

HE DREAMED OF THEBES AND CAMELOT,

AND PRIAM'S NEIGHBORS.

—EDWARD ARLINGTON ROBINSON, "MINIVER CHEEVY" (1910)

Have you ever seen that poster in the children's section of bookstores showing a couple of bears flying through the air, clutching the strings of a colorful balloon, beneath the words: "Books Take You to Wonderful Places"? It always makes me wonder how long those unfortunate bears have got left before they come crashing back down to earth.

It's true, stories can take you to wonderful places. What the posters don't tell you is that you can't stay there, and for those children who spent their early years in the otherworld of literature, real life can come as a rotten letdown. For these children, books should come with a warning label: "Beware! Reading This Book May Cause Severe Disappointment with Reality."

According to psychologist James Hillman, if you read a lot of stories as a child, or had them read to you, you're "in better shape and have a better prognosis than those to whom story must be introduced." For Hillman, these first readings become "something lived in and lived through," which, he claims, is "a way in which the soul finds itself in life."

This may be true for the lucky ones. But for others, I'm afraid, reading leads to nothing but trouble. Recall the words of Ecclesiastes: "For as wisdom grows, vexation grows; to increase learning is to increase heartache" (1:18). Take a look at poor old Jean-Paul Sartre. In his memoirs, the famous philosopher describes spending hour after hour as a child absorbed in his Encyclopedia Larousse, fascinated by each volume's colorful evocations of fauna and flora, only to have all this wonder dissolve the day he first visited the Luxembourg gardens, and saw how impoverished *REAL* plants and animals were in comparison. After all his reading, he found, "the apes in the zoo were less ape, the people in the Luxembourg gardens were less people." In retrospect, Sartre realized that he passed from "real" knowledge to its subject, finding more "reality" in the idea of a thing than in the thing itself. "It was in books that I encountered the universe," he recalls, "digested, classified, labelled, mediated, still formidable." In contrast, the world outside books appeared messy, disorganized, and unimpressive. Could it ever possibly compete with the beautifully patterned, ordered universe contained in a favorite set of encyclopedias?

For me, the intoxicating moment came when I learned that books could take you to horrible places—horrible, that is, in a thrilling way: places on the other side of the looking glass where unimaginable nightmares came true, where little girls like me were kept in cages, had their heads chopped off, were cooked and eaten for breakfast. These scary stories both frightened me and aroused a strange, dark appetite that was difficult to satisfy. The nastier the stories, the more I liked them. Like all magic spells, I found books could enchant my life, which, compared to the lives I read about, seemed increasingly flat and dull. I read hungrily, thoughtlessly, books that were far beyond my grasp. It didn't matter that I couldn't understand or appreciate them; I just let the images flow through my head. I read some of them so many times that I came to know long passages by heart—Shakespeare's *Macbeth*, for example, and certain tales of Poe. I'd whisper their lines to myself during the day, like private spells or incantations; it didn't

matter that I didn't know what they meant. What mattered was how they sounded, the images they conjured up, the way they made the hairs on the back of my neck stand on end. I'd heard of this before, but I hadn't known it could actually happen.

Horror stories were my favorite; I couldn't get enough of them. I loved the way they took me out of my own story, where nothing ever happened. It wasn't so much that they put my own life in the context of others' as that they annihilated it completely—at least, that's how it felt. They were the key to a secret door, the gateway to a fabulous landscape of fear. I read every scary story and horror comic I could find, from H. P. Lovecraft to *Lady Vampire*, from *Titus Andronicus* to "Tales from the Crypt"—all the better if they included rats, ghouls, voodoo, vampires, and bodies chopped up and hidden under the floor. I became something of a ghoul myself, buried all day in my bedroom, the door barred with a piece of stair rail that had broken off the wall, making the stairs up to my attic bedroom a bit dodgy to climb. Which was fine, because the only

people I wanted to see were already there: my friends Jekyll and Hyde, Mephisto, Dr. Strange, the Crypt Keeper, and—my closest pal—Melmoth the Wanderer, the protagonist of a three-volume Gothic novel by Charles Robert Maturin, first published in 1820, specially ordered from the library down the street. I never gave a second thought to the fact that the protagonists of these stories were all male. One of the great thrills of reading, for me, was to slip off the mantle of my identity and assume one that was far more exciting and unpredictable. I had no interest in "transparent" prose. I didn't read to see a reflection of my own world; I wanted another world entirely, one that had no counterpart outside fiction. What I most loved was literature that showed me another life, completely separate from the one I lived in, connected to it only by tentative forms and traces.

Eventually, my mother gave up trying to coax me downstairs for meals, and, apart from school, the only time I left my bedroom during the day was to renew my library books.

You may be wondering why I chose such morbid, archaic, and unfashionable reading matter. Wasn't I getting enough of that kind of thing at school?

A sore point. Whoever designed my school's English syllabus had decided, quite reasonably, that the best way to get kids reading at an early age was to reassure them that it didn't have to be hard work. It didn't have to be all old-fashioned words and long-winded stories about people in the past. The idea, I suppose, was to show us that literature could be relevant, up-to-date, and engaging, that it could be about ordinary people with everyday problems—that's right, people just like us.

Here's a sample of what they made us read:

Barry Hines, *A Kestrel for a Knave*—Young Yorkshire boy with problems at home and school finds meaning in his relationship with a tame kestrel. (Everybody in our school had to read the book at least once because it was by a local author.)

Stan Barstow, *A Kind of Loving*—Young Yorkshire couple is forced to marry when the girl gets pregnant. A play, which meant we were given parts to read aloud, preferably in Yorkshire accents. (Another local author.)

J. B. Priestley, *An Inspector Calls*—Suicide of a young shop girl leads to the undoing of a self-satisfied middle-class Yorkshire family. (Yet *another* local author.)

James Vance Marshall, *Walkabout*—Young brother and sister survive a plane crash in the Australian outback, and are guided to safety by a friendly Aborigine. (This book was especially popular with the boys because its cover, a still from the film, featured the young Jenny Agutter in a very short skirt.)

Clive King, *Stig of the Dump*—Young boy discovers a caveman living in his local dump.

Nicky Cruz, *Run Baby Run*—Young boy becomes a violent gang leader in Brooklyn, has lots of dangerous and exciting adventures, then halfway through the book converts to Christianity and starts behaving himself, at which point the book got so insufferable we refused to read any more.

William Golding, *Lord of the Flies*—A group of British schoolboys is stranded on an island after their plane is shot down. The priggish ones try to reproduce the rules of an organized society; the more adaptable, forward-thinking ones go native and have fun wearing war paint and killing pigs. When they're rescued, the conformists are honored and the adventurous boys made to feel guilty and ashamed.

I'm sure these were tried and tested choices for kids of our demographic: books that were relevant, uplifting, and appropriate. But what I wanted wasn't a window into the world, but a DISTRACTION from it. I didn't want to FIND myself in books—god forbid!—but to get away from myself, to disappear entirely. If I had to read about familiar experiences, I wanted them to be distorted beyond recognition, twisted into terrible nightmares with dead bodies and rats. Miserable shop girls, tame kestrels, and unplanned pregnancies weren't enough.

I'd always loved Edward Arlington Robinson's poem "Miniver Cheevy," from his collection *The Town Down the River*. The poem paints a brief vignette of a cynical drunk, a "child of scorn" who despairs of life in the "real world." Miniver, who loves Art, Romance, and other abstractions, spends his days dreaming of the glorious and romantic past:

> *Miniver cursed the commonplace,*
> *And eyed a khaki suit with loathing;*
> *He missed the medieval grace*
> *Of iron clothing.*

There was a girl in my class who made her own skirts and dresses on a sewing machine at home. When I was thirteen, I paid her to make me a vampire cloak in black velour, with a black lining, a large medallion clasp at the top, and a small, stiff collar. I loved that cloak. Sometimes, after dark, I'd put it on and go prowling round a disused neighborhood cemetery, all overgrown and neglected. When I went through its gates at night, I might have been walking into a book. It had a derelict church with a broken roof (rumored to be the meeting place of local Satanists), a gaunt mausoleum, a cluster of mossy crypts, a cobblestone alleyway, and a (fake) Victorian gas lamp. In my cloak I was Jack the Ripper, Mr. Hyde returning to his low door in the wall, Mephisto in search of Zarathos, Baron Mordo plotting the demise of the Ancient One. Like the narrator of Philip Larkin's poem "A Study of Reading Habits":

> *Me and my cloak and fangs*
> *Had ripping times in the dark.*

These were my private sanctuaries—my cemetery, my attic, and my books. I read aimlessly, dreamily, with no plan in mind but to get away from "real life." Compared with the books I read, "real life" didn't stand much of a chance—that is, what OTHERS referred to as "real life." To me, reading was as much a part of "real life" as any other activity, if not more so. At that age I hadn't read Proust, but I'd have been heartened to read the narrator's proclamation, in the last book of *In Search of Lost Time*, that "Real life, life at last laid bare and illuminated—the only life in consequence which can be said to be really lived—is literature." Proust himself, in fact, took the literary life as far as it could go—right to the very end. He retreated into writing as a psychic refuge, a way to reimagine the life he'd lived. As he grew more unhealthy, he began sleeping during the day and writing at night. As his work progressed, his physical existence declined. Shutting out all sound, light, and air, he began to dose himself with opium, caffeine, and barbital until, confined to bed, no longer able to receive visitors, he wrote himself to death.

I wonder: Is it possible to READ yourself to death?

Here's another question: Why do we privilege the world of the body over nonbodily forms of experience—dreams, memories, fantasies, movies, or stories we've experienced "only" in imagination? If we can see it, touch it, smell it, or hear it, does that make it more "real" than if we "just" dream or imagine it? If we can't separate reality from memory, fantasy, dreams, and stories, does that make us crazy? We privilege information from the senses, believing "external reality" is of a higher order than the imagination, but perhaps we're just outfoxed by their vivid feedback, by the need for a consensus reality that's stable and solid, one we share with others. Still, doesn't reading also involve a shared reality, a relationship between the reader's mind and the author's voice?

But then, shared experiences quickly become memories too; in fact they're always in the process of becoming memories, even while we're experiencing them. And memory, of course, isn't susceptible to rigorous proof, being itself notoriously subject to repression and denial, not to mention invisible editing. Was my vampire cloak really black velour, or was it dark blue plaid? Was I really thirteen, or a little older? If I'd been, say, fourteen or fifteen, would my nighttime prowling have seemed less cute and funny than embarrassing and bizarre? What we like to call "remembering" is more of a creative, reconstructive process than any kind of "exact record" of the past. We "remember" things that happened to us by telling ourselves stories, which always involve distortions of one kind or another. We might omit details that aren't consistent with the theme, for example, or insert bits to match our retrospective expectations. We also do this with memories of books we've read, embellishing and altering them in retrospect, so it's impossible for us to have an "objective" memory of stories we read once upon a time.

If we've been raised on movies and television, we tend to replay our memories through an inner repertoire of close-ups, long shots, various camera angles, and the undetectable special effects of the unconscious: egotism, repression, consistency of self-perception, and more. In other words, we think of the past as more "real" than dreams and fantasies, but essentially, they're all composed from the same, insubstantial ether of the imagination. When we incorporate memories into our preexisting belief systems, what happens to the parts that don't fit, that can't be integrated with our prior assumptions and expectations about the past?

I'm sure I'm not the only person whose memories of books, films, dreams, and fantasies are more vivid than those of my own bodily experiences, which is natural when you consider that their emotional impact has been much more intense than anything I've lived through in "real life." I don't have many "real" memories of my teenage years, for example, because I spent so much time reading, but I can clearly remember scenes from the stories I read—not the author's actual words (at least, not all of them), but the images that played out in my head, images that are now part of me, like the prints of a fossil embedded in rock.

Once, from the attic staircase, I overheard my parents arguing about the fact that I spent all my time locked in the attic reading.

My mother was trying to defend me.

"There's nothing wrong with it," she was saying. "It's good for children to read."

"Yes," yelled my dad. "But it's bloody SHAKESPEARE!!"

A couple of years later, I asked my mother if she'd give me a ride to a church hall to see a local production of *Twelfth Night*. I was thirteen. I told her it was a school trip, and that we were meeting outside the church. If I'd have told the truth, that there was no school trip, it's not that she wouldn't have let me go, it's just that it would have led to more mockery and teasing, maybe more worrying about what was wrong with me. By then, I'd learned to keep my Shakespeare to myself.

When I think about my teenage years, I think of myself lying on my bed in the attic reading (shot from above, with a wide-angle lens). I think of myself prowling around the cemetery (black-and-white footage, grainy stock). But I also think of Mr. Hyde trampling on a child in the street (my own Mr. Hyde, black-and-white footage, with maybe a touch of influence from the 1932 film version with Frederic March), Heathcliff (my own) with his sneer rigid in death, Jonathan Harker's letters from Castle Dracula (close-up shot of ornate Victorian handwriting). Next to this, "real life" was bleak and empty; the more I read, the more pathetic "reality" seemed. It's hardly surprising that I tried to avoid spending time there. I don't think my experience was so unusual. Nothing happens in our lives most of the time, and so we make things up, we tell stories—to ourselves, and to each other. It's a human trait we all share—the desire to have an effect on our environment, to make things happen, to change things. This, after all, is the point of any distraction—including art, music, sports, drugs, and religion. Like many children who don't know any better, my drug of choice was reading.

I wanted to get further and further away from the world I was living in, to get out of it completely, if such a thing were possible. This led to an enormous disparity between the world surrounding me, the limitations of my physical body, and the endless possibilities of the imagination, through which, in a different body, I could live a different life—any number of lives, in fact. But while reading may have expanded my imagination and broadened my inner life, it also narrowed my outer one, turning me from an ordinary, introspective teenager into a barely functional recluse. Although I hardly noticed it, buried in the attic with my books, at some point during my teenage years my dad moved out, my brothers dropped out of school and left home, and my mother rented out their empty rooms. It all passed me by—I wasn't interested. Looking back, I now see all those stories of premature burial as romantic versions of my own predicament. While I had my nose stuck in Poe, my own home, like the House of Usher, had split apart, turning me into a living relic of a former age, a madwoman in the attic, a Miss Havisham at sixteen, hidden, overlooked, buried alive like Madeleine Usher.

We had put her living in the tomb!

At least, this is the narrative I tell myself, the story I've made out of disparate needs, memories, and beliefs. It's a plausible tale, after all, with me at the center, a passably sympathetic, if not exactly lovable, heroine. It explains a thing or two.

Even so, is it really any more than just another creepy story?

the awkward age

There's no question that, in terms of emotional development, books didn't help me at all. For one thing, they gave me ridiculous ideas about romance.

The first book that had a really powerful impact on me was *Wuthering Heights*. It wasn't the first book to make me cry (like most children, I wept copiously and predictably through *Charlotte's Web*, *Watership Down*, and other books in which animals died), but *Wuthering Heights* was the first book to make me cry adult tears—not the instinctive tears of childhood, but tears caused by something, at age fifteen, I'd never experienced: broken love, if "love" was the right word for it. Whatever it was between Catherine and Heathcliff, I was utterly transfixed by it—a passionate connection, however sexless and spiritualized, that was stronger and more lasting than death, that couldn't end or be destroyed because it was part of nature, "like the eternal rocks beneath," as Catherine says to the housemaid, Nelly. I started crying when I read this speech; I sobbed when Catherine went mad after her husband banned Heathcliff from the Grange; I blubbered and wailed when she

begged Nelly to open the window to get just one breath of the wind blowing from the moor, where Heathcliff lay buried.

It seems odd that I remember *Wuthering Heights* as a great love story, because when I read it again recently, it didn't seem to be about love at all, but the pleasures of cruelty and violence. In fact, it's horribly sadistic, full of frail, imperious children being made to sleep on rough sacks and fed with watery porridge until death puts an end to their whining. It's actually a book about human cruelty and nastiness, with a touch of spite or malice in every chapter. Heathcliff is vengeful,

Cathy capricious, and the setting is bleak, cold, and brutal. People are always pinching one another until they're black and blue, getting thrashed to within an inch of their lives, idly hanging a puppy or a brace of rabbits, or grinding little girls' wrists into broken glass. Even Catherine and Heath-cliff seem to fight and quarrel far more than they ever express affection, but then I suppose cruelty is a form of love, too.

I often try to make sense of the impact this book has had on me, and why I was so stirred by it. When I first read it, I thought nothing was quite as rousing as a passion so strong you'd die for it. I was devoted to the idea of a doomed, hopeless love that was too late, no good, couldn't work, but went on anyway because it just couldn't be stopped. Looking back, I can see how this impractical, otherworldly all-or-nothingness has a special appeal to inexperienced teenage girls. But at the time, when I was all wrapped up in it, what I wanted to know was whether things like this could really happen. I'd lie in bed and wonder: Did they happen in *this* world, the "real world," the same world I lived in? I had no reason to think so. There was no evidence for it. It was only in books that people felt that way. In real life, people just got tired of one another, drifted apart, did their best, and got on with things. Personally, I hadn't even met anybody worth going downstairs for—forget about dying. I was perfectly happy as long as I lived in the world of books, but whenever I tried to enter the real world, the spell was broken:

> *"The curse has come upon me,"*
> *Said the Lady of Shallott.*

In "real life," things were very different. For the first nineteen years of my life, if any human boy (other than my brothers) was aware of my existence, he would have known me as that weird girl who read books OUTSIDE SCHOOL. The only one who ever liked me was a boy everyone called "Fungus Face" due to a mossy, greenish growth that sprouted up round his chin. To divert attention from this facial lichen, he somehow managed to grow a full beard at seventeen; he also had a head of prema-turely gray hair (already receding), and—at least, according to a persistent rumor that seemed too likely to be untrue—webbed feet.

He wasn't exactly Heathcliff.

Books got me into this mess. I'd been spoiled, not only by *Wuthering Heights*, but also by other love stories, including the plain girls' bible, *Jane*

Eyre. *Jane Eyre* is the perfect book to ruin the lives of solitary girls in attics everywhere, girls who feel they've been given a raw deal, overlooked just because they're not pretty. At sixteen, with my greasy skin and tragic hair, I was immediately drawn to the inner life of the much-abused Jane, quietly watching Mr. Rochester being seduced by the empty nonsense of a frilly debutante. Drab and kind in her sensible smocks, Jane meekly carries on

serving tea and being nice to everybody, cherishing "in her bosom" the secret hope that in the end, she'll be loved for her homely virtues and quiet intelligence, for who she is—modest and penniless.

In the end, all her years of pain and suffering pay off and Mr. Rochester finally appreciates the special qualities of the bookish girl nobody ever looked at twice. In fact—rather miraculously—he's been in love with her all along. That's the money shot in *Jane Eyre*—the sadistic glee of the moment when Mr. Rochester takes for his wife not Blanche Ingram, the superficially more appealing girl (as everyone expects), but his daughter's governess, Jane, with her gray smocks, low forehead, and "plain figure" (does that mean flat-chested?).

Wrongheaded as I was, reading *Jane Eyre* convinced me that, if it could happen to Jane, it could happen to me. The book's ending gave me the same nasty thrill I got when I imagined my own funeral (THAT'LL show them!). I'd find a Mr. Rochester to take me away from all that grease, a smart young gent who loved books as much as I did; maybe not books like *Jane Eyre*, but whatever the boys' equivalent was.

Well, it didn't happen. In fact, things only got worse.

Perhaps you're starting to suspect it wasn't READING that was my problem, but the books I chose. Perhaps I should have known you can't trust books, because in the books I read, excessive reading wasn't an issue. Girls who read too much were still appealing; men would still fall in love with them. There was even something endearing about it, in a gauche, bookwormy kind of way. Catherine Morland in Jane Austen's *Northanger Abbey* was a great favorite with me. She gets so carried away by her addiction to Gothic novels that she sees ghosts round every corner, and—much to the annoyance of her family and friends—makes each social encounter into a supernatural melodrama.

A voracious reader, Catherine is so wound up by horror stories that she comes to see herself as a heroine in the Gothic mode, and loses track of what's actually going on around her. She starts fantasizing wildly about her friend Henry Tilney and his family, falls madly in love, and dreams up all kinds of improbable crimes and scandals. But her inexperience with life outside books means she has no perceptiveness at all, especially in understanding other people, and her inexperience starts to cloud her judgment. She has no idea that her best friend, Isabella Thorpe, is madly in love with her brother James, for example, or that James feels the same way about Isabella. She tries to read other people by using examples from books, which leads to all kinds of sensational fantasies and embarrassing misunderstandings. She starts to believe that Henry is actually a murderer—and secretly hopes she's right. Things finally turn around when Catherine realizes that Henry's been in love with her all along. She gladly accepts his marriage proposal, and promises, charmingly, never to let her imagination run away with her again.

Needless to say, nobody ever asked for my hand in marriage. Nobody even called me on the phone. I was caught in a vicious, self-perpetuating cycle: the more real life disappointed me, the more I buried myself in books; and the longer I spent reading, the more remote grew the possibility of actual escape. Private fantasies were all I had, and the hours I spent locked up in the attic started to take their toll. I grew ill-looking and white, etiolated, like a plant without sunlight. It might be all the rage now to be pale and thin, but at the time it was the fashion to be rosy and tanned, not sick and waxy like me. My hair was a veil of grease hiding a sour, miserable expression. I started to suspect that even Fungus Face would have turned me down.

To make matters worse, I started to dress like Jane Eyre, in plain, gray pinafores over prim, high-collared blouses, thick woolly tights, and lace-up ankle boots or, when it rained (which was much of the time in Sheffield), a pair of bright blue Wellington boots. Among my classmates,

"...BOYS KEPT THEIR DISTANCE. EVEN GIRLS STEERED CLEAR."

with their tight ankle skirts and winkle-pickers, black eyeliner and ripped fishnets, I looked like a teenage nun on a fishing trip. No wonder boys kept their distance. Even girls steered clear.

Perhaps it's true that things might have been different if, instead of the novels of Jane Austen and the Brontë sisters, I'd read books in which readers DON'T come off so well. I didn't heed the cautionary tale of Miniver Cheevy, but I could have learned a lot from Don Quixote, whose absorption in chivalric romances drives him mad. I should have paid attention to the way Emma Bovary destroys her life by reading the way I was reading, without taste, discrimination, or a flicker of higher thought. I should have read books about the dangerous effects of an improper education on an impressionable mind, books about the misapprehensions and predilections acquired from excessive reading. But I didn't—or, if I did, I didn't fully understand them, and certainly didn't think they might apply to ME. I read about Dorian Gray without realizing that his ruin lies in the intoxicating novel given him by Lord Henry, which convinces him he wants a life of sensual pleasure, whatever it costs. I loved to read, but maybe if I'd paid close attention to Melville's Bartleby, destroyed by the misery of dead letters, I'd have preferred not to.

To put it simply, I'd have been much better off if I'd listened to my dad and spent more time in the company of other human beings. All those years in the attic would have been far better spent learning vital skills: how to socialize, how to engage with others, how to be physical, how to live in the world. Without this knowledge, I grew alienated, detached from society and culture, adrift even from family and friends.

If you're a balanced, discriminating reader, the books you read can make you more interested in moral and political questions, more active, articulate, and engaged. Ideally, reading can help negotiate the tension between self and other, help establish a balance between you, the reader, as an individual, and absorption in the group. With me, it was the opposite. I read unconsciously, almost involuntarily. My inner life was rich and complex, but it all stayed inside. I didn't talk about the books I read because I didn't know how. There was no balance, no fusion between inner and outer worlds. I could write, albeit in a fussy and pretentious style (which I can't seem to entirely shake off, as you may have noticed), but orally, I was virtually inarticulate. My reading vocabulary was expansive, but I spoke only a tiny fraction of it. To actually talk about what I read, I'd have needed a different voice, one that could cross over from private to public, from inner to outer worlds. In fact, I hardly had a voice at all. I went days without speaking. It was as though I'd been turned inside out. Like a mute or a victim of locked-in syndrome, my mind was always busy, but on the surface I might as well have been a zombie. It was as though I read and wrote in a dead language like ancient Latin or Aramaic, a language nobody spoke. Like a Victorian hysteric, I was paralyzed by fantasy, crippled by self-loathing, self-doubting inhibition—a problem that's never completely disappeared, and probably never will.

the outsider

If any of this sounds familiar, maybe you recognize the feeling of alienation that's common among those who read too much as children, and which, in the most extreme cases, can have irreversible consequences. The sad life of the book-hungry child has often been described, but few modern writers have summed up the damage done by reading quite so perceptively as Richard Rodriguez, author of *Hunger of Memory: The Education of Richard Rodriguez* (1983). Rodriguez, the son of Mexican immigrants, recalls how his passion for reading began when he was in fourth grade. He read everything he could get his hands on, but there was no satisfying his hunger. "Despite my best efforts," he recalls, "there seemed to be more and more books I needed to read. At the library I would literally tremble as I came upon whole shelves of books I hadn't read. So I read and I read and I read."

Rodriguez's journey was a painful one. As he explains in *Hunger of Memory*, his early drive to read marked the beginning of his transformation from socially disadvantaged immigrant to fully assimilated American, a transformation that occurred at the expense of a gradual separation from his past, family, and culture. He recalls:

> After dinner I would rush to a bedroom with papers and books. As often as possible, I resisted parental pleas to "save lights" by coming to the kitchen to work. I kept so much, so often to myself . . . I hoarded the pleasures of learning. Alone for hours . . . I rarely looked away from my books—or back on my memories. Nights when

relatives visited and the front rooms were warmed by Spanish sounds, I slipped quietly out of the house.

Rodriguez quickly began to achieve academic success, winning full scholarships to university and then to graduate school, but, looking back, he can now see how these honors took their toll: They distanced him from a people and a language that he loved—even, in the end, from his own memories of himself. After so much time spent reading books in English, Rodriguez explains, he found himself unable to translate his new thoughts and ideas into Spanish because he didn't have the words for them, and so he lost his voice, and—at home—became mute. "Silence! Instead of the flood of intimate sounds that had once flowed smoothly between us, there was this silence." No longer able to communicate with his family, Rodriguez also began to lose the connection to his story, his ancestors, and their traditions. "The family's quiet was partly due to the fact that, as we children learned more and more English, we shared fewer and fewer words with our parents . . . The child would need to repeat himself . . . The young voice, frustrated, would end up saying, 'Never mind.' The subject was closed."

In a later book, *Days of Obligation: An Argument with my Mexican Father*, Rodriguez discusses his belief that, though he now has a rare ability to navigate the intricacies of the English language, his "success" may have come at too high a price. The book follows his attempts to recapture his connection to his family and culture by relearning Spanish, working to reestablish the bonds of the past, to rediscover his pride in himself, his Mexican heritage, his ancestry, his origins. Yet, as he admits, language is so intimately tied to who we are, how we think, and how we view the world, that once the words have been lost, these bonds can be difficult to reforge.

In this respect, literature causes more damage than subjects like science, math, or business, because it's mainly by reading fiction that we acquire a facility with language that can be quite at odds with the way people around us express themselves. If you're an avid reader of fiction, you'll already be aware that one of the things novels teach us is to appreciate very subtle nuances of thought, emotion, and language, so it's unsurprising that people you know can start to seem flat and empty compared to the characters in books, causing you to turn gradually away from your parents and toward writers as figures of authority. Perhaps you start keeping a book with you at all times, even during meals, so you can escape into it when things look dire.

Instead of saying whatever comes into your head, as you used to do when you were a child, you start to wonder how to express yourself, rehearsing your words internally before you speak. Perhaps, more often than not, you decide against speaking out loud, in case people make fun of you, or just don't understand what you mean. You start to appreciate the value of reflection and privacy, choosing isolation and solitude over social situations, which become increasingly awkward and difficult to endure. You start to anticipate and avoid occasions that make you bored or frustrated, those in which you're forced to get involved, where you can't retreat to the corner with a book. You get used to uncertainty, detachment, and silence, and turn to reading all the more, to make yourself feel less lonely.

Maybe the other kids think you're rude and stuck up, and make fun of you for reading all the time. If you're a boy, you're teased for being a nerd; if you're a girl, you're a bluestocking or a bookworm. Eventually, even teachers start to seem limited and narrow-minded, and you start to lose confidence in them. At first you feel angry and irritated at other people's lack of interest in the books and ideas you find so fascinating. For a while you're deeply embarrassed by your parents, but as you grow further away from them emotionally, you start to feel more anxious and awkward. A terrible struggle develops. The fact that you're ashamed of your family fills you with guilt, because they probably love you unconditionally; perhaps they've sacrificed everything to give you the very education that's turned you against them. Most heartbreaking of all, they know you're ashamed of them, they understand, and they've forgiven you already.

A classic case is the anguish experienced by Pip in Dickens's *Great Expectations*, when Joe Gargery, his childhood guardian, comes to visit him in his rooms in London, after Pip has "become a gentleman." Pip listens to Joe's slow, heavy footsteps on the staircase with an excruciating mixture of love, guilt, and shame that grows more intense as he hears Joe pausing on each floor to catch his breath. Pip confesses the feelings with which he anticipates Joe's visit. "Not with pleasure, though I was bound to him by so many ties; no, with considerable disturbance, some mortification, and a keen sense of incongruity. If I could have kept him away by paying money, I certainly would have paid money."

Great Expectations was written at exactly the time when anxieties about reading were becoming a matter of urgent debate—when, for the first time in history, literacy was no longer a privilege of the upper and middle classes. The argument made by the Victorian intellectual elite—that even

a rudimentary education would make the masses dissatisfied with their ordained position in life, causing them frustration and disappointment at their miserable lot—may seem absurd to us today, but it's part of what happens to Pip. In a very different time and place, it's also what happened to Richard Rodriguez. It happened to me, as well. Maybe it happened to you.

You see, the old superstitions about books aren't groundless. They CAN cast a spell on you. Like a genie from a magic lantern, they can change your life completely, but—as the genie always warns you—you should be careful what you wish for. Once you've changed, you can't go back, which often means you can't help finding real-life experience more and more disappointing. The children's poster doesn't tell the whole story. Yes, books can take you to wonderful places, but they can also leave you stranded there, alienated and unemployable, lonely and classless, isolated from other human beings, even from your own memory, your own experience of yourself.

And let me tell you, there's nothing wonderful about that.

AND MOVING THROUGH A MIRROR CLEAR

THAT HANGS BEFORE HER ALL THE YEAR,

SHADOWS OF THE WORLD APPEAR.

—ALFRED, LORD TENNYSON, "THE LADY OF SHALOTT"

Even if they're no longer the only repositories of knowledge available to us, even if they're never taken off the shelves and dusted down, books are deeply comforting to have around. What can be more appealing than shelves packed full of familiar books?

Can you really be unhappy in a book-filled room?

Is there any style of home décor more timeless, more sophisticated, than stacks of book-lined shelves reaching all the way to the ceiling?

In grander homes, a room lined with books may still be referred to as "the library," but as a matter of fact, books aren't immediately visible in modern libraries, most of which are designed for easy access, with wide-open spaces, rows of computer stations, and lots of light and glass. Even older libraries tend to keep most of their books out of sight, down in the stacks. I've always been drawn to the backs, attics, and cellars of buildings—their lofts, basements, and rear staircases, their dark, secret parts. Library stacks are among the most private of public places. Generally located underground, like bunkers or dungeons, some are accessible only by tight stairwells, others by creaky elevators with iron gates. In these dusty rooms, long-neglected volumes of obscurities languish in rusty cages, like dying animals. Call it what you like—revisiting the womb, or anticipating the grave—but I've always found windowless rooms very reassuring. There's something special about being closed in on all sides, especially down in a basement or up in an attic, far from the world outside. When a library's stacks are off-limits to the public, when you need a special card or pass to go down there, they become a secret place that can only be reached through a crack in the earth's surface.

As a student at Oxford, I spent most afternoons in the Bodleian, one of the biggest libraries in the world. The main building—including the Sheldonian Theater, built originally in 1602—resembles a sort of square castle surrounding a cobbled courtyard. Every term, I'd choose a different room to nestle in. I enjoyed the grand, Gothic chambers with their arched ceilings, but I liked the smaller, less ornate rooms as well. Behind the high-ceilinged halls with their Corinthian columns, I found a whole underworld of wood-paneled burrows, surprising stairways, and galleries hidden from public view.

Along with Cambridge University Library and the British Library in London, the Bodleian is England's library of legal deposit, which means that, by law, it has to receive a copy of every work published in the U.K. and Ireland, from dry scholarly monographs to low-carb cookbooks. It currently contains more than eight million printed items (not including its many maps and manuscripts); at the time of writing, the catalogue is being made accessible online. As you might expect, the Bodleian has miles of stacks, many of them underground, and some in a holding facility a few miles outside the town. Of course, as with most research libraries, you're not allowed to check anything out, and hardly any books are kept on the open shelves. This means that any book you order can take up to two days to arrive (not counting weekends).

The stacks at the Bodleian—not accessible to students—are eleven stories deep, connected by underground passageways. The process of retrieving a book, like some occult ritual from the heyday of séances and spiritualism, began with the librarian putting a copy of your order slip in a sealed tube and sending it whizzing down a pressurized vacuum chute to the basement. Next, one of the workers down there sorted out the slips according to the level on which the book was stored (all the books were classified according to size to save space), and sent them to that floor through the same network of tubes. Finally, another person wandered into the vast stacks, retrieved the book and loaded it onto a little train, which delivered it back to the sorting depot, from which it was sent up to the appropriate reading room on a kind of creaky dumbwaiter.

I learned about all this from talking to the librarians; you're not actually allowed to go down into the stacks. Tours are offered, but I never took one; I didn't want to lose my fantasy that the people who worked down there looked like dwarfs or Oompah Loompahs, pale from lack of sunlight, like the albino rats that are supposed to live in the New York sewers, or the blind, mutant tribe of Mole Men living deep beneath the Earth that I'd read about in *Fantastic Four.* I pictured them as a race of book people, inbred, never glimpsing the day, speaking a language made from the Dewey Decimal System, resembling the race of cannibals living in the London subway in the movie *Death Line* (1973), who know only one phrase of human speech: "Mind the Gap!"

There really are people who live in library stacks, at least for a time. While public libraries are common hangouts for the homeless, everybody has to leave at closing time; university libraries, however, often stay open all night. A librarian at Columbia University's Butler Library told me that every so often, students, unable to afford New York's exorbitant rents, can be found nestled down in sleeping bags deep in the bowels of the stacks. More fortunate graduate students will sometimes be given their own carrel—a tiny office the size of a changing room, just big enough for a desk and chair—but with a door that locks. I knew a graduate student at Oxford, a philosopher, who, while writing up his doctoral thesis on Emmanuel Kant, lived in his library carrel for over a month, peeing into an empty milk carton he kept under his desk. Other shady things also go on in the secret depths of college libraries, the most obvious of which is sex, for which a lockable carrel must come in handy. Librarians have told me all kinds of stories about things they've found in the stacks, from the predictable (condoms, porno mags) to the perplexing (a dead rabbit, a voodoo doll).

These days, I assume, library stacks are growing less and less necessary, except as storage space, now that so much material is available online, but I must have spent weeks, maybe even months of my life in them, usually in the darkest corners of the dustiest rooms, sniffing out obscure books that were last checked out in 1932. I love library stacks, but they also frustrate me, the way bookstores frustrate me, even online bookstores. There's something anxiety-inducing about being surrounded by all those different thoughts and voices, reminding me that however long I might live, I'll never get to read even the tiniest fraction of the books that already exist, never mind the hundreds of new ones being published everyday. Thinking about it can be exhausting and depressing; it reminds me that every thought I have, every unusual combination of ideas that comes to mind, however oblique and idiosyncratic, has, in another place and time, already been thought, felt, expressed, published, and analyzed, more eloquently than I ever could. Miserable and depressed, I'll reach for *Suicide and Life-Threatening Behavior*, only to discover that somebody has already tried even my unique plan for a painless death, anticipated its flaws, and overcome them.

On the subject of suicides, libraries seem to attract a surprising number of them, though it's perhaps less surprising when you consider that library suicides generally take place in college settings, where there's a higher proportion of suicides in general. Not too long ago, New York University had a mini-epidemic on its hands; between September 2003 and September 2004, six students jumped to their deaths from various university buildings, the first two from the tenth floor of NYU's Bobst Library. Designed by architect Philip Johnson, the Bobst Library is early 1960s modern, with a central atrium surrounded by circular walkways, and an Op-art floor below. Some say this floor was purposely designed to discourage suicidal jumpers, since if you stand on any of the upper floors and look down, the atrium seems to be full of faraway spikes—though why this would deter rather than encourage would-be suicides isn't clear to me. (The atrium was actually inspired by Escher's drawing *Depth*.) The original barriers round the edge of the upper-floor walkways were startlingly low, but since the recent suicides the university has installed glass panels around them.

On September 12, 2003, John D. Skolnik, a troubled junior from Evanston, Illinois, stepped over the rails of the top-floor walkway and plummeted to the marble base of the atrium, landing with such force that students studying three stories below ground said they'd felt the impact. A month later, on October 10, 2003, on the way to a late Chinatown lunch with two friends, Stephen Bohler, age twenty, suggested he and his pals stop at the Bobst Library and ride the elevator to the top floor. When they got out of the elevator, while his two friends looked over the rail, Bohler went right up to the edge, deliberately stepped over, and fell into the open space of the atrium. The autopsy showed he was tripping on mushrooms, so his death was classed as an "accident" (a convenient way to make sense of this perplexing turn of events). Naturally, people connected Bohler's death with Skolnik's, and blamed the lure of Bobst's "atrium of death." But the library wasn't to blame. NYU has a higher than average suicide rate anyway, partly due to the special stress of living in a city the size of New York. Any public or semi-public building with a deep and accessible atrium will inevitably become a focal point for suicide, or speculations about it. According to NYU officials, Skolnik's was the Bobst's first suicide in the library's thirty-year history, and the first at the university since 1996.

Still, it doesn't seem far-fetched to forge a symbolic connection between libraries and death. That's part of their appeal, after all; there's a mausoleum-like feel to those dusty, underground stacks that could easily begin to drain you of the will to live. What can make the process of reading fiction so intoxicating, in part, is the way it engages the death drive; indeed, we talk about "losing ourselves" in a book, being "carried away" by a story. Libraries, like books, are places where we can escape from the demands and pressures of daily life, of our bodily needs and desires. Perhaps some time in the future, when physical books have become obsolete, those miles of underground passages beneath the Bodleian can be sold off as crypts to wealthy Oxford alumni, who might well fancy the notion of spending eternity in the stacks. In the ancient Egyptian *Book of the Dead*, the jackal-headed god Anubis escorts the spirit of the deceased down its sacred path to the underworld. In certain accounts of near-death experiences, collected at the Web site Near Death, this journey includes a visit to a heavenly structure with wide halls and curving staircases that closely resembles a library, whose rooms are lined with books containing all the knowledge of the universe:

> I was in a vast old traditional building, containing all the wisdom of the ages, everything ever said or written. Room upon room, shelf upon shelf of books stretched as far as the eye could see . . . I knew in my heart it was home.

> I was in a library in an ethereal temple or atrium, similar to ancient Greek or Roman villas. Everything was airy and light.

> At first I was taken up through the tunnel into a place of learning (library) into the glorious light at the one end of this almost infinite tunnel.

> I realized in the distance there was an open library. A library in the sky without walls . . .

of human bondage

Dreams of death among books are perhaps less common than fantasies of a life among them, but then, not everyone who loves books loves them in the same way. In the wide and varied world of readers, you occasionally come across a type of man (rarely, in my experience, a woman), usually over forty, who appears to be, let's say, "overly involved" with his books. Perhaps you know the type. He's often associated in a peripheral way with the world of books—he may be an author, critic, bookseller, or librarian—but he may just as well be someone you'd never suspect: a farmer, engineer, accountant, or taxi driver. For this man, the love of reading has been overtaken by the love of books as things, just as, for the sexual fetishist, erotic desire is displaced from the person to one of their parts or possessions—shoes, buttocks, hair. Upon first acquaintance, the book fetishist, or bibliomaniac, as he's also known, may give every appearance of being a real man of letters, a devoted reader, but if you come to know him further, you'll soon discover that he is, in fact, little more than a barren hoarder of books.

Of course, not all book collectors make fetishes out of their books, and there can be biblio maniacs with very small libraries. The vital difference is this: that, to the bibliomaniac, owning a book is more important than actually reading it. As with similar conditions, bibliomania occurs in a variety of forms, from the very mild to the crippling and incurable, but once it's set in, the sufferer tends to go downhill fast, so it always pays to keep your wits about you if you know someone who might be showing any of the following signs.

In its mildest forms, which are not always malignant, the bibliomaniac is inordinately fond of the object's physicality. He may love the way a book looks and feels; he may sniff its pages with a glint in his eye; he may fondle its dust jacket lovingly. He may have hard and fast rules about the way books should be treated. He may, for example, strongly disapprove of underlining and marginal notes (especially in ink), dog-eared pages, coffee stains, or worn edges. The refusal to lend books is a common symptom, as is the tendency to constantly rearrange them according to different systems, some more or less logical (alphabetical or Dewey Decimal), and others idiosyncratic (according to color, size, series imprint, or publication date). Bibliomaniacs often have a special interest in collecting volumes in a particular set. They generally favor hardbacks and first editions, and can be sneeringly dismissive of cheap versions, new imprints, or translations they deem "second-rate." They're irrationally preoccupied with what they refer to as "authenticity," and can be proud Luddites, often expressing disdain for the Internet and computers in general, as well as for e-books, self-published texts, graphic novels, and other literary forms that—in their minds, at least—simply don't "count."

Author and booklover Nicholas A. Basbanes, who's been described as "the Pied Piper of bibliophiles," refers to book collecting as "a gentle madness," presumably in contrast to the more violent forms of insanity, but I'm not sure it's always the harmless eccentricity Mr. Basbanes considers it to be. In an interesting article published in 1930 in *The International Journal of Psychoanalysis* called "Some Unconscious Factors in Reading," James Strachey, Sigmund Freud's English translator and a psychoanalyst himself, drew attention to a number of cases he'd dealt with in which ordinary reading habits became pathological. These include the case of a book-loving patient who talked at great length about literature and "constantly interlarded his conversation with quotations," yet Strachey believed that this man "had scarcely ever read a book through, and had never read more than a dozen consecutive pages at a single sitting." In my experience, bibliomania is one of those rare conditions where the sufferer's placid exterior can conceal a pathology so ingrained as to make the occasional burst of psychosis seem like a mere tic in comparison. For a classic example, get to know Peter Kien, the protagonist of Elias Canetti's bleak and depressing novel *Auto-da-Fé* (1935); alternatively, check out some bibliomaniac "porn," like the documentaries *Book Wars* (2000) and *The Stone Reader* (2002).

Should he give free rein to his desires, the bibliomaniac can ruin his life, along with the lives of his loved ones. He'll often take better care of his books than of his own health; he'll spend more on fiction than he does on food; he'll be more interested in his library than in his relationships, and, since few people are prepared to live in a place where every available surface is covered with piles of books, he'll often find himself alone, perhaps in the company of a neglected and malnourished cat. When he dies, all but forgotten, his body might fester for days before a curious neighbor grows concerned about the smell.

A perfect specimen of the bibliomaniac is Art Garfunkel. Yes, that's right, Art Garfunkel. You remember—the fuzzy-haired part of Simon and Garfunkel. Or, at least, that's how most of us know him; but then, most of us are blindly oblivious to the existence of the Garfunkel Library, a chronological online list of every book the erudite songster has read over the last thirty-eight years—almost a thousand of them—including the month and year of reading, the date of first publication, and the number of pages they contain. As the Web site boasts, Garfunkel is a "voracious reader," who gets through, on average, around twenty-five books a year—a lot more than most people, without question. For example, between June 1968 and

April 1970—golden years for Simon and Garfunkel, remember—he got through forty books, including *War and Peace* and *The Brothers Karamazov*. And these were the sixties! You'd imagine, at the height of his fame, Mr. Garfunkel would have had more exciting things to do than staying home with his nose in a depressing Russian novel, but apparently not.

If you're already thinking of poking around in the Garfunkel Library for a cheap snicker at an aging hippie's Carlos Castaneda collection— think again, friend. The Garfunkel Library is not to be sniffed at; indeed, its shelves are positively groaning with heavyweight tomes. There's no pulp here; there's not even any popular fiction. Well, almost none. No more immune to hype than the rest of us, it appears Art couldn't resist checking out *Jaws* in August 1974; *Interview with the Vampire* in July 1981; *Harry Potter and the Sorcerer's Stone* in December 2001, and *The Da Vinci Code* in February 2004. Apart from these rare off-notes, however, the Garfunkel Library consists mostly of classic editions of literature, history, and philosophy, including numerous volumes of Shakespeare, Freud, Proust, Dostoevsky, and Tolstoy. No Carlos Castaneda (though he does admit to reading *Jonathan Livingston Seagull* in 1972).

As a matter of fact, rather than giving you a cheap laugh, your first visit to the Garfunkel Library might leave you humbled, ready to doff your hat in shame. The more time you spend there, however, the more curious it all starts to seem. Most people, I think, tend to read eclectically, one book leading to the next in peripheral but connected ways. Mr. Garfunkel, on the other hand, seems to be following some kind of system that permits him to read only books that have been critically esteemed. He never seems to have given up any book halfway through, when he got sick of it, or when he misplaced his reading glasses—or if he did, he doesn't mention it. And then, what are we to make of the fact that in April 1984, he read Strunk and White's *Elements of Style* cover to cover—TWICE? Or that in March 1993 he claims to have read through the entire *Random House Dictionary of the English Language*—all 1,664 pages of it? Or that, according to those who've conducted interviews at his New York home, each book in the Garfunkel Library, after being read, is wrapped in protective plastic and shelved in the order of reading?

Without venturing to psychoanalyze Mr. Garfunkel's unconscious fixations, I'd say there are times that you can, in fact, tell a book by its cover—and one of them is when it's covered in protective plastic. And while it's not impossible to understand why someone would want to keep a careful record of the books they've read, why would they keep note of the number of pages, rather than, say, the edition, or the translation, or, oh I don't know, what they thought of it? This isn't just rigid, it's anal (and Garfunkel might even agree—after all, in August 1973 he read Irving Bieber's *Homosexuality, a Psychoanalytic Survey*, and in June 1987 he read Freud's *The Ego and the Id*).

Most revealing, however, aren't the books that ARE listed, but those that AREN'T. According to the site's author, "We are pleased to present a listing of every book Art has read over the last thirty years." That's right, EVERY BOOK, do you hear? This means that, although he's a poet himself, Garfunkel has only ever read four or five volumes of poetry—one of which, read in October 1989, was his own (*Still Water—Prose Poems* by Art Garfunkel). It means that when his wife, Kim, was pregnant in 1990, he read nothing in preparation—no *What to Expect When You're Expecting*, no *Official Lamaze Guide*. It means that, when he walked across America in 1984, and later on across Europe, he did so without the aid of travel books. It means he read nothing he could share with his son, born in 1991 (unless you count Louise Ames's *Your Five-Year-Old* in 1996). It means he read no books about healing and forgiveness in the buildup to his much-vaunted reunion with Paul Simon (unless that explains *You Just Don't Understand*, in August 1996). More recently, in January 2006, Art and his wife had a second son, born to a surrogate mother. You'd think he could have found something more pertinent to read in preparation for this emotion-laden event than Henri Pirenne's *Economic and Social History of Medieval Europe*.

Garfunkel's completism suggests a tendency toward pompous self-importance reinforced by the site's stuffy tone, in phrases like: "We also present the following list of books which have been designated by Mr. Garfunkel as his favorites." In short, Garfunkel seems to have reached the advanced stages of "Sir Elton Syndrome," characterized by the insistence that a pop star is oh so much more than that. Far from being merely a POP STAR, why, Mr. Garfunkel is a poet, a composer, a philanthropist, a humanitarian, and, above all, an INTELLECTUAL—certainly not a balding man-child with too much time on his hands.

Still, we shouldn't be too hasty to judge. There's a big difference between a bibliomaniac and an ordinary book collector, and while accepting that some book lovers can go to extremes, you also have to realize that, if you've been a reader all your life, you can't help feeling that books have a symbolic value. Plenty of people who are far from full-blown fetishists have developed private rituals around the reading process, including very careful rules about what they can and can't read. My friend Neil, for example, enjoys listening to audio books on his long drive to work, but has a rule that he'll only listen to books he's read before, because he feels that listening to a book is a very different thing from reading it, and "doesn't count." Some people think that reading a book in a modern translation "doesn't count," either; others will only read books in the original language. These people remind me of those cinephiles who won't watch films on video or DVD, and can't concentrate if the film is in the wrong aspect ratio, or if the print has been dubbed, or altered to fit the screen.

If you've been a reader all your life, your reading habits are probably so ingrained as to be virtually unconscious, so it can be an interesting experiment to foreground them for a moment. To do so, consider the following questions. Do you read footnotes as you go, when you've finished, or not at all? Do you read the introductory essays and all the back matter, or do you consider the "book" to be the text itself, which ends with the final chapter? Do you try not to "contaminate" your experience by avoiding the synopsis, blurb, or praise from critics on the back cover? Perhaps you won't read anything at all until you're familiar with the critical consensus. Do you have a number of books on the stove at the same time, so to speak—a work of fiction, another of philosophy, another of religion, and perhaps some poetry? Do you feel uneasy if you haven't spent at least a few minutes reading everyday?

Rituals around reading can be as personal and as private as saying your prayers. I have my own habits, like everybody else, though I've tried to discard the more irrational, time-consuming, and judgmental ones. In the past, for example, whenever I found myself in somebody else's home, like many people, I'd always have a brief glance at the shelves, and I'd feel a bit disturbed if they contained not books, but family photographs, whimsical knick-knacks, or porcelain figurines.

I remember once being particularly bothered by a visit to the home of an English professor, a colleague who was terribly proud of her new house, which she'd just finished decorating in a rustic style, with old-fashioned agricultural implements lining the walls. Let's call her Miss H. At the time, I couldn't help feeling that Miss H. was typical of a common type of academic in that she saw her books as tools of the trade, for use in teaching and planning courses, as well as for easy reference at work. Her living space, on the other hand, was a *Better Homes and Gardens* showpiece model whose ersatz farmhouse theme had no room for shelves of clashing, modern textbooks. As many people do, she divided her work from her home life. Miss H. didn't need her books around her. She may have been a dedicated reader, but she clearly never had the urge to dip in and out of her books on a daily basis, reread a favorite essay, or follow up a footnote just for fun. I tried not to, but I used to feel a streak of contempt for those like Miss H., for whom teaching literature was a career you "trained" for, the way you might train to become a lawyer or a car mechanic—something you might have an aptitude for, perhaps, rather than a vocation, a way of life. I used to feel, rather smugly, that an English teacher with no books at home was like a vicar whose Bible was kept for show on the church altar, not for use, at home by his bed.

These days, I try to be less judgmental. What business was it of mine, after all, whether Miss H. kept her books at home or at work? For all I knew, she had thousands of books in the attic, or in her bedroom, or in the garage, or online.

As for the bibliomaniac, of course there's nothing inherently WRONG with collecting books. As habits go, it's got to be better than smoking, or shopping for shoes, or doing crystal meth. I suppose the major difference is that we don't assume that somebody who collects shoes is necessarily a great walker, but some of us do have the misconception that owning a lot of books is the same thing as being a great reader, or knowing a lot, whereas the truth is, of course, a love of the physical presence of books doesn't in itself constitute any form of cultural acumen, any more than wearing a white coat gives you a knowledge of medicine. Most book collectors no doubt came to their hobby through an early love of reading, but as they grow older, they often come to indulge their obsession for its own sake, like all collectors, and it really makes no difference whether the objects in question are books, Toby jugs, porcelain elephants, or *Star Trek* figurines.

No doubt the bibliomaniac will bristle at this suggestion, arguing that his books are not mere objects for decoration and display, but a genuine working library—a defense that only works for those who don't have Internet access (although as I said, a lot of bibliomaniacs are dyed-in-the-wool technophobes), since, as everybody knows, it's so much faster and easier to Google a query than to actually get up and search for a book on your shelves (as Miss H. may have discovered long ago). But genuine working libraries are rare, and though I fight the tendency, I can't help being a bit suspicious of professionals—lawyers, academics, psychiatrists, consultants—whose offices are lined with shelves of heavy, leather-bound hardbacks, no doubt the classics of their field, whose presence implies the office is used not only for seeing clients, but for writing and researching, away from the hustle and bustle of the family home. I always wonder whether the books weren't bought for college, years ago, or perhaps inherited, and kept not to be consulted, but to confer status and authority (just look what a clever fellow I am, how much knowledge I've accumulated!), like the doctor's framed certificates, or the banker's gold-tipped pen.

So you see, here I am knocking one person for having no books on her shelves, and disparaging others for having shelves full of them. But old habits die hard, and it's about as difficult not to judge someone by the books (or lack of them) on their shelves as it is not to judge a book by its cover. Still I keep trying, and I think I'm getting better at not jumping to conclusions. After all, books can be all kinds of things to all kinds of people—they can be tools, guides, investments, manuals, home décor, work, produce, or just a messy pile of clutter. I try to remember, too, that not all readers accumulate books. Some see no point in keeping books after they've read them, and will sell them, or give them away. More and more people are getting into the habit of reading e-books on their laptops or BlackBerrys, and more and more libraries are being converted to electronic form. Though it may well turn out that the portable, private form of the book—the kind we can hold in our hands, and cradle in our lap—continues to provide, for most people, the ideal fulfillment of immersion in another world, this doesn't mean it's the only way this need can be satisfied. Deep immersion is a style of reading which, in itself, is a by-product of the growth of the novel—traditionally considered to be a grand, fictional creation to be read at a leisurely pace, and in a private setting. Novel reading is certainly well suited to the lap or the bed, but other kinds of reading require different postures. You'd find it hard to do much active reading in bed—that is, reading that requires a lot of note-taking, or marginal comments. We don't browse a lot in bed, or survey things, or flick through them. Some books are to be read from cover to cover, without missing a word; others are written for browsing, ambling, or idling in.

I also try to bear in mind that for most people, books have always represented something more like obligation than pleasure, which helps to explain the need for all those national reading campaigns. To the hypothetical "pure" reader, the text justifies its existence in the act of reading, with no ulterior motive, not even that of "entertainment" (since the notion of pleasure is implied in the carrying out of the act). This "pure" reader would look down on those who need a "motive" in order to read—to learn, or apply something, for example—for whom the text is merely a vehicle toward another function. But be warned: This tendency on the part of some readers to feel superior to others, however harmless it may seem, involves two flawed assumptions: first, that the physical presence or absence of books can tell us something very important about a person, and second, that some ways of reading are better than others.

the real thing

The most common form of bibliomania is an obsession with the physicality of the book, rather than its contents, but bibliomania isn't the only form of book-based pathology you may come across; in fact, there are quite a few. Another that crops up from time to time is bibliolatry, also known as the "sacred book mentality"—the "original intentism" professed by traditional upholders of the U.S. Constitution, or the literalism expressed by certain religious groups, including fundamentalist Christians and Hebrew Cabbalists.

For many years, orthodox rabbis have expressed outrage at the various translations of the Cabbala that are now available to all and sundry (including gentiles), just as they bemoan the co-opting of the Cabbala by New Age enthusiasts and celebrity converts (Madonna, Demi Moore, Ashton Kutcher, and Britney Spears are just a few of the stars who've been spotted wearing red string "Cabbala bracelets," now available to everyone at the mall). Bibliolaters usually believe their sacred book should be read in the original language whenever possible, and, when this isn't feasible (when the original language is an ancient one, for example), the responsible reader should seek out not the most elegant, accessible, or up-to-date translation, but the most "accurate." This is a long-established superstition. Samuel Johnson believed, "A translator is to be like his author. It is not his business to excel him."

King James I was so concerned about "corrupt" versions of the Bible—which, in the sixteenth century, was available in a whole range of different translations—that, in order to ensure his subjects were all on the same page, he commissioned a translation of his own that was answerable directly to the "truth" of the original. These days, however, the King James

Bible is regarded as misleadingly ornate by bibliolaters in search of the "true meaning" of the book "as intended by the author" (whatever that means), who prefer a strict, unimaginative translation that allows them to understand the "plain truth" without distortion, embellishment, or inaccuracy. Bibliolaters generally regard interpretation as a process of logic and equivalency, leaving no room for special considerations such as figurative forms like poetry and metaphor, or the possibility of creative license. Some religions take the idea of the sacred book quite literally, punishing those who handle it with disrespect—a punishment often imposed by the very people who harshly condemn any preoccupation with material objects.

Perhaps the most ancient and deeply rooted form of bibliolatry is the belief in a book that holds the "truth," as some believe of the U.S. Constitution, others of the Cabbala, the Koran, or the Bible. It's easy to see the appeal of this notion; it helps explain why, in every culture, certain texts have always held enormous symbolic weight. Many people still rely for guidance on opening the Bible at a random page; in early history, this method was even used to determine the guilt or innocence of an accused party, a form of bibliomancy (using books for magic purposes). More recently, during the "Satanic abuse" scares of the early 1980s, occult "experts" would advise police investigators to read synopses or substitutes rather than the actual "Satanic books" themselves, in case the honest cops should be "drawn in" by evil words (fear of books is known as "bibliophobia").

It's deeply comforting to believe that, whatever questions or anxieties you might have, there's a book that holds all the answers, whose teachings apply at all times and in every situation—a book you must handle tenderly, to honor its special powers. Equally reassuring is the idea that there are unique ways of reading this book that only certain holy, learned, or chosen people can understand, thereby establishing a hierarchy of readers, from the magus to the cognoscenti to the acolytes to the apprentices and ordinary practitioners right down to the common hoi polloi (women, peasants), who aren't even allowed to set eyes on it. Like all superstitions, these beliefs serve a number of important social functions, but in the end, they have little to do with the book itself, and everything to do with submission, fear, authority, and prejudice, along with the interests of certain social groups and centers of power.

as you like it

Not many of us get through school, not to mention college, without developing our own imperatives and superstitions around reading and the feelings associated with it, whether they're feelings of pleasure, affection, guilt, dread, anxiety, or simple indifference. As we grow older, these feelings tend to linger unconsciously, whether we continue reading avidly, or recoil at the very sight of a book. No one has more insight into the confluence between reading and memory than Marcel Proust, and no one has written so well on the subject, or at such length. In this passage from the *Time Regained* volume of *Remembrance of Things Past* (1913–1922), the narrator describes the effect of this synergy:

> A book which we read at a certain period does not merely remain forever conjoined to what existed around us; it remains also faithfully united to what we ourselves then were and thereafter it can be handled only by the sensibility, the personality that were then ours. If, even in thought, I pick up from the bookshelf *François le Champi*, immediately there rises within me a child who takes my place, who alone has the right to spell out the title *François le Champi*, and who reads it as he read it once before, with the same impression of what the weather was like then in the garden, the same dreams that were then shaping themselves in his mind about the different countries and about life, and the same anguish about the next day.

Memories of reading can often be far more complex than memories of "real" events, since, as Proust explains, they combine "factual" memories, like your personal situation and social context at the time of reading, with the power of an aesthetic experience. So when you think of a book that had a profound impact on you, you often can't help but remember what you were doing and where you were when you first read it. The same is also true, conversely, of life-changing events or circumstances that occurred while you were reading a certain book; your memories of the book and your reading of it can become woven together like the colored threads in a rug. In her poignantly eloquent memoir *Reading Lolita in Tehran*,

Iranian author Azar Nafisi describes how the experience of reading during air raid sirens has forever colored her feelings about the books she was engaged with at the time. "If a sound can be preserved in the same manner as a leaf or a butterfly," she writes, "I would say that within the pages of my *Pride and Prejudice*, that most polyphonic of all novels, . . . is hidden like an autumn leaf the sound of that siren."

How do you remember what you read? Think about a work of fiction you read a long time ago—what scenes, images, or characters come to mind? Do you see visual images of the story you're reading as it unfolds? If so, do you base the characters on people you know—friends, family, famous people, or composites of all three, as in dreams, or are they totally original? Are the images in color or black-and-white? Are they consistent or do they come and go? For some, reading fiction can engage other sensory responses, as well as the visual, like smell, sound, taste—and . . . well, I'm sure we've all had the experience of being sexually aroused by a fictional scene or a character description. Some people say they have rich sensory experiences, as intense and realistic as an IMAX movie, that radiate outward from a verbal text, while others, including those who've been blind from birth, have experiences that are more conceptual. I wonder if these images are retained, stored in our memory long after we've finished reading, and whether, by focusing carefully, we're bringing them back to the surface of consciousness, or whether we're actually creating them anew every time.

Some people regularly make friends with fictional characters, or even fall in love with them, or with their authors. Some can't keep from skipping to the end to find out what happens. Some feel compelled to read especially resonant passages aloud, to themselves or to others. Have you ever had the strange experience of reading a book you hate—but seem unable to stop? Have you ever read a book that left a bitter taste in your mouth? What about a book you love to death, but nobody else seems to GET?

If you've never paid much attention to your reading habits, maybe you should stop and think for a moment; there's a lot to be learned from foregrounding your daily habits, focusing on the things you normally take for granted. Ask yourself the following questions, and compare your responses to those of the fifty-six adult readers I surveyed (of all ages, equal parts British and American, male and female, academics and "laymen").

1. What book are you currently reading?

Of my fifty-six respondents, only one said he wasn't reading a book at the moment. A few people could give me a title, but not an author. About sixteen said they were reading two or more books at the same time; fourteen were reading history or biography, and the rest were reading fiction, mostly by contemporary best-selling authors like Dan Brown, J. K. Rowling, Dean Koontz, Stephen King, John Grisham, James Patterson, or Danielle Steele. One person (a poet) said she was reading poetry.

2. How do you decide what book to read next?

How flexible or schematic are you in your reading habits? Every reader has some kind of system, however unacknowledged or unconscious. Think about it. Do you go for a long time between books, marking time till something strikes your fancy, waiting to be given something by friends or family, or do you go directly from one book to the next? Do you make reading lists (on paper, on your computer, or in your head), and, if so, how strictly do you stick to them? Do you know exactly what you like? Are you one of those people who consistently reads the work of particular authors, or a certain genre? Maybe you never read anything but sword-and-sandal fiction, detective stories, literary "classics," historical novels, or Harlequin romances. Do you go through phases? (In the last couple of years alone, I've had a true crime phase, a biography phase, a Philip Roth phase, and a binge on campus novels.)

Twenty-two of my respondents said that when it comes to picking up a new book, they rely on reviews in the Sunday papers, or recommendations from family and friends. Eighteen said they just pick up whatever catches their eye on their bookshelves at home, at the bookshop, at a friend's house, or in the library—and people who love books know right away what they're going to like. One reader said:

> I often choose books based on the setting—if I pick up a book I like the look of, turn it over, and see the name St. Cloud or Topeka, I buy it and never have to read another word of the blurb. I love books set in U.S. towns. If I see the words "murder" or "bones" or "marshes" or any group of words depicting a lonely woman on a book, I get it.

The other respondents varied considerably. Some people said they have a small group of favorite authors whose work they follow closely, buying each new book as soon as it comes out. Others said they have a bedside stack to work through, sometimes systematically, sometimes at random. (I always have a stack of around ten books, and unless they're review books, I'll almost never take them out of order, however tempting they may look—but then, I also have very few qualms about giving up on a book if it doesn't engage me.) Some said they like to read books that correspond with their current situation—European novels while traveling in Europe, romance fiction when they're in love, and so on. Some said they visit bookstores to find something to read, picking up different books and reading their first pages; some pay more attention to price. For others, it's entirely a matter of serendipity—or, as one person described it, "a mysterious coalescence of urges and interests."

3. Do you always finish books, or do you give up on them? If you give up on them, how many pages does it usually take?

Of the fifty-six readers I surveyed, only three said they never, ever gave up on a book (and even then, I'm not sure I believe them). One commented: "I only start books I know I'm going to like"; another claimed, "Even in high school, I read every assigned book cover to cover"; and the third said, "If I'm going to hate something, I want to hate it thoroughly and completely." Everybody else admitted to giving up on a book from time to time, though some confessed to feeling guilty about doing so (why do so many people force themselves to read books they don't enjoy?), either because they find themselves struggling and losing interest, because something more interesting comes along, or for an unrelated reason ("I put it down for too long," "I'll start something else and forget to go back to it," "I'll mislay my reading glasses," "It's due back at the library," "I'll put them down and forget where I've put them"). Some people will give up after ten pages or "one bad chapter," others draw the line at three chapters, thirty to sixty pages, a hundred and fifty pages, or "about halfway."

The last book I gave up on was Samuel Beckett's *Molloy*, which I added to my stack after my boyfriend recommended it. He went on to read the other works in the same volume—*Malone Dies* and *The Unnamable*—and found them all engrossing, "in an odd, monomaniacal way." I first gave up on it after sixty or so pages, then a couple of days later I decided I'd try again, and made it through another sixty pages before conceding defeat. When I asked my readers to name a book they recall giving up on, titles mentioned more than once included *Moby-Dick*, *Don Quixote*, *As I Lay Dying*, *A Clockwork Orange*, *Midnight's Children*, *Foucault's Pendulum*, *Breakfast of Champions*, *The Three Musketeers*, *White Noise*, *Gravity's Rainbow*, and—thank you—*Molloy*.

Incidentally, a recent issue of the art and culture journal *Cabinet* included, as a free gift, two cardboard bookmarks to be placed "in books you will abandon." The bookmarks read: "You have reached the page on which this book's previous owner decided to give up," with a space at the bottom for the date and your signature.

4. Do you generally separate your reading into "work" and "fun"?

This question was mainly directed at the academics, but I thought it would be interesting to find out whether this was a common distinction. It may be surprising to some people to discover that those whose work involved "literary" reading—writers, literature students, journalists, academics in the humanities—did not, as a rule, separate their reading into "work" and "fun," which makes sense, because after all, we choose to work with books because we love to read in the first place. As one of my respondents commented, "There's no separation between work and interest—I work out of interest." Those who did make a clear distinction between "work" and "fun" were generally engaged in administrative or managerial positions, where "work reading" consisted of reports and other business-related documents, so, as one person said, "Most of my reading away from the office is fun—novels, newspapers, etc. I tend to do *work* reading at work." A couple of exceptions were a woman doing a PhD in history, who said "The reading I do for work and the reading I do for fun are so completely different, I consider them different activities," and a philosophy professor who made the comment, "I don't read pulp just to relax. TV is for that."

5. Do you ever reread books you love? If so, how often? Please give examples, if possible.

While some people feel there are just too many great books out there to go back and reread those they've read before, most people, it seems, reread their favorite books on a semi-regular basis, from every year without fail to once every four or five years. About a quarter of my respondents said they'd reread classics like *The Iliad, The Odyssey, Ulysses, Jane Eyre,* and *The Great Gatsby,* although my survey did include a heavy weighting of English teachers like myself, who reread books with a view to refreshing their memory for upcoming courses or for similar reasons, like background research. Others reread mainly stories, poems, and sections of longer novels. A lot of people said they like to reread their favorite contemporary novels, especially science fiction and fantasy—titles mentioned were *Catch-22, Portnoy's Complaint, Lord of the Rings, The Hobbit, The Silmarillion, Dune, Blood Meridian,* and the Harry Potter series. I was interested to find that seventeen of my respondents said they regularly returned to books they'd enjoyed in their childhood; particular favorites were *Catcher in the Rye*; *Watership Down*; *The Plague Dogs*; *That Was Then, This is Now*; *Forever*; *Where the Wild Things Are*; *The Secret Garden*; and "anything by Dr. Seuss."

6. Can you read books in noisy places (e.g., on trains and buses)?

I tend to be a very relaxed reader, able to lose myself in a book whatever the circumstances around me, but my friend Mark can't read anything, not even a newspaper, if there are people talking nearby (his new method is to wear a pair of Bose headphones and listen to white noise on his iPod). From the readers I interviewed, there seem to be more people like myself than like Mark. Only nine of my respondents said they couldn't read in noisy places. While many people said they preferred quiet, most people seem to have no problem tuning out external noise and absorbing themselves in their books. One person commented, "I have even read under shell fire. It kept the fear from becoming overwhelming."

A few people mentioned feeling uncomfortable and restless if they found themselves on public transportation without having a book to read. I know this feeling well. Since I'm lucky enough to be able to read pretty much anywhere, regardless of circumstance, and since books are a part of my academic work, I rarely leave home without something to dip in and out of during the day. Even if I'm going out for dinner or to a movie, there are still a few moments when I might find myself alone, waiting for a friend, or for the lights to go down, and it's difficult for me to simply sit still without getting restless. I read on the train and the subway—I can even read standing up, if it's not too crowded—and while walking down the street. Of course, I'll read in all the usual places, too—the little gaps in the day—in waiting rooms and in between appointments, and while eating lunch (I know, Mother, it's not polite).

For the most part, our notion of what reading is, and what it involves, still appears to be defined by the physical and economic restraints the reading process grew out of, from the texture of paper to the geography of libraries and bookstores. These notions generally depend on the material form of "real" books—but for some up-to-date types, these constraints no longer apply. None of my respondents said as much, but as I've noted, some people have moved away from "real" books, preferring to read books on their laptops or BlackBerrys, especially at work, when they can snatch only the occasional reading break. This is a natural side effect of our changing habits. We're busier than ever today, and, due to the increased pace of our lives, we tend to read in very short "spurts" compared to the readers of two or three generations ago. These days, when we pick up a book, it's usually for ten or fifteen minutes rather than an hour or so, a fact that some people attribute to the influence of the media, especially television, with its commercial breaks every twelve minutes and its six-second shots.

7. Can you remember if a book has ever made you laugh out loud, or shed tears? If so, please give examples.

Everyone I interviewed could remember laughing out loud while reading. Some could remember the book, and a few could even recall specific passages. *Portnoy's Complaint* and *Catch-22* got the most mentions, followed by *The Corrections*, *The World According to Garp*, *Bridget Jones's Diary*, *Fear and Loathing in Las Vegas*, *Much Ado About Nothing*; "anything by P. G. Wodehouse," "anything by Terry Pratchett," and *Marley and Me: My Life with the World's Worst Dog*. There were a few surprises here, too; for example, a psychiatrist confessed that she found herself laughing out loud at Dilbert cartoons and a book called *How to be a Jewish Mother*; and a fiction writer mentioned laughing out loud at his own work. Personally, I was surprised to realize that, although I often find things I read very funny, the pleasure always remains internal; I rarely laugh aloud at something I'm reading, unless it's being read to me by someone else who's laughing, and then I might join in, but it tends to be social or "performance" laughter. I'm sure I wouldn't laugh out loud at the same passage if I came across it myself.

Crying is a bit more complicated, since most people don't cry as readily as they laugh; there's more of a taboo about shedding tears, especially for men (although plenty of people happily admitted they'll "bawl at anything and everything"). Still, tears seem more permeable, more labile than laughter. If you're already upset, or grieving, or brokenhearted, the slightest thing can set you off, though some books will make you cry no matter what mood you're in (certain parts of *Lolita* do it to me every time). Twenty-six of my respondents (nineteen of them men) said that, while they know they've felt sad or emotionally moved by a book, they couldn't recall actually shedding tears. Others said they cry at "anything sentimental," or "anything involving animals suffering." Titles mentioned were eclectic, and included *The Pianist, Metamorphosis, A Child Called It, Jude the Obscure,* "the last few pages of *Finnegans Wake,*" *The Corrections, Little Women,* and *Marley and Me* (from the same person who said it made her laugh out loud). Personally, I'll never forget the odd experience of crying helplessly over *Beloved* while absolutely hating the book. I call it odd because, like most readers, I generally find the experience of crying over a book to be pleasurably cathartic.

A couple of men made interesting connections between passages that made them cry and their own emotional pressure points:

> The last two books that made me cry out loud were Coetzee's *Disgrace* and Chang-Rae Lee's *Aloft*. Now that I think about it, both are about the collapse of their patriarch protagonist's life-worlds; that probably says loads. Toward the end of *Aloft* I just couldn't take it anymore. I think it's the only time I had to take a few deep breaths before continuing to read.

> I remember crying when reading the end of Turgenev's *Fathers and Sons*. I found my mother finishing it in the kitchen one morning. She almost never read novels at this time. But here she was all red-eyed over this book. I read the novel after that. She handed it to me. I was about twenty-three then; I was having problems figuring out what to do in life, and I was butting heads with my father. I identified with the predicaments of the young men in the novel, the conflicts, and the complex bonds—sometimes unacknowledged—with the "fathers."

Of course, where you read is going to affect how you read. If you mostly read in public or semipublic places, and if you tend to read in ten or fifteen-minute intervals during your workday, then, unless you're a very gifted reader, it's going to be hard for you to get deeply involved in your book. If you're reading fiction, it's difficult to identify with characters and keep up with the nuances of a complex plot when you have to stop reading every few minutes, and not many of us feel comfortable laughing aloud or shedding tears in public. One reader confessed to feeling overcome at the closing chapter of *Brick Lane* by Monica Ali: "I was on the subway and had to stop reading it due to tears!" Another recalled, "At school we had an hour a week of private reading time. I remember bringing in Spike Milligan's war memoirs and being nearly thrown out of class because I couldn't read it without laughing."

8. Where do you buy most of your books? How much do you spend on books each year?

While online book buying seems to be more and more common, according to my survey, most people still also buy from bookstores, and even when buying online, prefer new books to used ones. A number of people commented on how much they used to enjoy hunting for bargains in secondhand bookstores, and how sad they felt that the Internet had "put an end to all that," since now "everybody knows exactly how much any book is worth." I was surprised to learn how little even the most prolific readers seem to spend on books (though it's also possible that people were underestimating their expenditures). Nobody, not even the academics, believed they spent more than $1,500 a year on books, and the average estimate was between $150 and $200. A lot of people said they rarely bought books at all, borrowing them instead from libraries, friends, and family, or relying on desk or review copies; a lot of other people said they get all their books from thrift stores, charity shops, swap meets, and library sales.

9. Do you use bookmarks, or dog-ear the pages of your books? Do you make marginal notes? If so, do you use pencil or pen?

Those who tend in the direction of fetishism responded to this question with expressions of mock (or perhaps genuine) outrage, perplexity, or disapproval ("Bah god no! . . . I'd seriously punch someone who dog-eared my books," "Turning pages down makes me cringe. NO MARGIN NOTES . . . Why would I make notes in the margins?" "Dog-earing is to be frowned upon. It is analogous to twisting the arm of a child").

Personally, as long as the book in question belongs to me, I have little restraint about dog-earing corners (but then, I'm often tempted to twist the arms of children). Since I buy my books used whenever possible, I also tend to make notes in the margins in pen, so basically, I'm with the person who said of his books, "I don't mind how they look, as long as they're stuck together." Surprisingly, we dog-earers are in the majority. Most people, including those you might expect to have fetishizing tendencies, like writers and literature professors, said they usually dog-ear page corners to keep their place, and often make notes in the margins. Others said they keep their place with bookmarks, Post-its, note cards, pens, pencils, loose book covers, hairpins, hatpins, subway cards, candy wrappers, sticky tabs, receipts, plane tickets, photographs, paper clips, or other idiosyncratic devices:

> I have these bookmarks that I make from torn pieces of paper . . . when I am finished with a book . . . it can have as many as forty of these bits of paper sticking out at the top—like some kind of headdress or rooster's comb. It's totally inefficient and ridiculous and I will probably never quit sticking these papers in.

For anyone interested in further reading on the subject, Nicholas Basbanes, in his latest work, *Every Book its Reader*, includes a long discussion of—among related topics—the habit of making marginal notes, of which the apparent master was the poet Samuel Taylor Coleridge. This is a topic also addressed by Ben Schott, of *Schott's Miscellany*, who in an article in the *New York Times Book Review* in March 2007 entitled "Confessions of a Book Abuser," draws the reader's attention to the marginalia of Pierre de Fermat, who in 1637 jotted in his copy of the *Arithmetica of Diophantus*, "I have a truly marvelous proof of this proposition that this margin is too narrow to contain." Without Fermat's marginal comments, Schott notes, mathematics would be considerably poorer—which highlights the ambivalent attitude libraries express toward such scribbling. Schott explains:

On the one hand, they quite properly object to people defacing their property. Cambridge University Library has a chamber of horrors displaying "marginalia and other crimes," including damage done by "animals, small children, and birds," not to mention the far from innocuous Post-it note. On the other hand, libraries cannot suppress a flush of pride on acquiring an ancient text "annotated" by someone famous. Like graffiti, marginalia acquires respectability through age (and, sometimes, wit).

Schott concludes by reassuring fellow dog-earers that treating books in a cavalier manner is not the beginning of the slippery slope to book-burning, that "the businessman who tears off and discards the chunk of John Grisham he has already read before boarding a plane may lack finesse, but he is not a Nazi." Reassuringly, he believes that "those who abuse their own books through manhandling or marginalia are often those who love books best," and "surely the dystopia of *Fahrenheit 451* is more likely avoided through the loving abuse of books than through their sterile reverence."

Still, anyone who reads a lot will probably recognize that, over the years, they've picked up a few funny habits, which makes it a bit easier to understand how some people come to be fussy about their books (Schott calls such people "biblioprudes"). Think carefully for a moment. Do you have any unusual tendencies while reading? For example, I have an odd habit—odd but perhaps not so unusual—of checking the page numbers every time I turn over a new leaf. I'm not sure what I'm checking for; just to be sure that they're in the right order, I suppose, though I've yet to come across any that aren't (and even if I did, what would I do then? Write a letter to the *Times*?). Also, I usually check how long the chapter is before I start it. I'm not exactly sure why I do this, though I suppose it has something to do with my need to be in control, since I find it very hard to stop reading at random. Books without chapters, or books with uneven chapters, annoy me very much, though it's unclear why I should turn myself over like this to the power of the book. After all, I could stop anywhere, wherever I wanted to (couldn't I . . . ?) Apparently, habits like these are not uncommon. As psychoanalyst James Strachey explains, "Even approximately normal people are sometimes overcome by a feeling that they have 'missed' something in a paragraph they have just been reading, and feel obliged to go through it again." He refers to two cases where this behavior had become obsessive. The first involved a man who had "the most terrible difficulties" reading, who "read with a pencil in his hand, and after going through each page with the utmost care and attention, and after convincing himself that he had understood it, he would put a tick at the bottom. He would then go through it again 'to confirm it' and put a cross stroke through the tail of the tick." The second involved a professional proofreader "who was perpetually haunted by the feeling of having 'missed' some misprint of a disastrous sort."

10. How quickly do you read? Do you skim through pages at top speed, or do you stop to savor the sentences along the way?

I'm sure we've all had the experience of not being able to put a book down, but for some people this seems to be the norm: "I will read a book obsessively in a single sitting, doing nothing else all day," said one person; another commented, "When I'm really reading a book, that's all I do until it's over!"

Personally, I've noticed that, with books I'm especially enjoying, I have a tendency to want to draw out the pleasure as long as I can by allowing myself only a few pages at a time, and reading with extra care, taking my time, enjoying the foreplay, as it were. But then, when I come to the last few chapters I find it hard to restrain myself, and once I know the end is in sight I charge ahead to the climax in one long session, unable to stop, rather like the way some people let themselves slurp, guzzle, and smack their lips when coming to the end of their dinner. Strachey has a lot to say about the oral components of reading, pointing out that "we speak of 'a voracious reader' or of 'an omnivorous reader'; of 'an unwholesome book' or of 'a stodgy book' or of a book being 'rather strong meat'; or, again, we talk of . . . finding a book 'indigestible', or of 'devouring' its pages."

And finally . . .

11. Where, and when, do you do your best reading?

When truly absorbed in a book, you're in an interesting kind of liminal zone between inner and outer worlds—awake but unaware, inwardly focused but, ideally, without the slightest bit of self-consciousness. The reader who's totally engrossed has no notion of time or place, no bodily sensations, no existence outside the book. This is why books can be so vital for those in dire circumstances—those who are bedridden, for example, or in prison or in the hospital. Books can remove you, however temporarily, from your current ordeal.

According to Freud, reading, like art and creative writing, is a kind of daydreaming, childish and retrogressive; those with happy, fulfilled, distracting lives should have no need to escape into fiction. But most readers seem to feel that, in moderation at least, fiction enhances their lives, making their time on earth richer and more interesting. Almost everyone who's in the habit of reading tries to carve out some time everyday to spend with a book, even if it's just a few minutes at night, before falling asleep. In fact, morning and night—the edges on both sides of the day—are the times most people seem to spend reading.

The etiquette of reading when you're not alone can be quite a touchy subject. Some people feel it's rude to read in company, and of course this is often true, but it all depends on the company, and on how comfortable you feel. For example, when you're in the first stages of a love affair, it would seem absolutely inconceivable to get out a book and read; you have no interest in anything except being with your lover. Even waiting in a bar or restaurant, you're a mass of nerves, hardly able to order a drink, unable to focus, incapable even of reading a menu. But there comes a time when there's nothing more natural than for you and your lover to spend the evening together absorbed in your separate books.

Getting to this stage, however, can be a delicate process. How many nights do you have to spend with a new lover before it's acceptable to reach out and take a book from the nightstand? In doing so, you're tacitly admitting you've reached a stage when your lover's presence is less interesting to you, at least for a while, than printed words on a page. It's a sensitive moment, not to be undertaken without a clear knowledge of the risks involved. Will your new lover recoil with dismay at your thoughtless indifference, or smile agreeably, and reach for a book too? And what if your lover reaches for a book too soon, too early in the relationship, before you're ready, before it feels right? Is there anything you can do? Should you say something, or should you just take it as a sign that the honeymoon is over?

And then, think about this: How many people do you know in whose company you'd feel comfortable losing yourself in a book? On one hand, it's hard to imagine any more blatant signal that you're not interested in other people's conversation, and there are times—if you took out your book during a dinner party, for example, or in the middle of a first date—when no other interpretation could be possible. In different circumstances, though, settling down with a book can show how completely at ease you are with somebody, feeling no obligation to make small talk, no need to stand upon ceremony.

The readers I interviewed came up with a wide variety of responses to the question of where they do their best reading, from the general ("anywhere," "at home," "on vacation") to the very specific ("lying on my BACK with my head propped up," "on the lounge chair with my feet up, something to drink, and a cigarette," "on a blanket or towel, in nature, with a glass of sauvignon blanc," "lying curled up on the sofa with my cat"). People seem to have all kinds of favorite spots for reading: "in the chair in my office," "at the pool," "in Starbucks," "on trains," "on the beach," "in my backyard, on a folding chair," "in the library," "in Central Park," "on planes," "on the sofa," "in my easy chair," "in the back seat of the car," "in coffeehouses," "in trees," "in the hot tub." And while lots of people freely admitted to reading in the bath, it's odd that nobody mentioned reading on the loo. They probably just didn't want to admit it. Strachey describes "the particular and widespread habit of reading while defecating," and recalls at least one case "in which 'something to read' was the *sine qua non* of successful defecation."

Psychoanalyst Edward Glover, in his "Notes on Oral Character Formation," refers to the common habit of reading oneself to sleep. "Sleep can in such instances," he writes, "be successfully wooed after a certain amount of reading. This amount varies considerably, but in certain cases a fixed dose is ingested regularly before sleep, a 'nightcap,' the directly oral equivalent of which is familiar to all." Whether at night or in the morning, most people seem to agree that the best place for intensive leisure reading is in bed. You can burrow down into the covers with your book or plump the pillows and sit up in your pj's like a dainty invalid. You can stretch out, curl up, or snuggle under the quilt. If you feel guilty about staying in bed, or if it makes you antsy to look at the clock, you can lie on top of the covers and do some leg lifts while you read. You can make a nice pot of tea for the bedside table (it's even better if you can get somebody to make it for you). Of course, there are other places that are more commonly associated with reading—airport lounges, long flights, and hospitals—but here we tend to read by necessity, as a way of passing the time, or to keep our minds off nasty things.

Lying stretched out in bed, everyone seems to agree, is the ideal place to read, the most conducive to immersion in the richness and complexity of another world.

THAT'S ALL HE DOES—READ, WRITE, AND READ,

AND SMOKE THAT NASTY PIPE WHICH STINKS:

HE NEVER TAKES THE SLIGHTEST HEED

HOW ANY OF US FEELS OR THINKS.

—JAMES THOMSON, "IN THE ROOM"

Chapter Three:
On the Shelf

Be totally honest for a moment—just between us. Have you ever pretended to be familiar with a work of literature you haven't actually read? Have you found yourself joining in conversations about Captain Ahab, Ophelia, or Leopold Bloom, without actually having read *Moby-Dick*, *Hamlet*, or *Ulysses*? Come on—I bet you have. If so, you're not alone. We've all done it, whether it's to impress a date by agreeing with them about the latest Philip Roth, or to appear blasé by arguing that Dickens is overrated, though we may never have managed to finish one of his novels. It's odd how many otherwise honest, decent people should feel so insecure about what they haven't read that they're willing to lie about it. What for? You wouldn't pretend to know your way around Chicago if you've never been there, or to have tasted ostrich eggs if you've never had the chance.

But then, there's no social assumption that knowing your way round Chicago makes you a more educated person, or that to be truly cultured, you "ought" to have tasted ostrich eggs. When it comes to literature, it's a different matter. "Classics" like *Moby-Dick*, *Hamlet*, and *Ulysses* are generally considered to be works that all smart, sophisticated people "ought" to have read. And, since most of us like to think of ourselves as smart and sophisticated, we feel we "ought" to have read them, as well.

If your best friend has just finished a great book and thinks you'd enjoy it too, she'll say you've "got to" read it, or you'll "love" reading it, or you "have to" read it, which all suggest the experience will be pleasurable. But when somebody tells you there's a book you "ought" to read, it usually means something rather different. "Ought" is used for obligations, things you feel you should do, despite your inclinations: You want to wear pink but you "ought" to wear black; you want bacon and eggs for breakfast, but you "ought" to have granola. In most cases, these are things you need to do for your own good, even though you might not want to. You "ought" to say thank you; you "ought" to call your mother; you "ought" to get going.

Books you feel you "ought" to read aren't usually books you expect to enjoy, in the short term, at least. Rather, they're books that will be "good for you" to have read in the long run; they'll make you more educated, more sophisticated—or, at least, they'll make you feel that way, which is almost as good. Books you think you "ought" to read are usually books you once started but

didn't finish, books you were supposed to read for a literature class but bought the CliffsNotes for instead, or books some well-meaning friend bought for you that you've never got round to reading, though they look impressive on your shelf. In each case, if they were really compelling, don't you think you'd have read them long ago?

Let me make it plain: There are no books you "ought" to read. Take my advice—if it bores you, if you don't get it, if it puts you to sleep or gives you a headache, put it down and read something else instead. Even this book: If you're not interested, stop reading right now! Put it down, get your money back, give it to a friend, or toss it out of the window. Honestly, I won't mind. There's no point forcing you to read something you don't find engaging. The truth is, if you're not interested in what you read, you'll get nothing out of it, and you'll probably forget it the moment you've finished. What have you got to gain from struggling to read something against your will? Maybe you'll be able to catch a reference to the book if it's mentioned in a movie or play; maybe you'll be able to hold your own at a fancy dinner party, but then, you could probably do the same thing by just reading the back cover. And let's face it, these days no one's going to be less successful or looked down upon because they haven't read *War and Peace*.

Most of the books people think they "ought" to read are those works generally known as "literary classics." These books have a reputation for being difficult to engage with, but it's important to remember that most "classics" were written for a very different age from ours, and for very different readers from you and me. Before the twentieth century, fiction was the main form of public entertainment (and even then, only a few people had access to it). There was, needless to say, no TV, no movies, and no Internet, and very few people actually owned books. What we now call "classic" novels were generally published in installments, or in magazines, so, like today's soap operas, they could be drawn out for as long as they held the public's attention. As a result, they couldn't be closely structured in advance; "plot" (as we know it now) was far less central than it is today, which helps explain why, used to the fast pace of modern media, many people get bored with "classic" fiction, just as they find it difficult to get into silent movies or films with subtitles. It doesn't mean they're less smart; it just means they're used to a different pace and style.

For readers today, it's a lot more difficult to get hooked by one of these "classics" than by modern writing; their slow, gradual unfolding demands the kind of time and attention few busy people are willing to devote to a relaxing, recreational activity like reading fiction. So the only time most of us ever read these books, or try to read them, is at school or college, when they're "assigned reading" in mandatory English courses. It's often said that being made to read literature in the classroom kills the joy of it. What's less often discussed is how many people continue to harbor guilt and shame about books they've never read (and to bluff about reading them, too).

Have you ever wondered why these books are supposed to be so brilliant, when you've tried to read them, and found they neither hook you in, nor inspire your curiosity, nor foster your pleasure, nor get you involved, nor keep you engaged? Perhaps you've decided that reading "classic" fiction is one of those cultural experiences, like opera, ballet, or avant-garde theater, in which, to really appreciate its subtleties, you have to be an expert, a real connoisseur, because obviously, there are people who (claim to) find these books riveting, compelling, and impossible to put down. And these people can't all be bluffing, can they?

CAN they??

Well, not all of them, but some might be. There's a scene in David Lodge's campus novel *Changing Places* in which a group of English professors, after too many drinks, plays a game they call "Humiliation," in which each person names a book he hasn't actually read (but assumes all the others have), and scores a point for every person who's read it. In other words, the winner is the person who humiliates himself the most. One of the eminent highbrows reveals that he's never read Longfellow's "Hiawatha"; another confesses he's never been able to get through Milton's epic poem "Paradise Regained." The titles get more and more familiar, but the game only ends when one of them, in a moment of drunken honesty, slams down his palm on the table and yells, "*Hamlet!*" He wins the game, of course, but the next day the news creeps out, ending up as a brief item in the university newspaper, and before long the sheepish professor has been turned down for tenure and forced to resign.

While the scene is obviously exaggerated, like most comedy, it hits on an important truth, which is that nobody's read everything, even English professors, and it's very common for people to give the impression—even to genuinely believe—they've read far more than they actually have. A lot of literary knowledge is picked up by accretion; you don't actually have to have read "Paradise Regained," or "Hiawatha," or even *Hamlet*, to be familiar with their plots, characters, and perhaps a few of their famous lines. Similarly, lots of fictional characters have passed into public consciousness

as archetypes, metaphors, or embodiments of particular kinds of behavior. By calling somebody a "Scrooge" or a "Don Juan," you're not actually claiming to have read the works by Dickens or Molière that feature these characters, just as you wouldn't assume someone who described their ex-boyfriend as a "Lothario" would necessarily be familiar with Nicholas Rowe's *The Fair Penitent*, the little-known 1703 Restoration drama in which this character appears.

While some people are very conscious of gaps in their literary knowledge, many others are not. In fact, they're often convinced they've read something even when they haven't, or haven't REALLY, which raises the question of what it actually means to have "read" a book. Not all the books we read stay with us, perhaps not even most of them, and if you've read a book but can't remember anything about it, how can you be sure you've "really" read it? Lionel Trilling once famously told Edward Said that he thought the Columbia University humanities core, one of the early "great books" curricula, "has the virtue of giving Columbia students a common basis in reading, and if they later forgot the books (as many always do) at least they would have forgotten the same ones."

I remember feeling terribly proud of myself in college for managing to "read" the whole of Edmund Spenser's *The Faerie Queene*—over a thousand interminable-seeming pages of it—but while I may have sat at my desk with the book in front of me, taken in each word with my eyes, and turned over every page, I remember so little about it that to say I've "read" it means nothing at all. (I'm not alone; when he was reading English at Oxford, poet Philip Larkin wrote the following note in his college library copy of *The Faerie Queene*: "First I thought *Troilus and Criseyde* was the most boring poem in English. Then I thought *Beowulf* was. Now I know that *The Faerie Queene* is the dullest thing out.") On the other hand, there are certain books I can remember so well that, even many years later, I can still recall the texture of the paper, the font, and the look of certain passages on the page.

A few years ago, when discussing Nabokov's *Lolita* in an undergraduate class, I was momentarily taken aback when one of my students, in defense of Humbert Humbert, mentioned all the gifts he bought Lolita, including a trunk full of clothes, a bicycle, and a DVD.

Wait . . . a DVD?

"*The Little Mermaid*," she reminded me, indicating the reference on her page, highlighted in fluorescent pink. She was right, Humbert does buy Lolita a copy of *The Little Mermaid* for her birthday, but it's not a DVD, it's a book by Hans Christian Andersen, "a de luxe volume with commercially 'beautiful' illustrations." I was a bit shocked to realize that my student knew *The Little Mermaid* only as an animated Disney movie, but I've had so many similar experiences since then that I'm starting to get used to them. Not long ago, one of my smartest students asked me if she could write a paper on "the character of the Cheshire Cat"; when I agreed, I didn't realize that, knowing nothing of Lewis Carroll, she was planning to write about a Disney cartoon. Just a few weeks ago, when I asked my freshman students what they thought of "The Courtship of Mr. Lyon," Angela Carter's updated retelling of the Beauty and the Beast myth, a number of them accused her indignantly of "plagiarizing from the movie."

Simply put, the students I teach are far more familiar with movies than with books—and why not? It's through movies that most people today come to know literary "classics." Many more people watch films than read books; in fact, cinema today is what literature was to the readers of earlier centuries: the most accessible form of culture (I'd probably have a much better memory of *The Faerie Queene* if they'd made it into a film). I'd far prefer my students were familiar with a movie version of something than not knowing it at all. It works both ways—I was pleasantly surprised, not long ago, when my whole class proved coolly knowledgeable about the history of Troy (they'd just seen the Brad Pitt movie, it turned out)—a nice contrast to the student who, when I asked him which Dickens he'd read, replied confidently: "Charles."

If you can manage to get hooked by a classic novel, by all means go ahead and read it, but if not, remember, you can always watch the movie. There are some tremendous film versions available, like *The Little Mermaid*, on DVD. My personal favorites include Robert Z. Leonard's *Pride and Prejudice*, Stanley Kubrick's *Barry Lyndon*, Jack Conway's *A Tale of Two Cities*, and James Ivory's *Howard's End*. There are also some great television adaptations you can order from Netflix, including first-rate versions of the best-known works of Charles Dickens, Jane Austen, George Eliot, and E. M. Forster, all particularly recommended for anybody who's having trouble with the originals.

Some especially interesting movies have been made from the works of Shakespeare. While Shakespeare's poetry is the best of its kind, I know a lot of people find the archaic language difficult to understand, and this often prevents them from appreciating its power. If you have a problem with Shakespeare, I suggest you pick up a modern translation, and then, once you've got a sense of the plot (not a difficult task—Shakespeare isn't really about the plot), find a good movie version to get a feel for the language, then try the original again. Particular favorites of mine—all loyal to the word and spirit of the original, and visually compelling in their own right—are Franco Zeffirelli's dark *Hamlet*, Roman Polanski's blood-drenched *Macbeth*, Michael Radford's lavish *Merchant of Venice*, and Julie Taymor's apocalyptic *Titus*.

much ado about nothing

There are lots of reasons why people believe in books you "ought" to read, but I suspect most of them come down to intellectual insecurity, snobbery, residual class anxieties, egotism, and a kind of superstitious folklore rooted in tradition and nationalism, reinforced by cultural and academic turf wars, and played out in school and college curricula. When I was "reading" English at Oxford, for example, the syllabus seemed designed around notions of "English" and "literature" that seemed to have been provided by the English heritage industry. Chronologically, the curriculum ran—as they put it—from *Beowulf* to Virginia Woolf, ending around 1930, and if you weren't English, you weren't on the list. The definition of "English" was nonnegotiable, by the way. Even "naturalized colonials" made it only by the skin of their teeth, depending on how "English" they were considered to be; so Henry James and T. S. Eliot were acceptable, but Ezra Pound was out.

You could spend your whole life reading classics—in fact, some people do—but it's not enough just to read avidly, you should also read widely. Otherwise, you run the risk of getting stuck in a rut, arrested at a certain stage in your development, with the corresponding danger that your own writing could remain a frozen replica of those early models.

The books we read at Oxford were supposed to be the "best" English literature, which meant, by implication, literature itself. At nineteen, I believed what they told me, unaware of how narrowly the subject was being defined. Only after two years of mandatory courses, including Anglo-Saxon grammar, were we finally allowed a choice of "special topics"—a choice that included, among various other options, "American literature from its beginnings to the present day." I went for it, and was enormously surprised to learn that America had its own literary history, as rich and complex as the "English" canon I knew. I began to understand that what I'd believed to be the only kind of literature there was, or the only kind that mattered, was actually only one variety among a near-infinite number of others. It was as though I'd been living on bread and jam all my life, and, believing there to be nothing else to eat, I'd cultivated a connoisseur's palate for subtle distinctions between different varieties of bread and flavors of jam—and then I'd suddenly stumbled into Harrods Food Hall.

I reacted by going to the opposite extreme, and reading nothing but the antithesis of the "classics" that made up the genteel Oxford curriculum. Like lots of other twenty-one-year-olds, I fell in love with Jack Kerouac's *On the Road*—not part of our syllabus, needless to say. Under the mad spell of Dean Moriarty, I urged myself to make up for lost time, to try everything, to live only in the truth of experience. I devoted myself to the quest for adventure, looking for people who could bring me closer to world-waking enlightenment. I'd never known books like this, literature that was both transcendent and worldly at the same time, packed with combustible truths loaded into a cannon of speeding words and FIRED. I hadn't been raised according to any religion, had hardly ever been to church, but *On the Road* made me realize that reading could be a transcendent experience, an opening of the spirit. The Oxford dons may have turned up their noses at Kerouac, but I didn't care. I couldn't imagine a more essential, more important book than this romantic hymn to the intoxicating pleasures of experience.

Still, compared to those of Dean Moriarty, my own adventures were pretty tame; I was still spending most of my time in the library. I did, however, manage to get myself a boyfriend, who'd also been ruined by reading, and he introduced me to all his favorite authors—William Burroughs, Jean Genet, the Marquis de Sade. His favorite book was *Last Exit to Brooklyn*, Hubert Selby Jr.'s raw, concentrated account of life on the New York streets. I read it and thought it was horrible and depraved; before long, it was my favorite, too. On first reading, I was shocked and galvanized by Selby's jagged, fragmented prose; on second reading, I came to see how carefully he'd stitched together these devastating tales of poverty, homelessness, prostitution, and brutality in the slums of postwar Brooklyn. The scenes of violence were so horribly real I couldn't read them without cringing in disgust, which had never happened with my Gothic novels. This kind of awfulness was true to life: a soldier getting crushed, beaten, and run over by a car just for fun; a transvestite groveling for affection; a man beating his wife just because she's a woman; a prostitute gang-raped and left for dead in the shell of an old car.

I suddenly felt as though I'd been living like a hermit, cloistered away reading nothing but Jane Austen and Emily Brontë. *Last Exit* was a kind of literature I'd never encountered before, never heard of. I found it profane and sublime at the same time, both terrible and poignant, but I knew immediately that it was as important and valuable as any other kind. It was a compendium of horror stories, but where the horror stories I was used to reading elevated their nastiness into something lofty and supernatural, *Last Exit* did the opposite, making ordinary people into human scapegoats, deliberately grinding your face into the dirt. It was like a veil lifting; it was a true revelation to me, that filth could also be sublime.

metamorphosis

With so many new books out there, why should anyone feel guilty about not having read the old ones? And why do the ranks of "classics" never seem to change?

These questions have vexed a lot of people for a long time. Some of the blame, it's true, rests with college reading lists, but to be fair, even in English departments, people no longer agree that there are certain books you "ought" to read, books that are more "valuable" than others, books that will enhance your social status, or make you a more well-rounded person. In most colleges these days, the notion of "great books" is mired in ideological struggles, and conflicts over race, class, and gender. Nevertheless, despite their reputation for liberal bias, English departments as a rule are obviously invested in the idea of a literary tradition based on certain difficult novels accessible only to a select, elite few. When, in 2003, Oprah announced that her book club would, in the future, be focusing solely on the "classics," the academic response was quite condescending, perhaps because the first books she chose—*Anna Karenina, East of Eden, As I Lay Dying*—were underscored by a tragic vision that conspicuously clashed with Oprah's upbeat, self-help ethos.

Still, it's not only universities that perpetuate the idea of books you "ought" to read. In the world of publishing, the "classics"—those impressive-looking volumes with scholarly introductions and period paintings on the front—are big business, and, more important, they're business that lasts. "Classics" from the past continue to be published because they're still making serious money, especially when they've recently been made into a Hollywood heritage picture starring Jeremy Irons, Hugh Grant, Kate Winslet, or the latest exportable Brit with straightened teeth. This explains the enormous range of editions on offer, from the fancy Oxfords and Nortons, with their introductory essays, annotations, and watercolors on the front, and the Penguins with their new covers by prominent graphic novelists, to the Wordsworths and Dovers at $5 a pop or less. In 2002, Jane Austen's *Pride and Prejudice* sold

110,000 copies, according to Nielsen BookScan (which excludes academic sales from its calculations, which means the numbers aren't inflated by all those reluctant students buying copies for their courses). In the long run, these sales are far greater than the best-sellers of any particular year, which are taken down from the store displays as soon as their brief moment of glory has passed. The shelves of "classics," however, carry the same books year in and year out, with no copyright fees to be paid, and a consistently high level of demand.

Since these books will always be read, will always stay on reading lists, and are praised far more often than they're disparaged, I want to put in a brief word of support for the devil's party, and warn you about some "classics" that are often required reading in college literature courses—books that I've read (or, at least, tried to read, usually more than once), and that, in my opinion, are generally unsatisfying, overrated, and unlikely to provide you with much more than a headache; in short, just between us, I've never understood why they're meant to be such a big deal. Fair warning: These are my own transitory, idiosyncratic, personal opinions; I'm offering them up in the hope that they'll inspire you to take your own approach to "the classics," and, perhaps, to free you from any residual guilt about books you haven't read.

First of all, it's important to remember that most of the ancient historical works touted as "classics" are, in fact, a pretty random selection of oddities that you're required to study purely because, through various accidents of circumstance, they happen to have survived. Their importance is historical, not literary; they have a lot to tell us about their time, but in my experience, that's not what most people are looking for in a work of fiction. You should also bear in mind that the notion of "originality" is a fairly modern one. Before the Enlightenment, all the best-known literature involved the retelling of well-known myths and legends, not the creation of new characters and plots.

If you're in college, you might be required to read some of these ancients—Sophocles, Aristophanes, Virgil, Ovid, Plato, and the like. Most readers find these authors a bit of a drag, though they might not admit it; some people even claim to find them funny, which is a bit hard to swallow. They tend to be best appreciated by philosophy professors, and perhaps by people who enjoy watching the History Channel. To the modern ear, the style of these writers seems heavy and repetitive; their idiom is so restricted, and their turns of phrase so predictable, that even in the most up-to-date translations they end up sounding like barren, senile versions of Dr. Seuss. Remember, most classical works are highly ritualized forms of writing, generally composed of action and dialogue, without commentary or analysis. If you're required to read one of these books and you really can't stand it, try picking up a copy of the CliffsNotes (or, if you're brave enough, distract your teacher with a discussion of why you're being asked to read this particular book, and exactly what you're supposed to be getting out of it).

I managed to get away without too much suffering over the ancient Greeks and Romans, but England has ancients enough of its own, though

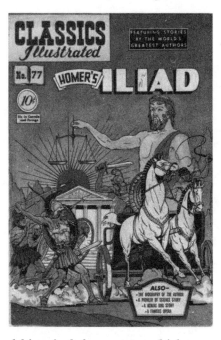

not as many. So few pieces of writing exist from Anglo-Saxon times that students are made to study any old rubbish. At least, that's how it seemed when I was at college; I sometimes think we'd have been asked to analyze King Arthur's laundry list, had it survived. Don't worry if you've never been able to get your teeth into *Beowulf*, *The Anglo-Saxon Chronicles*, *The Life of King Alfred*, *The Battle of Maldon*, or whatever else they ask you to read these days, because you're really not missing much; again, the importance of these works lies in their role as social and historical documents, which you can learn about without actually reading them. ("I can just about stand learning the filthy lingo it's written in," Philip Larkin wrote to his friend Kingsley Amis when they were undergraduates studying Old English at Oxford. "What gets me down is being expected to ADMIRE the bloody stuff.") The same goes for Middle English, including cringe-inducing Chaucer. The "Prologue" has some interesting little vignettes, it's true, but much of *The Canterbury Tales* is—let's be frank—tacky and vulgar, full of undeserved cuckolding and barbaric, ribald misogyny, like a medieval-themed episode of *The Benny Hill Show*. Malory can be interesting in parts, as poetry, but there are plenty more readable versions of the *Morte D'Arthur*, including T. H. White's Arthurian fantasy, *The Once and Future King*.

Can't stand poetry? Don't be ashamed to admit it; you're not alone. Sometimes it seems as though the only people who read poetry for pleasure are those who write it themselves. There's nothing wrong with poetry, of course—it can be tremendously meaningful when it works for you, when you find something that you really GET, but even then, it's best saved for special, private moments, when you've had a few drinks, maybe, and you're feeling thoughtful and lonely. Keep your favorite poetry books close by, on the table by your bed, to dip in and out of when you feel like it, not to read from cover to cover. My two personal rules for reading poetry are (i) the shorter the better; and (ii) let it rhyme. As for epic poetry, it's not impossible to read Milton and Spenser—in fact, it's quite manageable in short spurts, but once you've got the gist of it, there's no reason to plough through the whole thing unless you feel absolutely compelled, or want to impress somebody over cocktails. And speaking of cocktails, a lot of epic poetry produces the same kind of blackout as certain strong drinks—the morning after, you can't remember anything about it. Let's not forget that even one of the greatest readers of literature, Samuel Johnson, felt that "*Paradise Lost* is one of the books which the reader admires and puts down, and forgets to take up again. None ever wished it longer than it is."

As for the "classic" novels, some are just downright overrated. I've always felt that *Don Quixote*—considered by Harold Bloom still the "best novel ever written"—should be removed from all college reading lists. The first volume in particular is dull and meandering, reheating old stories from chivalric romance. It's really tough for today's reader to get absorbed in what is essentially a very basic plot, full of irrelevant, extraneous digressions that have nothing to do with the main characters and events. Even worse, whenever things start to get interesting, they always seem to be interrupted by one of Quixote's long, pedantic discourses on the virtues of chivalry. When Cervantes was writing, the novel form was still at such a primitive stage of development that no character's thoughts are ever internalized; every observation is spoken out loud, leading to page after page of conversation and interpretation, which quickly becomes tiring and hard to follow. On top of all this, the two horses—Quixote's poor old nag Rocinante, and Sancho Panza's nameless donkey—are constantly whipped and thrashed for no reason at all through the entire eight hundred pages, and I'm not sure why that's supposed to be funny.

But then, even when they don't contain cruelty to animals, early novels seem generally coarse to modern readers; it's hard for people today to get involved in implausible adventures like those recounted in eighteenth-century novels such as *Moll Flanders, Clarissa, Pamela,* and *Tom Jones.* Instead of the plot-based page-turners we're used to, these early novels are based on the model of the mock epic, explicitly undercutting and making fun of earlier, classical models, with which modern readers usually aren't familiar. In these

novels, plausibility isn't the point; the point is HOW each particular event happens. As with *Don Quixote,* English picaresque tales like *Tom Jones* tend to be heavy on commentary; the action is frequently interrupted by long digressions about art, philosophy, or politics. At the time these would have been regarded as a sign of additional respectability, but to the modern reader, they often signify a part you can skip without missing any action. I've never really gotten the point of *Tristram Shandy,* either, a book that was originally designed not as a novel, but a series of comic sermons. Its jokes and references are lost on me, perhaps because, in the opinion of author and critic Jane Smiley, "*Tristram Shandy* may be the most masculine novel ever written." In fact, in my opinion, the English novel doesn't really get interesting until Jane Austen, but some people find her scope too narrow, her style too genteel. Her works, as she herself described them, are like miniatures painted on ivory; her interest is not in depth or breadth, but in detail and precision.

Most of the Russian novelists—Tolstoy, Gogol, Chekhov, Dostoevsky— are too heavy and dour for readers today, too focused on the nature of "Russianness" and Russian history, though some people really love them (and not only Russians). Over time, I've come to understand and appreciate the shorter works of these writers (despite all those peasants, who always annoy me), but I'll never consider them page-turners, and until now, I've found the really enormous ones too intimidating a prospect (though I finally managed to finish *War and Peace*). Recently, however, feeling I "ought" to be at least familiar with *The Brothers Karamazov*, I tried listening to an audio version while I was driving. Be warned: This is definitely not the way to approach a long, difficult novel, especially one like *Karamazov*, which, in order to be fully appreciated, demands deep and prolonged exposure to the narrative *weltanschauung*. I drifted in and out, more out than in; I was put off by the story's forbidding scope and heaviness, its lack of wit and energy, not to mention the annoying way the reader pronounced the word "monk" (with a short "o," to rhyme with "honk"). Plus, I kept getting the characters mixed up. It's a real cliché, I know, but those Russian names are impossible, especially when you can't see them written down. I knew there were three variants of each name: the full name, the shortened version, and the nickname, but I'd still get confused. I couldn't stop thinking of Ivan and Vanya as two different characters; the same with Alexei and Alyosha. Scenes between two or three people would suddenly seem to be filled with a huge crowd, or someone would use a new variant of a nickname and I'd wonder where this new person had come from all of a sudden. It wasn't easy going. There were eight volumes, with six tapes in each volume. I didn't finish it. Somebody actually stole the last volume from the backseat after breaking the rear window of my car (remember, Baltimore is "The City That Reads")—and frankly, they were welcome to it.

Nineteenth-century literature is far more interesting as a whole, but still very limited; when people talk about the "Victorian novel," they're not usually talking about the period's women writers, but an intimidating set of English patriarchs, including Dickens, Gissing, Scott, Thackeray, Trollope, and Galsworthy. These authors are all very different, of course, and not at all *sui generis* (Trollope, whose work is never overly comic or melodramatic, called Dickens "Mr. Popular Sentiment" and thought he was pandering to the middle classes), but they have a number of things in common. Most significantly, beyond entertaining the reader, they're really interested in exploring daily life in nineteenth-century British society, through all its different classes and social levels, from the aristocracy and landed gentry to ordinary working folk. This ambition can sometimes lead to a tendency to deal in types rather than "real people," with the result that the reader can feel distanced from them. For example, despite all his emotional intensity and stylistic dexterity, Dickens has been widely criticized for his excess of sentiment, his use of melodrama, and his lack of psychological insight; his more broadly drawn characters can seem disconnected from life, which means we don't care about them as much. If plausibility and realism of character are more important to you than plot and style, you might find Dickens tough going. Bear in mind, too, that many of these authors wrote for serial publications (so you couldn't skip forward) and were paid by the word, so there always seems to be a hundred or so pages of every Victorian novel that a judicious editor would excise—subplots, digressions, minor "comic" characters, and page after page of details so dense and heavy that reading them can feel like wading through quicksand.

George Eliot is readable, but, like many other Victorian novelists, less interested in character psychology than in recounting details of day-to-day life at a certain place and time, implying that personality is limited and determined by social circumstances. Her particular focus is small town, agrarian life in the English Midlands in the years leading up to the 1832 Reform Act and the onset of the Industrial Revolution. It's useful to be aware that the strong points of novels like *Middlemarch* and *The Mill on the Floss* aren't to be found in character development, structure, or a lively, suspenseful plot, but in Eliot's social consciousness, the way she plays up the importance of hard work and a good nature, as well as virtue and morality. Personally, I find Eliot rather dry and unrewarding; she's a highly intellectual storyteller, a moralist rather than a psychologist, a trait she shares with Nathaniel Hawthorne, though Hawthorne's sensibility is thoroughly male. Despite his flat and dogmatic style, Hawthorne seems to be a perennial favorite in college English in the U.S.; I've been told it's hard to make it through college without someone asking you to read at least *The Scarlet Letter*, if not also *The House of the Seven Gables* and *The Marble Faun*—novels that I also find to be overrated; it's useful to remember they were far less popular in their day than they seem to be now.

Henry James is one of those tastes that adults acquire, like olives or anchovies. It's important to bear in mind that his main interest lies less in people than perspective, meaning the structured arrangement of characters' viewpoints in a series of carefully framed vignettes. One constant criticism that readers have made about James is that he's more interested in the integrity of form than development of character or movement of plot. He seems to be fascinated by abstractions, considering concrete

"...they were far less popular in their day than they seem to be now."

details beneath his dignity; his novels can be forbidding if you can't get used to his refined, metaphorical style.

When you get to the modern period, if you expect things to get more interesting as a matter of course, you're in for a big letdown. It took me quite a while to realize that a lot of twentieth-century novels are not novels at all, but something else wearing a novel's overcoat—philosophy, rhetoric, or an experiment in style. These works can be fascinating, and are often insightful and revealing, but don't expect to enjoy them the way you might enjoy a more familiar kind of book. I've never been able to get very excited about D. H. Lawrence, for example, who fundamentally strikes me as a man writing for other men. Short stories like "The Fox," "The Ladybird," and "The Rocking-Horse Winner" are difficult to escape, since they're so often anthologized, but I find them much more interesting than *Sons and Lovers* and *Women in Love*, which aren't actually novels so much as explorations of the morality, ideology, and politics of bourgeois life. In Virginia Woolf, this model is turned inside out; books like *Mrs. Dalloway* and *To the Lighthouse* focus not on social critique, or on any external circumstances at all, but only the dynamics of individual consciousness.

With "difficult" modernist writers like Woolf and (especially) James Joyce, the point of their work isn't so much to trace a linear plot than to travel through a single character's interior landscape, as they ruminate on a series of thoughts and events. Sometimes, as in *Finnegans Wake*, the style is deliberately structured to call attention to itself, and to the artificial nature of language in general, functioning as a sort of self-referential commentary on the idea that fiction somehow "represents" reality. *Finnegans Wake* is notoriously difficult; it's filled with obscure references and unclear allusions—appropriate for a novel meant to imitate a restless dream—and written in a highly abstract, nonlinear style. There's kind of mock grandeur about Joyce, too, as there is in the eighteenth-century picaresque, only in this case, the effect is more tragic than comic, as in *Ulysses*, where the most elegant and digressive narrative methods are applied to an ordinary day in the life of an ordinary man.

Some people believe that the best writing should, ideally, be invisible, like a clear pane of glass, allowing you to see straight through it to the events unfolding "on the other side." This is a good analogy for certain kinds of writing, like news reporting and journalism, but it doesn't hold true in every case. Sometimes the point isn't so much to tell you "what happened" as to explore or draw attention to something, like language itself, or the relation between writing and consciousness, or the failure of words, as in the plays of Samuel Beckett or David Mamet. A lot of modern writers, including playwrights like Eliot, Brecht, and Pinter, as well as novelists like William Burroughs, Thomas Pynchon, and Stanley Elkin, are often less interested in the traditional elements of their form than in juggling words and ideas, often weaving their themes into a complicated web of allusions and inferences, involving a very high level of abstraction, with no single character, image, or incident separable from the work as a whole. Think of them less as linear "stories" than as pieces of classical music, containing a variety of subtle themes and variations that ebb and flow as the work unfolds.

For many people, whether they go to college or not, once they've had the trauma of grappling with a painful "classic" at an early age, they never want to look at it again—or anything else of its kind. It's a sad truth that far too many "classic" (mostly Victorian) works generally considered "children's books," like those advertised in the *New York Post* promotion I described in my introduction, are truly appreciated only by sophisticated adults. If you read any of these books as a child, however you felt about them at the time (even if you loved them), I suggest you give them a second reading from an adult point of view: *Robinson Crusoe, Frankenstein, A Christmas Carol, Moby-Dick, Alice in Wonderland* and *Through the Looking Glass, Treasure Island, Dr. Jekyll and Mr. Hyde, The Jungle Book*, and anything by Edgar Allan Poe. There are also plenty of adult books that are best appreciated by children—but that's another story.

Despite what your English teacher may have told you, if a book doesn't really absorb you, you shouldn't be reading it—at least, not right now. You should only read books that give you pleasure. If you're feeling doubtful, here's a word of advice (and this applies to all books, not only "classics"): Make yourself a personal rule about the number of pages you're willing to give a book before you abandon it. For me, it's about sixty pages. I've learned that's enough time for me to get used to an author's style, to let myself be drawn in if I'm going to be, even if I'm not fully engaged at first. Your boredom threshold may be lower than mine, or you may be more tolerant; your rule might be arbitrary to begin with, but try to be aware, and

you'll soon come to have a sense of how much time it takes for you to settle in. Only YOU can decide what it means for you to be "hooked." Maybe it means you're merely curious enough to keep going; maybe it means you just can't stop reading. But if you apply your rule across the board, and give all books a fair chance, you should never feel you've abandoned a book you "ought" to have finished, and you can always go back to a book a few years later. After all, it will always be there on your shelf, waiting for you to try again, when you're ready for it. This way, when anyone asks, you can truthfully say, "Galsworthy? I've given him a try, but I'm afraid he's simply not my cup of tea."

So if there are no books you "ought" to read, are there any books you "ought not" to read? Are trashy mass-market paperbacks really just as "good for you" as literary fiction?

Or are they even better?

AT LAST THE SECRET IS OUT, AS IT ALWAYS MUST COME IN THE END,

THE DELICIOUS STORY IS RIPE TO TELL TO THE INTIMATE FRIEND.

—*W. H. AUDEN, "AT LAST THE SECRET IS OUT"*

iv. behind the scenes

In his book *The Story Species: Our Life-Literature Connection*, literary historian Joseph Gold argues that the ability to understand narrative—including the stories we tell about ourselves—is first and foremost a "species survival tool," unique to human beings. His basic argument is that storytelling has a role in human biology, namely "to foster diversity, build identity, support balance, nurture adaptation, and assist survival." By tracing the history of storytelling from oral traditions to the time of modern media, Gold makes the case that reading fiction is now in danger of being marginalized as an obscure, elite art, or a threat to the many forces that would discourage complex and independent thought. Never before, argues Gold, has the need for fiction been so great, or its ability to assist been so necessary, because never before has culture been so homogenized, and never before has the media had so much influence on individual identity.

These are all salient arguments. Reading can definitely help you understand people's inner experience, make meaning out of chaos, develop empathy, and encourage independent thought. But whenever the benefits of reading are trumpeted in this way, there's always an assumption, sometimes stated, often implicit, that "reading" really means "reading literature." Those who proclaim that reading is "good for you" rarely stop to explain why they think literature alone generates all these incredible capacities, rather than, say, genre fiction. Do Harlequin romances, for example, also teach us to generate empathy, to foster independent thought, to encourage meaning making and to develop all those other abundant virtues most often attributed exclusively to the holy grail of pure LITERATURE?

I don't see why not. If you enjoy what you read, I don't think you shouldn't feel guilty about it. I've never liked the phrase "guilty pleasure." I've noticed people use it to describe enjoying things they feel are "beneath them," things that are out of sync with how they perceive themselves. It's as wrong-headed, I think, as the idea of a split between "entertainment" and "education," as though something can only be one or the other, and never both at the same time. The books you read shouldn't embarrass you. I know it's a commonplace, but don't forget that Shakespeare and Dickens were the pop culture of their day. Today's genre fiction, partly because it's so easily overlooked, often contains original and radical perspectives on what's wrong with modern culture—the kind of progressive critiques of religion and government which, when concealed within the covers of a "bestseller," can have a forceful impact by sneaking under the radar of critical commentary. The popular success of Dan Brown's *The Da Vinci Code* is a good example; its heretical slant on Catholicism has gone widely unchallenged. It's often assumed that because a book is "entertaining" it can't also contain serious issues, and as a result there's more of a division today between "bestsellers" and "literary fiction" than at virtually any other time in history. When was the last time a literary prize was awarded to a genre novel? There's a lot of snobbery today about the cultural influence of "literary fiction," when, in fact, popular writing regularly exerts a far greater influence on the ordinary reader than any other kind.

To take just one example, fans of fantasy are often described, dismissively, as people who want to retreat from their everyday responsibilities into the sheltered, enchanted world of childhood. To many, fantasy books don't count as serious reading. But the fact that some novels are set in another world or time doesn't mean they're less applicable to modern life than those involving familiar, contemporary characters and situations. J. K. Rowling and J. R. R. Tolkien both address the same issues as Martin Amis and Philip Roth—personal loyalties, social conflicts, human crises—only they do so at a remove from modern life. This distance doesn't mean the books are any less pertinent to their readers' experience, however. No one wants to read a book that isn't, at some level, all about themselves. Plus, readers won't feel absorbed in a magical world unless that world contains believable characters for them to identify with. And when it works, this distancing can be very useful in its capacity to help readers consider various situations without feeling the need to be personally involved in them, which can come as a great relief.

The same is true of romance, which, at its best, can affirm our own state of mind, helping us realize we're not alone. Romance fiction, including so-called "chick lit," often brings up some really interesting ideas, both radical and conservative, about human nature and the state of being in love. It regularly tackles big problems, allowing readers to face such difficult issues as infidelity, sex, breakups, friendship dynamics, and the difficulty of juggling work and relationships. A lot of romance also deals with topical concerns like addiction, depression, abortion, and infertility, making it possible for us to examine these difficult subjects without being scared away, depressed, or intimidated.

If this is true of genre fiction, it's true of nonfiction as well. According to an article by Motoko Rich published in the *New York Times* on July 11, 2007, some reading experts claim that urging kids to read fiction in general might be a misplaced goal. "If you look at what most people need to read for their occupation, it's zero narrative," argues Michael L. Kamil, a professor of education at Stanford University. "I don't want to deny that you should be reading stories and literature. But we've overemphasized it." Kamil, coauthor of a 1997 Stanford University study on the subject, believes the overwhelming emphasis on story in education is misguided, and other kinds of texts are actually more useful in teaching children to read for information, which they can do on the Internet, for example.

Nor is it true, as many assume, that the opposite of fiction is page after page of dull, dry-as-dust facts. I'd like to suggest that nonfiction forms like biography, true crime, and celebrity confessionals can be far more useful than literary "classics" in that, at least for most of us, they contain information that can be of real use to us in our daily lives. In my own case, the literary fiction I once used as a refuge from reality led me to grow increasingly disillusioned with the outside world. The closer I looked at it, the more it seemed to be made up of lies.

The final straw came when I discovered *Hollywood Babylon*.

Let me explain.

man and superman

As a teenager, there was one thing I liked to do apart from reading, and that was watching old horror films on TV. On Friday and Saturday nights, when everybody was out and the house was empty, I'd creep downstairs in my dirty pink dressing gown and settle in the front room, itching for a scare. I loved black-and-white movies best of all, the older the better. This was before video, DVD, and cable, and I had to take whatever they happened to be showing on BBC1, BBC2, or ITV. I could usually find something creepy late at night on weekends, though a lot of it was admittedly rubbish. I had very particular tastes, too. I didn't enjoy looking at anything too familiar. I didn't really like anything made after 1970, and I far preferred American films to British ones. Compared to the great old black-and-white classics from Universal and RKO, I found the British Hammer movies especially depressing. Why would I want to look at the ferrety Peter Cushing, or the smarmy Christopher Lee, when I could be watching Boris Karloff or Bela Lugosi?

Bela Lugosi was my favorite—not only my favorite Dracula, but also my favorite actor. As a matter of fact, he was my favorite man. I had a poster of him in Tod Browning's 1931 *Dracula* on the wall above my bed. I loved his dark eyes, his widow's peak. His accent gave me goose bumps. Bela was a real gentleman, like Mr. Rochester, or—even better—Heathcliff in *Wuthering Heights*, who's actually referred to as a vampire, a ghoul, and a devil. In fact, when I saw Bela lying there in his coffin in *Dracula*, I thought of Heathcliff in rigor mortis with that "horrible sneer" on his face.

When I was thirteen, we had a "balloon debate" in history class, a kind of staged argument where you had to pretend to be a famous person from history. The premise of this game was that a number of important historical figures were passengers in a hot-air balloon that was rapidly losing steam, and only one could survive. You had to make the case why you were more important than the other people in the balloon, and everyone got to vote on who should be thrown overboard. I won the debate by a resounding majority, managing to convince

the rest of the class that I, Bela Lugosi, was of far more importance to the course of history than any of my fellow passengers, including Margaret Thatcher, Winston Churchill, Henry VIII, and Bob Marley.

I loved Bela, and I believed in him. Bela was more than a man. To me, he had glamour, in its original sense: the casting of a spell. Bela had me enraptured. I imagined going to stay with him in Castle Dracula. A coach would pull up outside my house, driven by a mystery coachman, all in black. Its door would open slowly. Nothing would be said. I'd climb inside, and be taken away from my dreary life forever.

Imagine my dismay, then, when the spell turned into a curse. One day, rooting through a used bookstore, I came across a copy of Kenneth Anger's scurrilous *Hollywood Babylon*, with its startling tabloid shots of a washed-up, gray-haired Lugosi. Aghast, disbelieving, I was devastated by Anger's bitchy, lubricious account of how Bela was so hard up when he died that his current wife and an ex-wife collectively could hardly scrape together the money for a funeral. He *was* a ghoul after all, it turned out; not a vampire but a dope fiend, fatally hooked on morphine. I'd imagined him living in a huge Gothic mansion in the Hollywood Hills, not unlike

Castle Dracula, but it turned out he lived in a cheap rented apartment in a dodgy part of Hollywood. Dracula was a junkie. I was sickened—not just by the seedy pictures, unassailable in their starkness, but by the sudden unwanted intrusion of real life into my private world, and by (of all things) a book. Books were my friends! Books were the fuel that fed my fantasies, not the source of their destruction. I had enough of that in real life.

Et tu, Brute?

I bought *Hollywood Babylon* on the spot, and read it so often I came to know the snide photo captions by heart. It was a book

of tremendous importance to me. It was the first book to stop me in my tracks, the first to make me reconsider things I'd always accepted without question. Instead of giving me refuge in a fantasy world, it helped me to see things as they really are, all the insects crawling under the stones.

Like most of us, perhaps, I'd taken it for granted that somewhere on earth was a place where rich people lived happy lives—a sort of Platonic realm populated solely by the gods, where everyone was beautiful, and had everything they could ever dream of. As I imagined it, this modern-day Mount Olympus was inhabited by an elite coterie of well-known people who'd been brought together through their involvement in the movies, and who shared the pleasures inherent in their celebrity status. While I realized this idyllic Shangri-La was more an existential state than a physical location, I also recognized its slightly flawed (but still fabulous) real-world embodiment every time I opened a magazine or watched a show about the lives of the rich and famous. I knew this place as Hollywood. To others, perhaps, it's Beverly Hills, Bermuda, Aspen, Cannes, Palm Springs, Monte Carlo, or simply America. Whatever name you know it by, it's the place people go to live when they've made it, the place where they sit round their swimming pools drinking champagne and chatting on the phone, sailing their yachts, playing roulette.

It was, I'd assumed, where Bela lived.

Like most people who grew up a long way from America (and like many Americans themselves, no doubt), I believed in Hollywood. I thought of it as a place where people unimaginably different from me lived enchanting, unpredictable lives, where everyone's needs were fulfilled, and where— unlike everywhere else in the world—you could never be bored, anxious, lonely, or miserable. I'd seen the photographs in magazines. I'd read about celebrities, how they lived. I'd watched them on television, those beautiful Americans, arriving at premieres and ceremonies, walking down the red carpet, people stretching out their hands to touch them as they once reached out to touch the hem of a saint's garment, or a hunchback's lucky hump. It seemed all too obvious that, due to their beauty, fame, and wealth, people who lived in Hollywood were happier than me.

And why not? Glamorous people cast a spell that makes us believe in them: a spell that works—we DO believe in them. We also assume that, along with their wealth and fame, celebrities are emotionally and personally fulfilled. We assume they must be better off than we are because their money can buy them the power to exert control over their lives, to avoid the kinds of setbacks that would trip up the rest of us, like waiting for a table at a restaurant, being convicted of a crime, or paying for an unexpected funeral.

As soon as I opened *Hollywood Babylon*, I realized we'd all been duped, which forced me to rethink all my former assumptions about other peoples' lives. I found this book so compelling, in fact, that I quickly developed an appetite for similar kinds of spill-all Hollywood confessionals and scandalous "true-life" tales of celebrity dysfunction. Compelled to discover the "real" stories behind the public façade, I began to unearth the most lurid and voyeuristic celebrity memoirs I could find, starting with *Mommie Dearest*, Christina Crawford's inglorious depiction of her movie-star parent, Joan. Other early favorites were *Haywire*, Brooke Hayward's chronicle of her life as the daughter of prima donna mother Margaret Sullavan, and Kitty Kelley's seamy biographies of Frank Sinatra, Jacqueline Onassis, Elizabeth Taylor, and the British royal family.

The stories in these books taught me things that were much more important than anything I could ever have learned from the Gothic novels I'd loved as a child. And yet, were they really so different? Looking back, the jump from Charlotte Brontë to Kitty Kelley seems less sudden and perplexing, more a change of degree than of subject. Like the Gothic tales in which I once immersed myself, these Hollywood horror stories told my own narrative, but on a grand, almost mythic scale. It was thrilling for me to discover that beautiful, wealthy people could be as miserable as me. Suddenly all I wanted to read about was people with horrible lives, but lives that were horrible in grand, interesting ways.

I wanted to read about people who were rich and beautiful, but still unhappy.

Before long, I'd become a connoisseur of books about the "dark side" of Hollywood. It was only *OLD* Hollywood that interested me at first. I'd always been fascinated by films from the classic period, the 1930s and '40s. The fact that people in the movie business today are drug addicts or alcoholics doesn't seem either surprising or particularly perverse. It was the wealth and glamour of the past that captivated me, but after reading about Bela, I was no longer interested in beautiful people and their daring love affairs if I couldn't also get a glimpse of their sordid underbelly—that world of greed, lust, jealousy, and shame. And I quickly learned that as long as there were fantasies of a rich elite living in a world of sparkle and style, as long as the movies fueled dreams of glamorous, sexually charged, thrill-packed lives, there were grotesque horror stories of intolerable pressures, violence, and catastrophe.

I especially came to love books detailing the legendary stresses that every celebrity has to face: the criticism, the hypocrisy, the backstabbing, the extravagance, the dramas and scandals, the searching inquisitions into private lives, the fabled rejection that follows the longed-for adoration. Not that I didn't care about the lavish homes and priceless jewelry—I did!—but I also wanted to know about the personal anxieties and emotional tensions that went with them, the drunken collapses and nervous breakdowns that inspired frenetic and distasteful outbreaks of gossip in the tabloids. I guzzled down tell-all biographies of Jerry Lewis, Frances Farmer, Bing Crosby, James Dean, Grace Kelly, Jayne Mansfield, Marilyn Monroe, and Judy Garland. I feasted on *Hollywood Cesspool* by evangelist Robert L. Sumner, a book published in 1955 by Sword of the Lord Publishers in Murfreesboro, Tennessee, proclaiming itself to be "A Startling Survey of Movieland Lives and Morals, Pictures, and Results" (the back cover advertised other books by the same author, including *The Blight of Booze*, *The Menace of Narcotics*, and *Hell Is No Joke*).

The coda to this epiphany came when I was a little older, and came across Nathanael West's great Hollywood novel, *The Day of the Locust*. I've never found a more vivid expression of the emotional fickleness of fans than the final scene of this remarkable book, when the crowd at a Hollywood premiere, after waiting for hours to catch a glimpse of the stars, runs amok and strikes out at random; the mass of worshippers suddenly becomes a lynch mob, their adoration transformed into a raging desire to KILL their idols. Tod Hacket, the novel's protagonist, sees the crowd's behavior as the only appropriate response of those who've been rewarded all their lives in the coin of the realm—celebrity—only to realize too late that the currency is worthless, and they've all been conned:

> They realize that they've been tricked and burn with resentment. Everyday of their lives they read the newspapers and went to the movies. Both fed them on lynchings, murder, sex crimes, explosions, wrecks, love nests, fires, miracles, revolutions, war . . . Nothing can ever be violent enough to make taut their slack minds and bodies. They have been cheated and betrayed.

Confirming Hacket's speculation about the frantic mob, French sociologist Edgar Morin, in his book *Les Stars*, claimed that the reason people have such an unquenchable appetite for celebrity stories is because what they ultimately want is to CONSUME their idols. "From the cannibal repasts in which the ancestor was eaten, and the totemic feasts in which the sacred animal was devoured, down to our own religious communion and receiving of the Eucharist, every god is created to be eaten," he wrote, making the convincing case that the first stage of this assimilation of our idols is the obsessive consumption of information about them through the vicarious voyeurism of the celebrity memoir.

let us now praise famous men

In the last few years, there's been a lot of talk about forging new ties between traditional literary disciplines and areas like philosophy, psychology, biochemistry, and the neurosciences. For example, there's a growing acknowledgment of the value of literature in medical education, because, it's argued, reading fiction can improve students' clinical skills. One of the claims made by those who advocate the teaching of literature in medical school is that narratives, especially those about illness and suffering, can help trainee doctors better understand the inner experience of their patients and, as a consequence, develop greater empathy. From this perspective, medical textbooks detailing the symptoms of a disease are like charts outlining the geography and geology of a country; only literature, or so they say, can provide a first-hand account of what it's like to actually live there.

More concretely, it's been suggested by neurologists that the nervous system is organized in such a way that the brain automatically clusters incoming stimuli into certain kinds of patterns or configurations, which we experience as "meaning." When reading, the information we take in has already been put in order, already made into a series of patterns. According to this theory, the more we read, the more we refine our ability to make meaning out of senseless experience, to find order and control, and so to get relief from the anxiety generated by all the senselessness and aimlessness around us, the helplessness and confusion we're bound to feel in the face of random, unpatterned events.

If this is true, then surely the kinds of books most likely to assuage our existential anxiety—our despair at the random emptiness of life—are not literary classics, are not fiction at all, in fact, but celebrity biographies and confessionals, today's demotic equivalent of the stories once told by Sophocles, Ovid, Virgil, Plato, and all those ancients they say you "ought" to read in school. We can empathize far more easily with narratives of illness and suffering when they're REAL, and when they're told on a grand scale, when their subjects are gods and goddesses, heroes and heroines, as the ancients knew perfectly well.

Celebrities are today's equivalent of these archetypes, embodying different ways of being in the world, of existing in a human body, providing us with patterns on which to model our own lives. Their stories fascinate us, at least in part, because they represent familiar, endlessly recurring responses to the human condition. This race of marvelous creatures comes alive in our fantasies and daydreams, emerging semiformed from the everyday world. Often of humble birth, they begin to display apparently extraordinary powers from their first years of life. Their stories are filled with trials, temptations, false prophets, and deadly enemies, all of which they must overcome, and if they do so, they can rediscover themselves and find inner peace, often in the arms of a loving partner, pet, charity, or social cause.

Celebrity narratives establish the main scripts, presentational props, conversational codes, and other source materials through which cultural relations are constructed today, at least in the West. They're social myths embodying the soul of our culture; they're one of the main ways of organizing recognition and belonging. So even if you never read celebrity confessionals, magazines, or tabloid newspapers, you still somehow have a sense that Richard Gere is serious and spiritual, Meg Ryan is fun and flirty, Tom Hanks is decent and hardworking, Jack Nicholson is sly and playful. You "know" these things not because you follow celebrity gossip, necessarily, but because they seem to make sense, because you watch movies in which these figures are cast in familiar roles, and because stories about them are filtered along to us through the ether of pop culture, the air we all breathe, whether we know it or not.

At certain times, as in ancient myths, particular figures will be in the ascendant as embodiments of their distinctive archetype. The warrior figure, for example, formerly played by Hercules, and later by leaders like Alexander and Genghis Khan, has been played in modern culture by actors like John Wayne, Arnold Schwarzenegger, Clint Eastwood, and Brad Pitt. The female beauty, embodied by the goddess Aphrodite, once played by actresses like Marilyn Monroe and Jane Russell, is now performed by the likes of Jennifer Lopez and Angelina Jolie. The role of the sacred fool or trickster—Hermes, Puck, Brer Rabbit, Wile E. Coyote—has been played by figures like Charlie Chaplin, Robin Williams, Adam Sandler, and Jack Black.

The mutability of this modern pantheon provides us with an ersatz, parasocial community—a group of familiar figures that we recognize, that we know will be there every time we open a magazine or pop in a DVD. They're familiar to us; they feel like our friends, no matter how remote we may be from their "civilization." These characters, in whatever incarnation they may appear, have a permanent home in our inner lives as well as existing "out there" in the world. Our constant faith in the power of celebrity is a magic force field that surrounds us, keeping us bound together. Membership in the celebrity community may change, but it remains intact, forming a kind of golden radiance, a collective emanation that will be there no matter what. Like the figures in fairy tales and the tarot deck, celebrities are physical manifestations of psychic models, the timeless inhabitants of the human unconscious. Their narratives, like those of Homer and Virgil, are retellings of ancient stories—and a story doesn't have to be original for us to get caught up in it. Just as *The Odyssey* and the Trojan War once captivated audiences, celebrity trials and tribulations continue to engage us (will A and B ever get back together? will C ever find true love? will D ever stop drinking?) even though we already know how the story ends.

When I first started to read celebrity confessionals, I was embarrassed by how much pleasure they gave me. I felt guilty for buying them, and even more for enjoying them; everyone else I knew dismissed them as trash. Instead of keeping them on the bookshelves with my Gothic novels and ten volumes of Swinburne, I hid them with my emergency chocolate, under my bed. I'd gorge them down in one sitting like a binge eater, ashamed of the time I was wasting, the junk I was consuming.

Now I know there's nothing to be ashamed of; these kinds of books might not be "great literature," but they're just as "good for you" as any other kind, perhaps even more, since they so vividly expose the lies we live by, showing us how the world really works. These confessionals have taught me a number of important lessons—some of which I'm going to share with you here—including the fact that celebrity is really all that matters. Yes, despite what they tell you in school, skill, talent, and "sheer hard work" do not dictate our scale of social value; the only real value is that of fame. This simple, straightforward hierarchy gives some order to the essential messiness of life, deflecting us from the unequal hands we've been dealt by nature. Even if you claim you don't "believe" in the value of fame, you don't really have a choice—it's about as valid an option as not "believing" in money. You might claim to know nothing about celebrity, but you can't help judging other people according to their relative celebrity in your own circles, and yours in theirs. We all pretend not to care, we all say we don't, but of course we all do. In fact, many of us care about little else.

A hierarchy like this is especially necessary in today's society, since the church lost its power long ago, and most royalty has no function anymore except a symbolic one. Most royal figures are simply minor celebrities, no more, no less. In some of the smaller European countries, in fact, they ride around on their bicycles unknown and unrecognized. It's just quaint social convention that still makes them kings and queens, since they have no power, relatively little money, and no real fame to speak of. The crude exception to this practice is the British royal family, which insists on remaining wealthy and in the public eye, and so is now largely regarded as a national embarrassment, an unsightly and expensive white elephant, like the Crystal Palace or the Millennium Dome. This helps to explain the popularity of lurid tell-all books like Kitty Kelley's *The Royals* and Andrew Morton's *Diana: Her Story*.

Like continental royalty, those with great skill and talent, however well known their names and works may be, are stuck on the bottom rung of the celebrity ladder as long as no one recognizes them in the street. As the nineteenth-century essayist William Hazlitt once observed, "the way to fame through merit alone, is the narrowest, the steepest, the longest, the hardest of all others." Today this path is closed to the public. It's no longer possible to achieve fame by merit alone; you also need, at the very least, a powerful agent, an image consultant, and an awful lot of strategic publicity. Merit, in fact, is probably something of a drawback; it's easier to become famous for committing crimes than for doing good deeds—and even then, there's no guarantee. If you live in a town small enough, you can probably still get your picture in the paper by pushing somebody under a train, but to achieve fame on a national level, you have to do something far more newsworthy.

Patriotic idealists and self-made millionaires might argue that America's scale of value is determined by capitalism—that those at the top of the social ladder are the people with the most money. Wealth, of course, is still an important way to judge a person's value, but wealth and celebrity have a peculiarly intimate relationship: We usually assume that celebrity is a function of prosperity, just as prosperity is taken to be a function of celebrity. This isn't always true, of course—there are plenty of unknown multimillionaires who guard their privacy very closely, and more than a few penniless celebrities. But these are special cases. Unless the rich go to great lengths to conceal their wealth, the splendor of their lifestyle will make them well known, and the penniless celebrity—with the possible exception of a few incarcerated criminals—is no longer a star. So while wealth alone doesn't necessarily lead to fame, it's typically the currency in which fame is measured; successful celebrities can turn their fame into money through sponsorship deals, just as moguls like Donald Trump can easily turn their wealth into fame.

Another fact I learned from celebrity confessionals is that celebrity IS religion. Forget all that nonsense about the separation of Church and State—celebrity is the officially endorsed religion of America. Like all religions, it has its own rites, myths, divine forms, sacred and venerated objects, consecrated men and women, holy places and rituals. Like tribal shamans, celebrities have the power to heal, to create ecstasy, to inspire swooning and hysteria in the crowds who clamor to see them (or their on-screen images). They can work magic, bringing hope to ailing children; they can live on nothing but grapefruit; they can appear years younger overnight; make comebacks or suddenly disappear from sight. They have a miraculous dimension to them even when they're photographed buying their own toilet paper or pumping their own gas: They're miraculously down-to-earth, miraculous in their desire to be "just like us."

We worship celebrities just as fervently as we once worshipped the gods. We make pilgrimages to their birthplaces and gravesites; we scour eBay for souvenirs, in the hope of coming closer to the hidden meaning of their lives. You might even say that relics are as important to the religion of celebrity as they were to the followers of medieval saints, only instead of offering you Christ's bones in a bottle, today's peddlers sell the discarded accessories of fame they've found by foraging through celebrity rubbish. This may be why celebrities are notoriously fussy about their trash. In *Mommie Dearest*, Christina Crawford recalls how, during a sanitation strike, her mother had all her trash put in Bergdorf Goodman boxes and wrapped with big purple bows before it was taken out.

I once read an article in the *National Enquirer* about the contents of Henry Kissinger's trashcan. The reporter who'd dug through the famous bigwig's rubbish came up with an empty vichyssoise can, some used packets of antacids, a couple of empty yogurt containers, two unread copies of the *New York Times*, a lot of empty cigarette boxes, and a prescription for Seconal. These inanimate artifacts, like saints' relics or fragments of Christ's true cross, enable supplicants like us to savor the proximity of our idols. I now know that books about celebrities are considered "trashy" only by people who don't understand the true value of trash.

The analogy is made explicit in the art of Barton Lidice Benes, whose best-known installations, *Reliquaries* and *Celebrity*, memorialized in his book *Curiosa*, are curiosity cabinets in which Benes displays his collection of remnants from celebrity lives. His fastidiously arranged inventory includes Roy Rogers's nasal douche, staples from Larry Hagman's gallstone surgery, Frank Sinatra's fingernail clippings, a small vial of Sylvester Stallone's urine, a heel from one of Elizabeth Taylor's shoes, Nancy Reagan's chocolate-stained table napkin, and Bill Clinton's half-sucked throat lozenge. Benes keeps and catalogues letters accompanying the objects sent to him, generally by intermediaries (his wide network of friends and acquaintances), which act as certificates of their "genuineness," just like the signatures on papal indulgences, or letters accompanying swatches from the shrouds of saints. Like genuine holy relics, these sacred gleanings are elevated to the saintly status of art once they've been framed, enclosed in curiosity cabinets, and exhibited in a gallery. To really appreciate their power, then, you have to believe in two different systems of magic: that of celebrity and

that of art. The equation becomes even more complex when the relics displayed are those of celebrity artists, like the swatch from Mark Rothko's tie, or his leftover medication.

If celebrity confessionals taught me that celebrity is religion, they also taught me that celebrity is politics. In the arena of politics today, image is everything. The success of celebrity politicians explicitly confirms the fact that imagery has finally subsumed the political realm. The line between politicians and other kinds of celebrities has become so blurred that celebrity scandals are often used for political purposes, and political scandal has been relegated to the level of "ordinary" celebrity gossip. Indeed, today's media seems devoted to pumping out an endless stream of "behind-the-scenes" exposés in the form of "news specials" that "investigate" the latest political crimes and scandals, providing a constant flow of speculation about the private lives of those in the seats of power.

In fact, to pretend the person we vote for is any more or less than a public face—to suggest anything else is at stake—now seems abject hypocrisy. In a way, I'm surprised it took so long to happen. It seems perfectly natural that stars like Ronald Reagan, Jesse Ventura, Clint Eastwood, and Arnold Schwarzenegger should have moved into the field of politics, since—politics being all about image and entertainment—they already have a solid constituency in their fan base. In fact, I think ALL politicians should start their careers as celebrities in some other realm; it's simply more honest. That way, we'd no longer have to go along with the charade that politicians are anything other than charismatic public figures. We could finally acknowledge that the real politics is conducted behind the scenes, as it's always been, among figures unseen by the public eye.

Another important lesson I learned from celebrity confessionals is that, behind the scenes, most celebrities—like most clowns, so they say—are rather unhappy. What I learned from *Hollywood Babylon*—something we all know, at some level, but continue to ignore, or repress—is this: Being a celebrity isn't fabulous, but can actually be horrible, nightmarish, devastating in its consequences. According to Pablo Picasso (in *Picasso in His Own Words*), of all the unpleasant things he'd known in life—poverty, disapproval, unhappiness—fame was not only the worst, it was worse than all the others put together. This is the story told by every celebrity confessional: That there IS no special place, no world of glamour and enchantment. Those homes we see in magazines, the ones filled with brilliant, charming, wealthy people—they're just a façade. Their physical form may exist, but what that form suggests is a sham. Those with beauty, wealth, and fame suffer as much self-doubt, depression, and grief as the rest of us—probably a whole lot more—and are all the more subject to petty squabbles, mood swings, dashed hopes, and disillusionment.

For example, in her book *Spend Spend Spend*, Vivian Nicholson, a British woman who became enormously wealthy overnight after winning the lottery, explains how, for her, the thrill of newly acquired wealth and fame wore off after two or three years, when she discovered that everybody suffered from exactly the same kinds of problems, and that even when she was rich and famous, she was still the same person she used to be, among others no different from herself. She also explains how, once her material goals had been satisfied after a year or so, she started to feel unfulfilled, even in the most basic terms. Larger, more obscure longings rose up to take the place of the old ones—longings that grew oddly exaggerated. Most of us have limited wealth, so this desire for excess is never roused in us, but in the rich it knows no bounds. From *The Most Beautiful Woman in the World*, Ellis Amburn's biography of Elizabeth Taylor, I learned that it sometimes takes the form of *nostalgie de la boue*—a search for novelty in the trappings of indigence or depravity, a romantic attraction to poverty. (It's never been completely out of fashion for the rich to go "slumming," as in the case of well-born women like Taylor, Margaret Trudeau, and Princess Stephanie, who repeatedly get involved with blue-collar men.)

Another lesson: While increased dissatisfaction with one's "inner self" is perhaps the best-known by-product of wealth and celebrity, the outer self is more easily corrected. Tab Hunter, in *Tab Hunter Confidential: The Making of a Movie Star*, explains how, in the early days of celebrity, newly signed talent would be taken directly from the studio to the dentist to have their teeth cleaned and straightened, even before they were given make-overs and new names. For the celebrity of today, on the contrary, it's seen as evidence of pride and integrity to stick with their original names (think of Marg Helgenberger, Jennifer Lopez, or Barbra Streisand), but the same is seldom true of appearance. The livelihood of the celebrity depends on being looked at, and those on both sides of the camera have acquired a clinical, critical eye for fine distinctions of physiology, scrutinizing the form and shape of the human face in Talmudic minuteness.

Through *A Little Work: Behind the Doors of a Park Avenue Plastic Surgeon*, Paul Z. Lorenc and Trish Hall taught me that today's trends in cosmetic reconstruction are much more advanced than the simple face-lifts and nose jobs of yesteryear. While procedures like breast enhancement, lipo-suction, and brow-lifts will always be popular, more advanced forms of surgery are now available for the man or woman who has everything. In ladies of a certain age, apparently, the most fashionable kind of procedure is vaginoplasty—the construction of a "designer vagina." According to Lorenc and Hall, "reduction surgery repairs stretched or oversized vaginas, preserving the rosy 'curled' edge of the labia. Surgery can also restore the elasticity that may have been lost after childbirth." Younger women favor abdominoplasty, the restructuring of the stomach and reshaping of the belly button, which fashion has made into an erogenous zone among the hard-bodied. This way, "outies" can be turned into "innies" (according to the authors of *A Little Work*, a "T-shape" is considered ideal). Feet can also be restructured to match your favorite shoes. If you never leave home without your Manolos, the pinkie toe can be amputated for a streamlined fit; if you prefer sandals or bare feet, the toes can be aligned to look neat and appealing in meditation and yoga classes.

I also learned why we follow these trends with such hubristic fascination: because cosmetic surgery gives the lie to evolution. Through her book *Survival of the Prettiest*, Nancy Etcoff, a psychologist at Harvard Medical School, taught me that beauty attracts us because symmetrical good looks are a reliable marker of healthy offspring who will live to procreate. Cosmetic surgery, she suggests, is the most fundamental lie you can tell to a potential breeding partner, implying that you're a fine, youthful breeder, belying the secret truth concealed in your genes. This helps to explain our obsessive dismay at the practice, and our gleeful fascination with those who take plastic surgery to extremes, apparently oblivious to the bizarre distortion of their features.

On the other hand, hypocrites that we are, we're also fascinated by celebrities who have, as the tabloids put it, "let themselves go." Nothing is more titillating than a candid shot of a star whose public appearance seems evidence of deep denial, whose response to pressure involves a mortification of the body—anorexia, weight gain, drug addiction, or public displays of drunkenness. Psychological problems provoke equal glee in the tabloids, particularly nervous breakdowns that come in the wake of habitual infidelities, drug abuse, depression, and physical illness. Psychologists Andrew Evans and Glenn D. Wilson, through their book *Fame—The Psychology of Stardom*, taught me that celebrities suffer an abnormally high incidence of mania, schizophrenia, paranoia, and psychopathic behavior, since these kinds of addictive, maniacal, and obsessive practices are the corollaries of helplessness and inauthenticity.

To those who are anxious about their appearance, the constant threat of public exposure can have a very damaging effect. Evans and Wilson claim some celebrities begin to experience a resistance to appearing in public: a particular form of burnout known as "reactive inhibition"

experienced only by the most successful stars. This syndrome is characterized by a feeling of having reached a plateau, of being at the top of your
game, where there's nothing more to be gained from repeating the same
old skills, singing the same old hit songs over and over again, shaking your
famous hips or wiggling your famous buttocks like a performing animal.
Some celebrities react to this stress by suicide; others take refuge in drink or
drugs; still others renounce the celebrity life altogether, wanting to become
an "ordinary" person again, which is often no longer possible.

I'm especially compelled by those moments when the truth about
celebrity leaks out, just a tiny bit, and I can't help catching a glimpse of the
machinery behind the scenes. I've sometimes hung around in the crowds
at film premieres waiting not for any celebrity in particular, but to see
whoever shows up. The feverish excitement of these crowds can make you
so sick and giddy that anyone arriving by limo who looks glamorous or
familiar can set off a chorus of shrieks and shoves, even if no one knows
who the "celebrity" actually is. So desperate can this feeling grow that after
hours and hours of waiting in the sun or rain, you can be driven to near-
hysteria by the appearance of the lowliest B-list celebrity—an aging game-
show host with a toothy smile, the child or parent of a famous person, a
long-forgotten character actor. These occasions always remind me of the
crowd scene in *The Day of the Locust*. There's something a bit nasty and
cynical about the mood of these crowds, whose excitement always seems
on the verge of turning into anger at not being presented with a more
convincing illusion.

pride and prejudice

Perhaps the most important thing I've learned from reading celebrity confessionals is that *schadenfreude*, in one form or another, is the force
that turns the wheels of American culture. While we may not all read
celebrity memoirs, we're all implicated, in one way or another. What's
capitalism, after all, but institutionalized *schadenfreude*—making money
at the expense of others? What's democracy but the struggle to see your
own values succeed, and those of others' fail? What's sport but watching
the best team win (and all others lose)? Our pleasure in seeing our ideals
upheld, and those of others come to ruin, is a corollary of the American
way of life, an emotional phenomenon that accompanies the successful

execution of secular justice, the laws of God, and the natural fluctuations of the market.

One of the most emotionally gripping aspects of the celebrity confessional is the fact that it can have genuine consequences for the celebrity's career. This is high-stakes voyeurism, involving the lives of real people. Unlike the rest of us, celebrities have no institutional means of public redress, which is why the sociologist Francesco Alberoni refers to them, in his essay of the same title, as "the powerless elite." If the gossip is vicious enough, in fact, they can actually be toppled from their places in the pantheon; it's hard for divinities to transgress their archetypal roles and emerge unscathed. Maybe this is our way of getting revenge on a star whom we see as having failed us, a way of cutting through the deluge of phony anecdotes, lies, PR campaigns, and airbrushing, and, just for a moment, making everybody turn and face the truth.

It's an old truism, of course, that the same fans that put celebrities on pedestals can't wait to knock them off. According to Daniel Boorstein in his book *The Image: A Guide to Pseudo-Events in America*, "The very agency which first makes the celebrity in the long run inevitably destroys him. He will be destroyed, as he was made, by publicity." In the main, stars are knocked off their pedestals when they make us look at the illusion too hard, or for too long, so it starts to split apart, and we can catch a glimpse of the truth showing through the seams. This isn't what we want to see! As voyeurs, we need the objects of our desire to reveal themselves from a distance, a little bit at a time. We want them airbrushed, blurred, wrapped in fur and jewels; we don't want them standing before us naked, warts and all. No real Peeping Tom wants to see everything at once. The pleasures of voyeurism are those of furtive spying, not sudden revelation.

Celebrity confessionals have also shown me that a culture of voyeurism is only possible in a nation of exhibitionists. Those who are disquieted by the confessional tendencies of modern society should bear in mind that we've always wanted to pry into other people's private lives; tell-all tales of infidelities and illicit behavior have long been our daily fare. It's a hallmark of the essentially conservative nature of our society, in fact, that the private goings-on of public figures like Michael Jackson or Bill Clinton can cause such a fuss. After all, if we were anything like the jaded, amoral cynics the pundits make us out to be, other people's private transgressions wouldn't interest us in the least. Instead, we insist on holding them accountable.

Another lesson I've learned from my reading: The power of gossip is severely underrated. Here's an example. The *Daily Mirror*, a British tabloid newspaper, recently dispatched a reporter, Ryan Parry, to penetrate daily life in Buckingham Palace in the guise of a footman. Among the details Parry revealed was that the Queen has cornflakes and oatmeal served in Tupperware containers for breakfast, and that she often eats her dinner alone, in front of the TV set, with her remote control on the tray. Her favorite show, apparently, is *EastEnders*, a popular soap about working class Londoners.

When the Queen criticized the newspaper's "revelations" (without denying them, natch), she referred to them as nothing more than "idle gossip." This phrase seems terribly old-fashioned to me—a throwback to the days of magic and superstition, witchcraft and ducking stools. Judeo-Christian moral codes condemn the practice, and various forms of punishment, including stocks and "scold's bridles," were designed to make a public exhibition of those who indulged in it. Even today, the common opinion of gossip is inclined to place it rather low on the scale of human behavior, associating it with trivial and superficial matters. Many people consider it a form of self-aggrandizement, a way of belittling other people, and a silly waste of time. Significantly, it's an activity associated mainly with women and gay men (straight men don't gossip, they "network," "banter," "shoot the breeze," or "talk shop"). Of course, there are also lots of people who claim to be totally bored by gossip—and they may be telling the truth. But it might be the case that many of those who disdain it do so because they feel it implies a certain criticism and condemnation. By gossiping, some feel, we're making moral judgments, we're looking down on people, or mocking them, because of their private behavior.

Still, while gossip itself is so widely condemned, there are an increasing number of people who love to be gossiped about. There are many in the public realm, I've learned, who enjoy nothing more than being the subject of a rumor or a piece of scandal, even if it lasts no more than a day. While this may not be true of the Queen of England, for B-list celebrities, being mentioned in the news—even for being turned away from a party, or filing for bankruptcy—is, to some degree or other, their *raison d'être*, their only means of wielding power in the public realm, as well, perhaps, as exercising private power over others. After all, many celebrities hire PR outfits to make sure they're gossiped about, and to plant gossip about them in the press. The power of fame seems to be undiluted by its proliferation: The public is adoring, but often undiscriminating. Largely because of television, many more people are famous today than ever before. The explosive propagation of cable channels engenders more celebrity lifestyle programs, more biographies, and more once-anonymous stars than at any other time in history. As a result, there's vastly more private information "out there" than there used to be, and far more gossip in circulation, giving us a much-needed glimpse into the increasingly image-controlled lives of our social icons and cultural authorities.

Celebrity confessionals have also taught me that where there's smoke, there's fire. While anyone can make up a piece of celebrity tittle-tattle, the rumor will never spread unless there's something to it—in other words, unless it seems plausible or reflects a symbolic truth. Most gossip that's interesting enough to be passed along either hits on something real about its target, or reflects current anxieties. The constant speculation about Tom Cruise's sexual orientation, for example, reflects a sense of disquiet about the obsessive control he exerts over his publicity, his consistent refusal to speak about his divorce from Nicole Kidman (don't we have a right to know what went wrong?), and his longtime membership in that wealthy and secretive Hollywood cult, the Church of Scientology. The rumors also tend to affirm our commitment to the existing social order, and to hetero-sexuality as the "norm" to be deviated from. It's partly through this kind of gossip that we learn what our culture demands of us, what sort of behavior is acceptable, and what to expect from our friends and neighbors.

These days, the Internet has superseded television as the richest, most accessible repository of gossip—not only gossip about others, but also gossip about ourselves, in confessional forums like Post Secret, Not Proud, E-admit, Group Hug, Daily Confession, and The Confessional. These sites appeal to the same voyeuristic curiosity that tempts us to read other people's diaries and steam open their mail. The anonymity of the participants means they're firing blanks, however; their confessions, even the most juicy, can't hurt a soul. The secrets unearthed in these sites are faux-secrets; any frisson they provide is impotent, even innocent. Art historian Kerr Houston notes, in a recent article on the subject, "online confessionals are revelations made to everybody but the one person who might want or need to hear the imparted information." He adds, however, that this has always been an aspect of confessions, which seek personal rehabilitation without the cost of complete disclosure.

I wonder who reads these anonymous confessions, when the Internet offers so many opportunities to unearth rumors and scandals with real names attached, unauthorized tidbits about public figures—a valuable currency in an age when the dish about celebrities is increasingly filtered through PR mills, and the gossip columnists of old Hollywood—Herb Caen, Irv Kupcinet, Hedda Hopper, Louella Parsons—have passed from the scene. The rise of independent Web sites devoted to rumor and gossip, like Gawker, Defamer, Awful Plastic Surgery, and The Drudge Report ("I don't call it journalism," says founder Matt Drudge, "I just go where the stink is") has made it increasingly easy for voyeurs to bypass the PR flak and root around in the dirt, like pigs on a truffle hunt.

Another lesson: What goes around, comes around. One of the best Internet sites for reading about celebrities is The Smoking Gun, a site now affiliated with Court TV, which displays reproductions of primary source documents dredged up from dusty archives and dingy clerks' offices—police reports, lawsuits, FBI memos, depositions, and other items of public record. A typical document reproduced in their archives is the statement of financial affairs from Burt Reynolds Productions, Inc., listing "Payments to Creditors within Last 90 Days Aggregating More Than $600" as part of a bankruptcy settlement. Among the payments listed are a whopping $5,647.20 to "Ed Katz Hair Design" and an additional $1,950.00 to "Apollo Hair Systems." There's something gleefully comforting about documents like this. It's great to be reminded that a person who has all the external trappings of "success"—fame, wealth, good looks—can suffer from serious financial problems just like anybody else, and isn't exempt from having his flaws and frailties recorded and exhibited. The Internet can make private things public through disconnection and secrecy, allowing us to speculate about personal matters, to interpret and assimilate them into what we already know about the celebrity in question. In this case, Burt Reynolds's hairpiece—excuse me, hair SYSTEM—may not have been much of a secret to anyone actively following his career, but this evidence of its five and a half thousand dollar price tag is an embarrassing comeuppance for a man who appears to have so lost touch with reality as to believe his hair loss mattered enough to require spending a significant chunk of his diminishing wealth to buy it off for a while. The exorbitant prices paid for these vanity products allow us to feel that our own small problems pale in comparison with the severe, costly mistakes often made by those in the public eye, and allow us to feel better about our own flawed, aging bodies, our own wrinkles, sagging flesh, and, yes, hair loss. There's also a delicious taste of hubris in the idea that jealously guarded secrets about the intimate lives of well-known figures can become public knowledge thanks to the research of a couple of mischievous reporters and the democratic potential of the Internet. If the mass media has really reduced the world to a global village, then The Smoking Gun is the global village stocks.

"A Culture of Voyeurism"

the way of all flesh

Essentially, I think we're driven to read about "real people" in an attempt to understand ourselves by balancing and measuring our lives against those of others. We live in a culture of storytelling, and much of what we think we know about ourselves—our memories and imaginative reminiscences—are fictions and fabrications. We'd be unable to exist without the make-believe that helps to create our sense of self. And so, naturally, we're fascinated by what goes on behind the curtain. A lot of us are less interested in the public facade than the machinery behind the scenes, the delicate process of constructing a coherent persona out of mental chaos. People like me, who love the celebrity confessional, enjoy seeking out those moments of flux that expose the complexity of human experience in the teeth of public image.

At the heart of voyeurism, I think, is not just prurient interest in other people's dirty laundry or envy of their public success—although those things might well be part of it—but a more perplexing question about the relationship between the public person and the private life. We all struggle to make coherent and intelligible logic out of the muddle of our inner lives. We're all driven to present, even to ourselves, a version of who we are that's necessarily incomplete, that conceals, forgets, represses, sublimates, and projects. Our drive to understand other people works, I believe, like a talisman to ward off the frightening fact that there's no such thing as the "true self," only different stories we tell ourselves (and each other) about who we are, and who we want to be.

This, at least, is one of the forces that drives us to read.

But what about those who are also driven to write? What kind of force could impel such a peculiar habit?

Read on, and you'll soon find out.

Oh, both my shoes are shiny new,

And pristine is my hat;

My dress is 1922 . . .

My life is all like that.

—Dorothy Parker, "Autobiography"

CHAPTER 5

BETWEEN THE LINES

For convenience, we tend to categorize people as "right-brained" or "left-brained," but in fact, there's a whole range of different kinds of thinking. People respond to the world around them in an enormous variety of ways, using each of their senses differently. Synaesthetic thinkers, of whom Nabokov was apparently one, see letters and words in visual terms; others see music this way. Some people are highly conscious of textures, arrangements, the juxtaposition of objects; others see mainly light, balance, and the interplay of colors. Some people are articulate speakers, but have great difficulty reading; others can predict the fluctuations of the market but seem unable to match their own socks. Plenty of people can speak many languages fluently, yet remain illiterate in them all.

"I love personal detail, all the more so if it's for its own sake...I love overhearing conversations when I'm on the bus or train..."

Let's consider that word: "illiterate." It's hard to imagine a greater stigma. Calling somebody "illiterate" is almost always an insult or a put-down, and is usually followed by a word like "peasant," "fool," "ape," or "thug." It's interesting how willingly—even proudly—people confess to all kinds of other failings: being tone deaf, having no sense of rhythm, no head for names or numbers. A person will happily admit to not being much of a talker, or being unable to draw a thing, or having no ear for languages, but have you ever heard anyone voluntarily confess to being illiterate?

In Bernhard Schlink's best-selling novel *The Reader*, the narrator's ex-lover, Hanna Schmitz, refuses to defend herself against charges of murder, choosing to spend the rest of her life in prison rather than publicly acknowledge that she doesn't know how to read or write. Hers is an extreme case, no doubt, but illiterates in fiction seldom turn out well. If you're familiar with *Portnoy's Complaint* by Philip Roth, you'll probably remember Portnoy's delirious and hateful descriptions of Mary Jane Reed, known as "The Monkey," a sexy model from the backwoods of Virginia. Portnoy finds himself irresistibly attracted to her, but he's horrified by her lack of education. In one scene, waiting in her apartment while Mary Jane is in the bathroom getting ready to go out, Portnoy notices a note someone has left on the coffee table:

> Has a child been here, I wonder. No, no, I am just face-to-face with my first specimen of the Monkey's hand-writing. A note to the cleaning lady. Though at first glance I imagine it must be a note *from* the cleaning lady . . . Three times I read the sentence through, and as happens with certain texts, each reading reveals new subtleties of meaning and implication . . . Oh that z, that z between the two e's of "pleze"—this is a mind with the depths of a movie marquee! And "furget"! Exactly how a prosti-tute would misspell that word! But it's something about the mangling of "dear," that tender syllable of affection now collapsed into three lower-case letters, that strikes me as hopelessly pathetic . . . This woman is ineducable and beyond reclamation.

Putting aside his denigration of cleaning ladies and prostitutes, we are reminded, by Portnoy's shock at this discovery, how literacy is taken for granted as the cornerstone of even the most basic education, with every-thing else—skills in math, music, art, and science—coming afterwards. In the light of this assumption, we should try to remember that most illit-erate people (approximately 18 percent of the world's population, most of them women) are unable to read because they've never had the privilege of being taught. It's true that most people in the West do learn to read at a basic level, but a lot of them may never use this skill except to follow traffic signs and read restaurant menus, which isn't to say they don't have highly developed minds. Some people are very proud of the fact that they don't read; they see reading as a waste of time, especially when there are so many other things that need taking care of. Nevertheless, many of us auto-matically, perhaps even unconsciously, associate advanced literacy with a highly developed mind; we assume the more literate you are, the more profound your self-knowledge, the deeper your sympathies. In this chapter, I want to refute this superstition by taking a close look at some well-known authors' private lives.

Whenever I start to get interested in a particular writer's work, I also start to grow curious about that writer as a person. I can easily satisfy this curiosity—literary biography is a thriving industry; more and more books about the lives of authors are published every year. The popularity of this genre, like that of confessional nonfiction, life writing, and autobiography, is based, I suspect, on the same impulse that compels us to unearth details of celebrity lives.

There are lots of differences between well-known authors and other kinds of celebrities, the most obvious and significant being the fact that, while everybody knows what film stars look like, many well-known writers prefer to remain out of the public eye, unwilling even to have a photo on the back of their book jackets. They might be world famous, but you could walk past them on the street without knowing it. You might imagine what they look like, you might create a version of them in your head, but more often than not, you'd be dead wrong. People can be shockingly different in the flesh than they appear on the page, as you'll know if you've ever met your pen pal, answered a lonely-hearts ad, or gotten together with somebody you met online. When I left college and started writing to my friends for the first time (this was in the days before e-mail), I was surprised how many of them turned out to have writing styles that were nothing at all like their everyday personalities. Down-to-earth pals seemed unusu-ally cold and pompous on paper; someone I'd known well for many years came across as pretentious and eager to impress; a witty and erudite chum proved virtually illiterate.

Still, despite this experience, whenever I get the chance to see writers (even if it's just on TV) whose work I know well, I can't help being taken aback by the difference between the flesh-and-blood individuals, and the written styles I've come to associate with their names. Sometimes the contrast will be so great that it's almost impossible to reconcile one with the other, and I can't help thinking to myself: "How could THIS possibly be the person who wrote THAT?" One example: A couple of years ago, I was at a ceremony where a prize was being presented to the author of a poignant, sophisticated new novel. I hadn't thought about it much, but I suppose I'd expected him to be frail and elderly, bespectacled and sad looking. When his name was announced, however, the man who stepped up to the podium was toned, muscular, and dressed in a flashy suit. His hair was carefully gelled; his telegenic chin displayed the calculated razor stubble of the infomercial actor. His appearance was so at odds with my expectations that it actually took me a few seconds to realize that this was, in fact, the author himself, and not someone who'd been sent to pick up the award in his place—his stylish younger brother, perhaps, or his gym instructor. When I told a writer friend of mine about this experience, he said he always felt there are two kinds of authors—those for whom their writing is an extension of an outgoing, charismatic, ego-driven personality, and those who shun publicity, for whom writing is a compensation, a substitute for existence in the larger world. Still, there's no sin in being attractive, as long as you're not also hopelessly vain, or worse.

Ever heard the maxim "never meet your heroes"? I think this injunction should apply more to literary heroes than any other kind, since, for the most part, all we have of authors is their prose. When I was younger, I used to idolize the authors whose work I admired. I'd go to great lengths to find out everything I could about them, only to discover, in almost every case, they were the most unpleasant of people. Nabokov has long been one of my favorite writers, for example, but even his best friends admit he was a narrow-minded snob and quite inarticulate in the flesh. One critic said of him, "He wrote like a genius, he thought like a man of letters, and he spoke like a child."

This makes me wonder—which is more "authentic": the flesh, or the words? We're often warned about dodgy strangers lurking on the Internet— weaselly con men who are "not who they seem to be," a distinction that depicts the online personality as a veneer of lies smoothing over the flawed "reality" of the bodily self. We take it for granted that the "real" self is the flesh, not the words—but why should this be the case? It might be worth considering how our written words say as much about us, if not even more, as our physical bodies, which, after all, are accidents of random genetic fusion beyond our control, and subject to all kinds of prejudice, however unintentional. Many people prefer to keep their relationships online for precisely this reason—so they can be who they "really are," rather than being judged by their age, gender, race, body type, or other markers of "personal identity."

As for people in the public eye, I think there's a case to be made that gossip about them is part of the deal, since they're usually compelled to do what they do by a need for attention, a desire to have their life, tastes, and appearance scrutinized by an appreciative audience. The question is a bit different, though, when it comes to gossip about those whose fame depends not upon their looks, acting ability, public charisma, or sporting prowess, but on their intellect: writers, critics, philosophers—the cultural cognoscenti. I know it's irrational, but I can't help feeling that people who devote their lives to the "higher faculties" (reason, logic, philosophy, analysis) should be more immune than the rest of us to those embarrassing failures, shameful mistakes, and humiliating lapses in judgment that make for all the best gossip. In the showbiz world, we've almost come to expect that the private secrets of collapsed marriages will eventually be made public, but details about the private lives of the cultural cognoscenti smell rather different.

I've come to realize, lately, that it's not only the writers I particularly admire who seem to have been irritating people; it's true of writers in general. Often, the more successful the work, the more small-minded, petty, and arrogant the author turns out to have been in private—according to their friends and neighbors, at least. As a result, it's hard for me to credit writing with the therapeutic potential so often attributed to it. For the talented author, all that time spent rendering and transforming personal experience doesn't seem to enhance self-awareness at all; for the untalented, then, it seems doubly self-indulgent to spend time on writing that will neither add to self-knowledge nor give pleasure to others. When we associate literacy with advanced thought, we're forgetting that, however talented an author may be at telling stories, theirs is an impractical skill, one with no applied function outside the text. Evolutionary psychologists have even suggested that the incentive to write, and the energy to do so, is a displacement of the "fight or flight" response fueled by the same rush of adrenaline that, in other people, may take the form of aggression, even violence. Paradoxically, perhaps, it seems to be the most sensitive and insightful writers who most often suffer from a failure of self-reflection, an inability to plumb their own depths, to understand their own motivating forces, as though there were an inverse ratio between the contemplation, observation, and psychological penetration of an author's work and the oblivious, self-destructive misery that dominates the private life. When the nasty Nabokov wrote, "There is nothing more exhilarating than philistine vulgarity," he was overlooking something even more peculiar and fascinating: the vulgarity of the cognoscenti.

the human comedy

Luckily, we have a sad litany of case histories to remind us that great writers are not only as fallible as the rest of us, but often a lot more so. In general, I've found these biographies and autobiographies to be more interesting and helpful, not to mention more readable, than the fiction written by their subjects, and so my advice to you if you're having trouble with a long, dull "classic" is to put it down, and pick up a book about the author's private life instead. You could very well learn a lot, and you'll certainly find it more engaging. Let me guide you through this fascinating territory and point out a few interesting sights along the way.

Some historians of literary biography claim the genre in its modern form began with Lytton Strachey's *Eminent Victorians*, first published in 1918, in which the author composed brief, ironic portraits intended to expose his subjects as they "truly were," without concealing any of their faults. But while such biographies can be fascinating, they're seldom as compelling as first-person memoirs, mainly because there's often something slightly disingenuous about the biography. Naturally, biographers want the stories they tell to be not only interesting, but valuable in a literary sense, in the connections they make between the life and the work, when the truth is, most writers lead pretty dull lives, spending up to fourteen hours a day on their own, sitting in front of a computer or a typewriter. As a result, the conscientious biographer may struggle to find some kind of fit between the writer's childhood experiences and family relationships on the one hand,

and the literary work on the other—connections that, more often than not, simply don't exist.

Still, not all authors are quiet and reclusive; some lead lives that seem far from dull—that have, in fact, proved too exciting or eccentric for the popular press to ignore (think of Fitzgerald, Hemingway, Kerouac, Mailer). The writer-as-celebrity is still atypical, but things are changing fast. These days, successful literary figures often have to act like movie stars, or to present themselves as such. While this is nothing new in itself—after all, plenty of fans flocked around Byron and bought tickets to hear Dickens read—it's now reached the stage where in some cases, the writing is almost an auxiliary to the life. These days, it's difficult to be a best-selling author if you're not glib and facile enough to do the round of talk shows and public appearances; it's even more difficult if you don't have a personal back-story, preferably involving a major failing or "life struggle" like alcoholism, drug addiction, depression, or some other burden that can be described at length in your best-selling memoir. This can be coy and discreet, or candid and shocking: It's up to you. You can serve up contrition on a plate, or you can be full of excuses, begging for understanding and forgiveness. I'm especially fond of those that promise startling revelations and lurid displays of candor; they seduce me with the offer of a rare, delicious treat: patho-logically self-destructive behavior, which is thrilling to read about, as long as it's described in honest and thoughtful prose, as long as it isn't solipsistic, tedious, tendentious, or self-indulgent.

Maybe the most traditional form of confessional is the kind we could call "My Foolish Former Life," which goes all the way back to the *Confes-sions* of St. Augustine and John Bunyan's *Grace Abounding* and is still popular today; recent examples include Martin Amis's *Experience* and Günter Grass's *Peeling the Onion*. Some people like memoirs that finish with a moral-izing lesson, like Augustine's *Confessions*, while others disdain the preachy flourish, preferring to draw their own instructions where they can. Every-body seems to like reading about other people's wild indulgences, espe-cially those that cause them to crash, burn, and repent, paving the way for a slow and painful recovery. There's little more stimulating than other people's failures. I'm particularly interested in the details of exactly how much these penitent authors used to drink, how much money they spent on drugs, or how they sabotaged once-in-a-lifetime opportunities through their arrogance and conceit. One of the things I love about these books is how physically healthy and emotionally stable they make me feel. My own excesses and indulgences suddenly seem so trivial that I start to think my one major failing is the fact that I find other people's problems so interesting. Part of me seems to feed vicariously on accounts of indulgence and excess. I wonder: Is this an ethical flaw? If so, the popularity of the memoir suggests I'm not the only one who suffers from it (although, suddenly, I feel rather naked in my confession).

I enjoy memoirs less when the author isn't properly embarrassed by former misdeeds. I don't mind so much if I catch just a slight sniff of the sinner's vestigial envy for a former, more colorful self, as long as they're older and wiser now, and, while not actually censoring bygone transgressions, are, in the main, ashamed of past indulgences, not simply out to impress. But when I suspect they don't really regret any of it, or they're only feigning embarrassment, the appeal is steeply diminished. For me, the pleasure of the confession is directly linked to the power of shame.

Less lubricious kinds of memoirs have charms of their own, of course, but none give me quite the same heady thrill as the tell-all confessional. Formal or academic essays sometimes lure me in with their shiny promise of personal revelation. I fall for the hook and start reading, only to find that, more often than not, the self-disclosure is only on the surface, and always slightly disingenuous, as if it's permitted only when done playfully, through oblique hints and clues. In the academic essay, there seems to be an unwritten rule that it's all right for you to bring up your own experience as long as you don't dwell too long on the personal stuff, and if you're going to use the first person, you have to play it for laughs, using a dismissively faux-humble, self-deprecating persona. You can use personal anecdotes only to embellish the body of the piece, not to provide substance for deep inquiry, or to form the core of the writing itself.

The confessional memoir is the naughty younger sister of the personal essay, a traditional form that found its first modern exponent in the early Victorian writer William Hazlitt, and is currently defended by well-respected practitioners like Cynthia Ozick, Joseph Epstein, Joan Didion, and Phillip Lopate. Ideally, it seems, if you're writing a personal essay, you're supposed to move subtly and thoughtfully from the personal to the universal, exploring common human experiences, rather than indulging in your own idiosyncrasies. You're supposed to describe your own circumstances in order to correlate them with shared thoughts and feelings, expressing general observations about human nature. The personal dimension of the essay is just to hook your readers, and once they're hooked, you can help them consider the wider human dimension of your experience. That's the idea, anyway.

Frankly, I don't see the appeal of the "wider human nature." What's wrong with personal details "for their own sake"? Why are they so often considered wasteful and sordid? Maybe it's the Anglo-American Puritan heritage that makes us reluctant to dwell seriously on the minutiae of human life and emotion—the imperative not to be too self-absorbed, to pay more attention to others. Good conversationalists, like well-behaved children, don't hog the limelight by assuming their anecdotes are more interesting than anyone else's, or that everybody wants to hear them. This injunction seems to cross over into writing, too. People often assume that to write consistently about themselves and their experiences, without exploring their larger connections, is in bad taste, tactless, hopelessly arrogant, and requires very little imagination.

Well I, for one, disagree. I love personal detail, all the more so if it's "for its own sake." To me, there's nothing more interesting than listening to people talk about themselves. I love overhearing conversations when I'm on the bus or train, or in the gym (and these days, with cell phones, you can't help it). Like my French bulldog, I'm all ears. And this is the same state I get into when I read. I'm at full attention, alert, totally focused; I turn myself over completely to the voice of the author. This is why I love the confessional: because it's monogamous; it gives me absolute personal commitment in return.

through the looking glass

A lot of people wonder why we need to know about the private lives of writers; they think a good piece of literature should stand on its own. Maybe that's true. I can only speak for myself, and in my case, when I like a work of fiction, I start to wonder where the author's ideas are coming from. I find myself wanting to know more about what poet John Berryman called "the stock of available reality" that the writer has access to, and I start to wonder about the autobiographical underpinnings of the work. Not everybody feels this way, as I've discovered. In fact, many people see this kind of speculation as, if not sordid, then at least irrelevant, nothing at all like scholarly biographies and "serious" literary criticism. A lot of people sneer at the thought of studying a work of fiction in the context of a writer's "real life"; they see it as gossip masquerading as something "higher." Some people think it's no different from the celebrity confessionals discussed in the previous chapter—the kind of writing, they assume, that's aimed at people who lack the imaginative ability to relate to a subject unless they see the flesh and blood behind the scenes.

Well, pardon me, but there must be an awful lot of unimaginative people around. Over the last few years, it's been a kind of mantra of agents, critics, and publishers that the novel is "over" and the role once played by fiction is now being played by the confessional memoir, which grows in popularity each year. This claim is often phrased as a lament, as though the public's fondness for the memoir were a symptom of the shameful decline of literacy, just as the form itself is often dismissed as irrelevant and self-indulgent.

For example, critic Charles Baxter, in his book *Burning Down the House*, claims the confessional trend has come at significant cost to both individuals and society. He argues that the collapse of boundaries between public and private life has led to a breakdown in social decorum. There's no longer any incentive, he claims, to bear difficult circumstances with uncomplaining dignity, to accept your lot in life, however bleak it may be. Baxter argues that this century has been driven by forces, from psychoanalysis to the social revolution of the 1960s, that have eroded the moral values of restraint and discretion, and the more people feel like making their private lives public, the more the publishing industry is ready to oblige them.

Critics like Baxter, who dislike confessional memoirs, usually do so either because they consider them "exploitative" of others, or because they regard the memoir as an "easy" kind of writing that doesn't impose the same kinds of creative and artistic demands as "real" fiction. While most people would agree that all books, whether fiction or nonfiction, are in some sense "about" their authors, those books that don't "go beyond" the purely confessional are more often felt to be indulgently narcissistic. The memoir itself, especially if it involves dysfunctional or self-destructive behavior, is generally seen as an emotion-laden, watery-eyed, "feminine" genre, as opposed to the rational, more masterfully objective, third person "masculine" form of literary fiction.

In brief, critics like Baxter generally assume the authors of confessionals are incapable of writing any other kind of book, which is obviously untrue in the case of fiction writers who've also written memoirs (including

Philip Roth, William Styron, Elias Canetti, and Primo Levi). More to the point, why assume a writer should "go beyond" memoir any more than they should "go beyond" any other genre, including literary fiction? After all, to dismiss the work of those who "confined themselves" to memoir would be to dismiss the work of Samuel Pepys, James Boswell, Casanova, John Evelyn, and Anne Frank, among many others.

Perhaps some people feel ambivalent about the current spate of "crisis memoirs" because, however much their authors claim to have been through, the very physical existence of the book bespeaks a certain amount of privilege. You have to have a decent amount of private time to be able to write a best-selling memoir—not only a room of your own, but time away from the demands of earning a wage and looking after your family. This kind of time, these days, is most often bought with the help of a well-connected agent and a hefty advance, which casts the crisis, however long ago it may have occurred, in the light of something lived through and left behind, something that's been overcome, analyzed, and relegated to a place in the past. To put it another way, would we have the same reverence for the diaries of Anne Frank if their author, instead of being sent to the gas chamber, had been offered a six-figure advance for a sequel?

On the other hand, I'm sure the crisis memoir does a lot to appease the envy of all those people who feel they have a book in them (which, according to the latest poll, is everybody), as well as all those unpublished authors, impoverished authors, and mid-list authors envious of the fame and attention lavished on the latest Johnny Spillguts. You might envy his advance, you might be jealous of his film deal, but if it came at the cost of going through what he's been through, of living his miserable, screwed-up, addiction-prone life, of BEING HIM, you wouldn't want it in a million years. And isn't it rather presumptuous to assume that any and all thinking people can situate themselves as actors within the plots of their own lives? The notion that confessing your private follies can help you make peace with your "true self" seems grotesque, perhaps even obscene, beside the work of writers like Czeslaw Milosz, E. M. Cioran, or Primo Levi—writers who've lived their entire lives in marginalized nations where borders are constantly being erased and redrawn; writers whose experience of national unrest has forced them to question the very existence of personal identity.

Be that as it may, I rarely feel I've got a real understanding of a fictional work unless I also have some knowledge of the personal and psychological circumstances that went into its creation. This makes sense, I think, with regard to the kind of work I find most compelling (expressionist, projective writing that seems to represent a personal manifestation of psychic experiences), but it's perhaps less necessary in the case of work that's widely considered to transcend the limits of motive cause and individual consciousness. Either way, it may not matter very much in the end, since in their personal lives, disappointingly, most authors turn out to be less like Hemingway and more like Henry James—that is to say, however wide and worldly their themes, most writers live in and through the books they read. Henry James, who called himself "The Master," is perhaps the quintessential example of the author who, despite the knowing, sophisticated tone of his novels, developed, as a result of his literary success, a boorish arrogance and a tendency to hold forth, assuming he knew far more than those around him. James talked about the "incomparable luxury of the artist," but in his daily life he seemed to forget he didn't have quite the same luxury. He was a real letdown in the flesh, at least according to his friend, the satirist Max Beerbohm, who, in one of his letters, describes running into "The Master" in a London bookshop and having to listen to the great novelist's interminable grousing. All Beerbohm wanted to do, he said, was go home

and read the book he'd just bought—which just happened to be the latest Henry James. It's one thing when your favorite author turns out to have been a bigot, a Nazi, or a fighting drunk, but it's quite another to discover he or she was just another tedious old windbag.

To discover such unpleasant things about an author you love can lead to disappointment, or even anger, but the feeling of violation is never justified. After all, when we summon up an impression of an author, as we all do as we read, we're actually creating a fictional persona. Some authors, mainly the kind for whom their writing is an extension of their personality, enjoy this fictional persona very much, and come to bask in its reflected glory. Others, mainly those for whom writing is a substitute for existence in a larger world, grow afraid of their persona, which they regard as an odd delusion, having nothing to do with them. Either way, every successful author eventually disappears behind his or her literary mask, which everyone except their personal friends actually believes to be them.

Beerbohm's anecdote, although perhaps exaggerated for comic effect, is a very tasty pinch of gossip, and gossip, to my mind, is the key ingredient in the literary biography—a genre that is, as a whole, less explicit and more serious than the personal confessional, mainly because juicy gossip about other people is often considered grounds for libel. This is why the best biographies are written when their subjects are dead, but freshly dead, still enough in the public eye to remain interesting (and marketable) subjects. It's a treat to find a really gossipy biography of a still-living fiction writer, partly because we sometimes get to witness their public indignation and attempts to "set the record straight" (although the most successful authors, after years of reviews, criticism, and public speculation, often develop a sort of bunker mentality about this sort of thing). Equally fascinating are literary biographies of subjects whose biographers, at least by the time they're through, don't seem to like them very much anymore—which appears to have been the case with Mark Schorer's life of Sinclair Lewis, Lawrence Roger Thompson's two-volume biography of Robert Frost, and, most famously, James Atlas's book about Saul Bellow.

If you're turned off by all this poking about behind the scenes, it might be because you feel that, for the writer, "real" experience isn't worth writing about until it's been "transformed" into art, so why should we waste our time digging up the dirt? While it's true that most "serious" literary biographers do prefer to avoid "idle gossip," focusing most intently on the development of a writer's form, style, and literary themes, there are plenty of others who aren't beholden to a priggish fear of details. One of the best of these is the essayist Brooke Allen, who, in her collection *Artistic License*, makes the claim that "The Western literary tradition seems to have been dominated by a sorry collection of alcoholics, compulsive gamblers, manic-depressives, sexual predators, and various combinations of two, three, or even all of the above." For example, of Hans Christian Andersen she writes, "As with so many artists, there was a bizarre contrast between Andersen's stunted personality and his work, which became ever more sophisticated and allusive"; "the obsequiousness, the eagerness to please, and the incessant craving for praise and attention were adolescent qualities that Andersen never outgrew, and they became ever more ridiculous as he aged." She would no doubt concur with Thomas Carlyle's remark about the novelist William Thackeray: "I wish I could persuade Thackeray that the test of a great man is not whether he would like to meet him at a tea party." In refreshing contrast to those readers who claim to have no interest in an author's private failings, who claim they'd prefer not to know about, say, Saul Bellow's misogyny or T. S. Eliot's anti-Semitism, Allen suggests that the nature of any form of art is somehow intrinsically connected to the flawed characters of those who make it, leading to the frightening paradox that might well be at the very heart of creative expression: the fact that good art is often made by "bad people."

Or at least—if this value judgment makes you shift uncomfortably in your seat—by deeply disturbed people. Let's say that many of the world's greatest writers suffered from what we'd now describe as psychological problems, including (but not limited to) manic depression, schizophrenia, obsessive-compulsive disorder, alcoholism, and various other addictions. Psychologists have estimated that the incidence of mental illness in authors (along with others in the creative arts) is at least three times that of the population at large, and this applies particularly to those who are most eminent, which puts paid to the notion that writing is, by its very nature, a therapeutic act. There's clearly a link between madness and creativity, albeit a very complex one, but I wonder if there's also a link between creativity and behavior that's annoying, self-obsessed, or just plain rude?

As Brooke Allen admits, literary biographies—especially the more revealing ones—get a lot of bad press. Their authors are sometimes characterized as vultures, feeding off the flesh of the dead, and sometimes as parasites, drawing sustenance from the life of the living. Freud believed that most biographers are contaminated by the infantile desire to idealize their subjects into unreality in order to build them up into all-powerful parental ideals. Clearly, Freud wasn't familiar with those biographies that, far from idealizing their subjects, bring them back down to size by ratting on all their secrets. In reference to a biography of the writer Jean Stafford, Joyce Carol Oates famously came up with the term "pathography" to describe this kind of book—the kind that focuses on its subject's defects and failings, whose motifs, as Oates put it, "are dysfunction and disaster, illnesses and pratfalls, failed marriages and failed careers, alcoholism and breakdowns and outrageous conduct. Its scenes are sensational, wallowing in squalor and foolishness; its dominant images are physical and deflating; its shrill theme is 'failed promise' if not outright 'tragedy.'"

This is the familiar lament of the staunch literary purist, who asks why we need biography at all, since, if a writer's life has been devoted to self-expression, if the basic sensations and critical events of their experiences have been used as material for their books, what more of significance can the biographer add to the record? The work is sacred. Why tarnish it with the profanity of private gossip?

Other, more moderate voices, without going so far as to disdain biography altogether, argue that most fiction writers, even those who don't lead humdrum lives, are presumably of interest to us because of the words they set down during the quiet interludes in between the turmoil. It then follows, or so the argument goes, that there are appropriate and inappropriate questions to be asked about an author's private affairs, and that it's possible, when studying a person's life, to separate the essential from the trivial. These are often the same people who like pointing out that biographers have a duty to tell the "essential truths" about their subjects, and that we should judge the writer on their body of work, not on the color of their underwear or how they treated their pets.

I think this is rubbish. Shouldn't I have a chance to decide for myself what's essential and what's trivial? And isn't the trivial also true? If an author slept on black satin sheets, kept cocaine in her purse, cried in his beer, or kicked her dog, then yes, please, I'd like to know about it. I can't imagine any detail so trivial that it doesn't grab my attention, doesn't make my ears prick up. In fact, I often think that the more trivial something is, the more interesting I find it; the trivial, so often overlooked, can be a special gateway into understanding.

This, returning to Freud, is the premise of free association, but Freud wasn't the only one with something to say about finding truth in trivia. It was also one of the major pursuits of the surrealists, articulated most clearly by the poet André Breton, who made the case in his semiconfessional novel *Nadja*, that "criticism . . . should confine itself to scholarly incursions upon the very realm supposedly barred to it, and which, separate from the work, is a realm where the author's personality, victimized by the petty events of daily life, expresses itself quite freely and in so distinctive a manner."

Like his fellow surrealists, Breton was fascinated by life's true riddles—its mysterious juxtapositions and unexpected revelations, its odd arrangements of objects. To the surrealist imagination, everything was connected, nothing was separate. Breton and his friends considered the individual detail, however apparently insignificant, as forming the core of their art. "I insist on knowing the names, on being interested only in books left ajar, like doors," he wrote. And in *Nadja* he was equally candid about the details of his own life, following up on his promise that "I myself shall continue living in my glass house where you can always see who comes to call; . . . where *who I am* will sooner or later appear etched by a diamond."

the painted veil

Gossip is no more—and no less—than the repetition of information about another person, usually of a private nature, without that person's explicit knowledge or consent. Our culture today seems fascinated by gossip, and with the intimate details and unflattering secrets it usually involves. In some ways, we seem to be increasingly compelled to find out everything we can about other people, especially people in the public eye—to peer underneath their skirts, to inspect their closets, to spy through their keyholes, to sniff their dirty sheets. Even if gossip reveals nothing very clear or specific about another person, its very existence is enticing, especially when it hints at secrets of a private and intimate nature. It functions as a kind of narrative striptease; pieces of gossip are like little windows through which we can peer into somebody else's private life. But instead of satisfying our curiosity, this arouses us even further, exciting all kinds of speculations and implications. We find ourselves absorbed by gossip, I believe, because it brings to life the story all of us share: the story of being human.

Gossip, of course, is not a modern phenomenon. In fact, though it's neither a biological function nor the fulfillment of a basic bodily need, gossiping is an activity that people have always engaged in to some extent, including many of those who profess to disapprove of it. Beneath the "official" current of lives and events, there's always been another, secret chronicle, made up of private whispers and personal reminiscences, rumors and innuendos that never appear in the history books.

Still, while there are few written records of early private gossip—Samuel Pepys's diary being perhaps the most famous example—anecdotal accounts of the personal lives of public figures go back as far as 100 AD, to Plutarch's *Lives of the Noble Greeks and Romans*. Each historical period had its own form and style of gossip, depending on the moral compass of the time. Political gossip, for example, has been used to disempower, to reveal hypocrisy, to destroy, to entertain, and to slander. The modern era of public gossip as we'd recognize it today began in 1704, when Daniel Defoe devised the world's first newspaper column that was devoted entirely to dishing out scandal, keeping first names secret (as in "K— was seen out on the town with B—"). Defoe was followed by columnists like John Evelyn and Edmund Yates, who in the 1870s began to use the personal voice ("I hear—" "I learn—" "I understand—") that today's columnists have imitated. Unlike modern gossip columnists, however, the set whose goings-on were chronicled in eighteenth- and nineteenth-century newspapers tended to be aristocrats, politicians, and lesser members of the nobility.

Gossip and literature have always been closely intertwined. In the twentieth century, many British newspapers attempted to give their gossip columns a patina of gentility by getting literary figures to do their dirty work. Newspaper magnates Lord Beaverbrook and Lord Rothmere, for example, hired a number of well-born writers to pen their columns, including Malcolm Muggeridge, who wrote for the *Evening Standard* and found his job "revoltingly futile and exhausting," and Sacheverell Sitwell, who wrote "Atticus" in the *Sunday Times* and likened it to "a truffle hunt." Nancy Mitford, on the other hand, loved her job as gossip columnist for *The Lady*, which she described as "a freeloader's dream."

"The thing about gossip," Miss Marple is fond of saying, "is that it is so often true." She's right. Not only can gossip foreground a much broader truth than that limited by "the facts," but it's also evident that memoirs, anecdotes, private details, and personal reminiscences are by far the most interesting, exciting, and compelling way of telling a story. Literary gossip, to me, isn't so much a vice as a rare skill—the ability to separate evidence from speculation, to plumb another's motives. To gossip about literature is to think deeply about authors—what they do, who they are, and how they relate to each other.

Today, the best sources for literary gossip about authors are book blogs like Bookslut, Booksquare, GalleyCat, Paper Cuts, and Return of the Reluctant, among many others, which contain the latest dish about well-known, big-name authors—their latest sales figures and royalty statements, their feuds, rivals, relationships, and reviews. As the ubiquity of such blogs testifies, gossip is everywhere, and it's absolutely free. Nobody can control which parts of their lives others can scrutinize, nor can they regulate the circulation of rumors—as many celebrities have discovered, much to their dismay. Perhaps the radical potential of gossip to resist authority helps explain just who is surrounded by anxiety and unease, why there are so many social sanctions against gossip, and why most people, when they do engage in it, do so in a guilty and secretive way.

Confessionals—the source of most literary gossip—come in many forms, including film, performance, painting, drama, and even poetry. The subjective voice played a particularly important part in the work of many American poets of the 1950s, including Sylvia Plath, Anne Sexton, Robert Lowell, Randall Jarrell, Theodore Roethke, Elizabeth Bishop, and Delmore Schwartz, all of whom specialized in first-person verse. Significantly, these poets all died prematurely. Some committed suicide; others died after an illness or accident. Either way, their early deaths were caused, at least in part, by strain imposed by the demands of their writing, and their general tendency toward self-destruction. An author's premature death unquestionably brings extra attention to the work, often from readers whose primary interest may not be the intellectual or emotional demands of the writing, but who may enjoy unearthing clues that give a glimpse into the writer's messy, complicated life. This isn't true only of authors, of course. Any untimely death—especially the desperate gesture of suicide—gives that person's life a kind of fascinating shape it wouldn't otherwise have, making it take on a certain retroactive gloss. Any successful writer or artist who commits suicide inevitably secures continuing critical attention for their work and its connection with the specific details of their life and death.

Sylvia Plath is perhaps the best-known example of a literary celebrity whose every written word—including her many private journals and letters—has, since her death at age thirty-four, been publicly analyzed. Most writers who die young give us little to go on other than their published work, but Plath's output of private writing, as well as poetry and fiction, was unusually prolific. Since her death, her every living moment, it seems, has been filtered, sifted, and studied in minute detail; everything she produced has since been recorded, published, and analyzed—not only her poetry and letters, but drafts of unpublished works, essays, photographs, journals, notes, sketches, and even doodles. Many of those who knew her have published their memories of the poet; others, who didn't know her, have published accounts of her dreams, her childhood fantasies, and her troubled marriage, ranging from the carefully biographical to the openly fictional.

How should we make sense of all this? Perhaps the trajectory of Plath's life and death contains an illusion of immortality, reminiscent of the adolescent fantasy that, after our death, every detail of our existence will be probed for its complex layers of meaning and presentiment by some of the world's greatest minds. Or perhaps it was Plath herself who sowed the seeds of her own posthumous fame. She was, after all, consumed by the drive to have her worth ratified by the wider community of critics and writers, to achieve literary celebrity (she wondered in her journal: "Why am I obsessed with the idea I can justify myself by getting manuscripts published?"). Or perhaps, as her state of mind deteriorated, her attempt to turn the confusion and neurosis of her life into poetry led Plath to a kind of violent despair, especially in the poems she wrote on the edge of suicide, which, like all suicide notes, insist on our full attention, all the more so in that they are addressed to nobody (and therefore everybody) in particular.

Of the many biographies of Sylvia Plath in print—and there are at least ten—most people agree the best is Anne Stevenson's *Bitter Fame*, published in 1998. To me, the most compelling part of this book is the series of appendices in which various people who knew Plath give their personal impressions of the poet. Among these reminiscences is a memorable essay by Dido Merwin, wife of another well-known poet, William (W. S.) Merwin, who came to be a close friend of Plath's husband, Ted Hughes. Unlike many other reminiscences of Plath, which tend to portray her as a tortured genius martyred by the demands of her narcissistic husband, Dido Merwin's essay is notably bitchy, despite (or perhaps because of) the fact that she was suffering from terminal cancer when she wrote it. As Sylvia Plath's own poetry testifies, people on the edge of death don't mince their words.

Mrs. Merwin recalls one occasion, for instance, when Sylvia and Ted were staying with the Merwins at their farmhouse in Spain; some trivial incident, long forgotten, had sent Sylvia into a huge sulk, and she insisted on staying at home while the others spent the day exploring the countryside. "What still remains a mystery," writes Dido Merwin, "is how she managed to put away the entire midday meal that I had left for her, Bill, and Ted. And that this Pantagruelian triple lunch in no way diminished the gusto with which she silently tucked into her dinner . . . As I watched Sylvia grimly downing the *Fons foie gras* for all the world as though it were 'Aunt Dot's meat loaf,' there was little doubt that we were in for a reign of, if not terror, then tiresomeness every bit as effective."

This anecdote illustrates another too-often overlooked aspect of the literary memoir—that choosing which details to include and which to leave out is a genuine skill. The best literary biographies are at the same time both gossipy and high-toned, both erudite and engaging; they're a pleasure to read. They're also brave, as with Dido Merwin's reminiscences, which go strongly against the grain of Plath's posthumous reputation. The most courageous memoir writers aren't afraid to venture into dangerous waters. They require both a keen memory for intimate details and the powerful imaginative ability to reconstruct a scene; they demand the creativity of a talented novelist and the persuasive qualities of an expensive lawyer. Dido Merwin's essay is a fine example of the perfectly toned biographical memoir; her little vignette paints a picture of Plath's sullen arrogance that's as vivid as any photograph.

comedy of errors

Another writer whose work draws very consciously from his personal life is the novelist Philip Roth. Well known for his consistent use of alter egos, most notably Nathan Zuckerman, Roth obviously enjoys insinuating biographical details into his fiction, playing games with the ambiguous nature of concepts like truth, confession, and identity. His method of writing, as he's often pointed out, involves working with his own experiences, and his fiction deals mainly with what he knows best: the Jewish American family, self-consciousness, the psychoanalytic process, and the complex web of relationships between human beings, especially between men and women. In fact, he often includes well-known facts about his own life in his novels. The protagonist of *Operation Shylock: A Confession*, for example, suffers a nervous breakdown partly induced by the soporific Halcyon, something that happened to Roth himself in 1988.

Incidentally, *Operation Shylock*—a novel about a doppelgänger—was, according to its author, inspired by an incident recalled by the mid-list novelist Richard Elman in his book *Name Dropping*. Elman—long accustomed to being taken for his much better known namesake, biographer Richard Ellman—describes spending the night with a beautiful fashion model, only to realize the next morning, much to his horror, that she slept with him because she believed him to be not Richard Ellman but Philip Roth (he allowed her to leave unenlightened). While Roth seems to have been amused by the story, the experience as Elman recalls it isn't funny at all—in fact, he found it sorely humiliating. After realizing what's happened, Elman admits that "tears came again to my eyes, masking my spurious joy, beneath which I felt the eerie calm of the imposter. My previous feelings of well-being after making love were being dragged down by a loopy mistake in identity; and I was afraid to destroy an illusion she had so carefully nurtured and sustained throughout our night of lovemaking." (It's hard to imagine this happening today—a beautiful model spending the night with a man she mistakes for Jonathan Lethem or Dave Eggers.)

Philip Roth, a Pulitzer Prize–winning novelist, is the author of *Portnoy's Complaint*, *The Ghost Writer*, *American Pastoral*, *The Human Stain*, and many other critically acclaimed and best-selling works of fiction. Now in his seventies, he's often described as the greatest living American man of letters, and is certainly one of the most important authors of the last fifty years. His relationships with women have played a crucial role in his fiction; his first wife, Margaret Martinson, has been described by Roth as the prototype for the barely literate Mary Jane Reed ("The Monkey") in *Portnoy's Complaint*, and for Maureen Johnson, the vengeful, castrating wife in *My Life as a Man*. Roth separated from his first wife in 1963, but their turbulent marriage remained undissolved until 1968, when Martinson was killed in a car accident.

Philip Roth was involved with a number of other women after the death of Margaret Martinson, but his most significant and lasting relationship was with the British actress Claire Bloom, who was his companion for fifteen years before the two finally married in 1990. Not long after their marriage, the relationship fell apart, and in 1996, after an acrimonious divorce, Bloom published *Leaving a Doll's House*, a tell-all memoir in which she described her life with the famous author. Two years later, in 1998, Roth retaliated with a fictionalized account of his second marriage in the novel *I Married a Communist*. The two books are so different in style and tone that to look at them side by side does neither of them justice, but it's a fascinating exercise, and not just in the comparison of revelations and counter-revelations. Roth's book was applauded as "extraordinary," "remarkable," "a wonderful novel, full of heart and soul"; Bloom's autobiography, on the other hand, received far less attention, and when it was reviewed at all, was generally dismissed as "dismal" and "uncomfortable." Personally, though I generally like Roth's work, I found Bloom's book far more compelling, partly because of its candor, honesty, and—at least in comparison with Roth's—its attempt to get at truth, at least as Bloom experienced it.

I hasten to point out here that Claire Bloom is an actress, not an author, and her style in *Leaving a Doll's House* is coy, wordy, and overdone in places, at least to my taste, as with her long, sentimental account of a wartime childhood which takes up the first section of the book. She then goes on to describe an illustrious stage career and two marriages, before getting to the relationship with Roth. *I Married a Communist*, on the other hand, is an urbane and sophisticated work that deals with the McCarthyite witch hunts of the 1950s, and the protagonist's marriage to a famous stage actress, Eve Frame. It includes three characters that all serve to some extent as stand-ins for Roth, each embodying a different facet of his personality.

In *Leaving a Doll's House*, Bloom sets herself up as a fragile and naive ingénue, inexperienced in the ways of the world, and inclined as a young woman to hide herself in dreams, melodrama, and romantic fantasy. The daughter of a middle-class British family, she explains how her childhood was scarred by her charming but irresponsible father, Eddie, who moved his wife and children from home to home before abandoning them altogether. Claire, her younger brother John, and their mother clung together in near poverty until Bloom's sudden rise to fame in the British theater after she won a starring role, at age nineteen, opposite Charlie Chaplin in the classic silent movie *Limelight*.

As Bloom tells it, her early years in the theater were characterized by a string of passionate and romantic but ultimately unsatisfying relationships with costars like Richard Burton, Laurence Olivier, Yul Brynner, and Anthony Quinn, most of them married, all of them deeply narcissistic and self-involved. In 1959 she married the American actor Rod Steiger, with whom she had her only child, Anna. In *I Married a Communist*, the Steiger role is played by a character Roth names Carlton Pennington, a "tall, slender, graceful man with hair as dark and sleek as a raven and a dark mustache." A marriage is arranged between Eve Frame and Pennington because "she and Pennington had made such a hit together, and she was so enamored of him, that the studio decided they ought to get married, that they ought to have a child. All to squelch the rumor that Pennington was gay. Which, of course, he was." Now, nobody who knew him has ever alleged that Rod Steiger was gay; nor is Roth doing so here. Still, Claire Bloom admits that her first marriage was undertaken more for companionship than for love ("The marriage offered us the shelter and affection we were seeking after errors in previous relationships," she writes. "If our priorities were more need than passion, our relationship gave us many years of supportive family happiness").

Eve Frame, in *I Married a Communist*, is described as a fragile, beautiful actress, a former silent movie star known for her impeccable style and refined accent—"A woman with pathos. A beautiful woman with pathos and a story to tell. A spiritual woman with décolletage." Ira, the novel's unsophisticated protagonist, is captivated by the forty-one-year-old Eve with her tender, exotic charm, and the two quickly fall in love. At first, theirs seems to be a magical, enchanting, unpredictable match; before long, the couple is married, and Ira has moved into Eve's East Village town house.

As Ira comes to know his new wife better, however, he begins to recognize some disturbing elements in her character, the most unpleasant of which is her barely repressed selective distaste for Jews. She has no problem with the accomplished Jews she's met in Hollywood, on Broadway, and in the radio business. Her contempt is reserved for "the garden-variety, the standard-issue Jew," particularly the elderly Jewish women who make up her largest group of fans, whom "she could not pass without a groan of disgust. 'Look at those faces!' she'd say with a shudder. 'Look at those hideous faces!'" What makes her disdain even more deplorable is the fact that she is herself Jewish—born, in Brooklyn, the humble Chava Fromkin.

Claire Bloom is also Jewish, and, although her father changed his name from Blumenthal to Blume, she's never made any attempt to hide her origins, unlike many Jewish actresses of her generation. Partly, she claims in her memoir, this is because her family never practiced any religion, and she experienced her Jewishness more as a feeling of foreignness than as a racial or religious difference. Anti-Semitism would be considered a far greater crime to Roth than to Bloom, since Roth is so closely identified with his Jewishness, and Bloom more by her Englishness, or her beauty, than her ethnic origins. In *Leaving a Doll's House*, Bloom says her husband vowed in 1988 that he'd never live in England again because "he now claimed to find the English anti-Semitic" (the couple had been spending six months of each year in London and six months in New York).

In *I Married a Communist*, Eve Frame has been married twice before Ira— she left Carlton Pennington for a close friend of his, a theatrical producer, real estate speculator, and rapacious capitalist named Jumbo Freedman. In Roth's novel, Freedman is a "sex clown" who makes enormous amounts of money from Broadway shows starring his new wife, then spends the proceeds on decadent luxuries, including a New York town house on West 11th Street fitted out in velvet grandeur, like a lavish brothel. "Being Eve," we're told, "she goes along with this guy's extravagance, acquiescing to his wild ways. Sometimes when Eve would start to cry out of nowhere and Ira would ask her why, she would tell him, 'The things he made me do . . .'"

If Jumbo Freedman sounds like a monster, his real-life counterpart is even more grotesque. In a chapter of *Leaving a Doll's House* called "The Unmentionable," Bloom names her second husband as Hillard Elkins, an agent and theatrical producer—his hits included *Oh Calcutta!*—who was originally a good friend of Rod Steiger's. Bloom describes him as "an average-built man with impeccably manicured nails and a perfectly trimmed goatee," who rides a motorcycle, uses a sunlamp, dresses like a teenager, and has "the frenetic air of a ringmaster added to a threatening and intimidating sexuality." She confesses frankly that, against her better judgment, she became intoxicated by this unappetizing Svengali, and wound up, at the age of thirty-eight, riding around on the back of his motorcycle, smoking pot, getting caught up in a swinging lifestyle, and finally leaving her husband to marry Elkins. Her description of life with "The Unmentionable" is open and self-revealing, though perhaps—like other episodes in the book—a little arch, especially in the air of naivety she retroactively gives herself (at thirty-eight). "Elkins's entire being was centered on sexual gratification; his fantasies were alternately voyeuristic and sadistic," she writes. "Inexperienced and sometimes apprehensive, I was a willing partner to his games, stretching the boundaries of physical experience."

The marriage lasted five years, but its effects on Bloom's daughter Anna were long lasting. Anna, claims her mother, was unprepared for her parents' divorce; her mother's remarriage to "The Unmentionable" came as a terrible shock, from which she never recovered. Bloom admits that, as a result, blame and recrimination on Anna's part, and overindulgence on Claire's, tainted her relationship with her daughter. "We became almost like sisters, arguing over our territorial rights, squabbling over clothes," she writes. "Our roles as mother and daughter were confused."

In *I Married a Communist*, it's Eve Frame's relationship with her daughter, Sylphid, a harp player, that finally causes the breakdown of the marriage between Eve and Ira. In Roth's novel, the ogre-like Sylphid has been so coddled and indulged by her mother that by the age of twenty-three she is a "big adult baby" still living at home, a "time bomb," an obese, angry monster who spends her days taunting and abusing her timid, passive mother. When Eve becomes pregnant by Ira, Sylphid calls her mother a "kike bitch" and forces her to get an abortion, threatening, "If you ever, ever try that again, I'll strangle the little idiot in its crib!" So monstrous and obnoxious is Sylphid that Ira eventually insists she move out of the house, and goes so far as to rent her an apartment in nearby Washington Square. But when Eve breaks this news to her daughter, Sylphid attacks her violently, and Ira discovers his wife "on her back screaming and crying, and Sylphid in her pajamas sitting astride her, also screaming, also crying, her strong harpist's hands pinning Eve's shoulders to the bed."

Eve's indulgent relationship with her grotesque daughter means that Ira spends much of his time taking Sylphid to recitals and carrying her huge harp up and down long flights of stairs. At home, he finds it difficult to work in her presence, and each night he's driven to bed early by Sylphid's music practice. After years of this torment, he finds himself seeking refuge in an affair with a friend of Sylphid's—an English girl, Pamela—who seduces him one night when the two of them are home together alone. When the affair is over, Pamela writes a letter to Eve claiming that Ira made unwanted sexual advances toward her, though she felt unable to tell this to Eve at the time. Finally, after her divorce, Eve publishes a tell-all book called *I Married a Communist*, denouncing Ira as a brainwashed leftist fanatic, ultimately destroying both his career and his life. Claire Bloom's version of her relationship with her daughter is, in keeping with the rest of her memoir, somewhat vague (possibly because Anna Steiger now has a career of her own, as an opera singer). She admits, however, that her relationship with her daughter was unnaturally close. "When Philip accused me of having an unhealthy preoccupation with Anna, neurotically attempting to make up for what I had failed to do in the past, he was correct," she writes. But she goes on to accuse Roth of harboring a jealous hatred of her daughter, forcing Anna out of the family home against her will. Terrified of losing her husband, Bloom complied, sending Anna to live in a nearby student hostel, a decision she still regrets. "I don't think Philip will ever understand what a monstrous episode that was," she commented in an interview with *People* magazine in 1996. "Many girls of 18 have left home, but Anna was wounded already, and this was very difficult." Even worse, after she and Roth had broken up, Bloom received a letter from a friend of Anna's, Rachael, claiming that in 1988, while Claire was away making a television film in Kenya and the two of them were alone in the house, Rachael had been subject to sexual advances from Roth.

After the nightmare of Roth's first marriage, chronicled at some length in his thinly veiled memoir *My Life as a Man*, he was understandably reluctant to remarry. But after fifteen years as his partner, Bloom wanted their relationship to be legally recognized, and Roth eventually consented—on the condition that Bloom sign a pre-nup giving him the right to terminate the marriage at will, with no further responsibility toward her. After the divorce, Bloom's lawyer managed to prove this agreement invalid (describing it, according to Bloom, as "the most brutal document of its kind he had ever encountered"). Roth, claims Bloom, was apoplectic, accusing her of betrayal (perhaps the impulse behind the choice of the name "Eve"), and faxes her a list of everything he's given her during the marriage that he now wants returned, including jewelry, assorted pieces of furniture, $28,500 per year in support, $100,000 worth of bonds, and an absurd $62 billion fine for her refusal to honor the pre-nup—a billion dollars for every year of her life. On top of this, she says, she discovered that her husband had, for some time, been having an affair with one of their mutual friends.

If *Leaving a Doll's House* and *I Married a Communist* are considered together, as responses to the same marriage, both husband and wife paint grotesque, outlandish portraits of one another. To her husband, according to his fictionalized account of their marriage, Bloom was hysterical and melodramatic, psychologically unstable, and unhealthily attached to her abusive daughter. In *I Married a Communist*, Eve's undoing is her want of character; she is "someone from whom life itself had escaped," "a woman whose deepest sense is her sense of incapacity." Her memoir *I Married a Communist*, which betrays and ruins Ira, is described as, if not ghost-written, then "the aging actress's last great career—shouting her hatred in the street." And yet Ira, who represents Roth only in part, is certainly complicit in his victimization. Ira's passionate communism is fueled by the same uncomprehending, self-destructive outrage that eventually causes his downfall. Although he portrays himself as simply a witness to the horrors going on in his household, Ira clearly bears some burden of responsibility for the breakdown of his marriage.

But Roth has disguised himself under the cover of fiction. According to his ex-wife, he was controlling, manipulative, and temperamental, wavering impulsively between overwhelming neediness and cold, distant anger. Still, it's hard to read *Leaving a Doll's House* without feeling impatient and exasperated with Bloom's mousy passivity, her seeming inability to come to terms with things. In a review of Bloom's book published in the *New Yorker*, author Daphne Merkin complained that Bloom asks for more sympathy than she deserves, casting doubt on her claim that she was helpless in the face of Roth's abuse. "One can discern," wrote Merkin, "through the pious gloss Bloom puts on the events of her life, the shrewd maneuverings of a stage brat."

Philip Roth describes his wife, in the fictional disguise of Eve Frame, as a bitter, hysterical woman, with nothing to redeem herself but her beauty and her acting talent. Even so, it's possible that Bloom got off lightly—in his novel *Deception*, Roth introduced a writer named "Philip" who has a series of affairs to relieve the tedium of his relationship with a middle-aged "Claire" (after Bloom threatened to sue, he changed the character's name).

Bloom's portrait of Roth is far more sympathetic, and, consequently, she comes out as the more appealing figure in this tangled web of thinly veiled fictions and fictionalized truths. Although she shows that Roth could be spiteful, vicious, and downright sadistic, she also makes very clear what she loved about him. She explains how she was drawn to his fierce wit, great humor, generosity, and intelligence, and loved talking to him about books. Even at the end of their marriage, she confesses that she still loved him and dreamed of their reconciling. Plus, she always claimed that Roth was worth the pain. "I thought I'd found the ideal father, lover, husband," she told *People* magazine. "And I had, for a long time . . . I had a devastatingly dreadful end to what had been in many ways a wonderful marriage, and I thought it might help me to write about it and help other women . . . Philip always said, 'Be private in your life, and shameless in your work.'"

Clearly, however, he believed that even shamelessness should have limits. On February 4, 1999, in the *New York Review of Books*, John Updike wrote, in reference to *Leaving a Doll's House*, that "Claire Bloom, as the wronged ex-wife of Philip Roth, alleges him to have been neurasthenic to the point of hospitalization, adulterous, callously selfish, and financially vindictive." Roth responded to his literary rival with a letter published in the same journal on March 4, 1999, criticizing Updike's lack of a "neutral tone," pointing out that he "adduces no evidence other than Miss Bloom's book," and complains, "over the past three years I have become accustomed to finding Miss Bloom's characterization of me taken at face value." Apart from this, Roth hasn't commented publicly on the memoir, but his friend Saul Bellow observed that it caused him "a lot of pain."

Saul Bellow's third wife, Susan Glassman, was angered by her husband's depiction of her as a nagging shrew in the form of a character in one of his novels; she described this borrowing as "ironic . . . at a time when the artist has attributed to him the magical properties of a priest." Glassman brings up an important ethical issue here: whether the use of "real people" in books like *I Married a Communist* at some point violates the privacy of those who've been used as models. There are clearly moral dilemmas involved in writing about "real people," but these are usually seen as "private" issues, separate from the work itself. This seems unfair to me. If writers as widely read as Roth and Bellow really have the right to put anyone they like into their fiction, don't their readers and critics also have the right to speculate about the biographical underpinnings of this work—and in print, if necessary?

Traditionally, of course, the writer's life has been the realm of the biographer, not of the humble reader or literary critic. It seems somehow not kosher for the ordinary reader like you or me to delve into *Madame Bovary* in order to speculate about Flaubert's relationship with Louise Colet, or to ruminate about D. H. Lawrence's sex life on the basis of *Sons and Lovers*. The role of the critic, too, it's widely assumed, is to focus on the literary attributes of a work of fiction; the highbrow critic isn't supposed to care (or even to notice) that the writing is based on "true-life" experience. Most literary critics, unless they're psychoanalytically inclined, would no doubt agree that it does the novel or story little service to trace its origins back to real, private incidents, and the investigation of an author's personal life is a wrong-headed approach to their works, since fiction writers use reality only in order to transcend it.

Well, I disagree. Even fantasy has to be drawn from "the stock of available reality" in a writer's life, and it's an inescapable truth that fictional characters are often based on people who are known, or have been known, to the author. Fiction is, among other things, a way of expressing real feelings about real people, a means of self-exploration, a coming to terms with past experience, sometimes even a way of settling scores. This, I think, makes fiction fair game, opens it up, allowing us, the readers, to sniff out connections between people in the novel and the "real" people in the fiction writer's life—wives, colleagues, childhood friends—who might have been used as "material." It seems inappropriate, really, to separate the realm of the text from that of the private life, especially since the best writers are often the greatest cannibals and scavengers, able to absorb all kinds of details, phrases, nuances of behavior, and private peccadilloes, then to transform and incorporate them seamlessly into their fiction.

I suspect that resistance to this sort of analysis is based on the fear that poking about in the source material will detract from the "magic" of the creative process. It's a common superstition that "we murder to dissect," that to explain something is to take away its essence or its power, the way a joke stops being funny as soon as you start to analyze it. In response, I'd say that you can't ever really know where "reality" stops and "the creative process" begins, any more than you can fully explain what makes something funny. The relationship between fiction and "real life" is elusive at best, often messy and slippery, never offering exact translations, never amenable to being pared down or deciphered to find what's "real life" and what's "made up." There's no way of reducing fiction to any ultimate or literal truth, even if we do believe in such a thing. After passing through the complex alchemy of the imaginative process, no scene, figure, or secret can remain untransformed.

So while I can sympathize with Philip Roth, at the same time I'm fascinated by the implication that his life, in its pattern of repetitive obsessions, seems to mimic those of his most troubled and troubling protagonists. The narrator of Proust's *In Search of Lost Time* explains that the writer is perhaps even more susceptible to emotional pain than others. "When it comes to his own passions," he says, "though he is as well acquainted as other people with the general laws that govern them, he is not so skillful at liberating himself from the personal suffering which they cause."

One of the main complaints made by Joyce Carol Oates about the "pathography" is that it so emphasizes the faults of its subject that it leaves unexplained how such an undistinguished life could produce such a distinguished body of work. But even as great a writer as Tolstoy, although revolted by what he saw as the great nastiness—even criminality—of his own life, felt his biographer would have to include all the awful things as well, because without them, his life story would be a lie. I don't believe it diminishes any writer's literary achievements to suggest that the main force behind creativity is rarely either deep intelligence or profound humanity, but, more often than not, an odd mixture of blind inspiration and unreflecting instinct.

People are mistaken, then, when they assume a connection between prolific reading or skillful writing on the one hand, and civilized manners and human instincts on the other. But while great writers are often badly behaved, it's usually in predictable ways involving run-of-the-mill transgressions, petty vanities, ordinary arrogance, and other minor follies. It's not as though they're mass murderers or serial killers. That sort of thing is all in the next chapter.

MY ACTIONS PUZZLE EVERYONE.

FRIENDS, I DO BUT LOAD A GUN.

EVERY WORD I WRITE'S INSPIRED,

THOUGH THE GUN IS NOT YET FIRED.

—*GEORGE D. PAINTER, THE ROAD TO SINODUN*

vi under the floorboards

I've suggested in this book that there are a lot of very smart, well-educated people living very functional and successful lives who not only don't like to read literature, but simply don't like to read at all—who never have, and probably never will.

There are plenty of people, in other words, for whom reading is anything but "fun-damental."

One of these people is Temple Grandin, a talented designer of agricultural equipment, featured in Oliver Sacks's book *An Anthropologist on Mars*. In her own book *Thinking in Pictures*, Grandin, who's autistic, explains how words are like a second language to her, and how, ever since an early age, she's taught herself to translate both written and spoken words into full-color movies, complete with sound, that run in her head. While she has no difficulty picturing complex architectural designs, even mapping out sophisticated blueprints and anticipating structural problems in her mind, she has difficulty understanding the kinds of abstractions she can't convert into pictures. Philosophy, for example, is incomprehensible to her, as is any kind of theoretical reasoning.

Grandin is what's sometimes known as a "visual-spatial thinker," the kind of person who tends to synthesize the whole rather than attending to details. These kinds of thinkers tend to make associations in parallels, or at tangents, so, for example, as children, they might say "dog" when they want to go outside, or refer to all cold drinks as "Sprites." These idiosyncratic associations can sometimes lead their thought processes to get sidetracked or stuck, causing their reasoning to seem irrational, and making it difficult for them to follow the sequential logic of others. Many (but by no means all) visual-spatial thinkers fall somewhere on the spectrum of autism. Some have a keen interest in aesthetic aspects of mathematics (geometry, algebra, tables, and so on) as well as computers; others have musical memories—they may be able to differentiate pitches, recall exact tones without aid, or name a certain note played in an instant. Others have "eidetic memory" (also known as photographic memory, or "total recall"): For example, chess grandmasters can memorize complex positions of pieces on a chessboard, due to their ability to mentally organize certain types of information. Others may have some degree of hyperthymesia—they may spend an abnormally large amount of time thinking about their personal past, and have an extraordinary capacity to recall specific events in detail.

Some people have amazing memories for names, numbers, languages, poker hands, dates, times, postal codes, bus timetables, or long lists of random words. Even within the range of those who read regularly, tastes can be very different. Some people like to read things that might seem eccentric to you and me—supply catalogues, etiquette handbooks, safety manuals, maps, lists, albums, vintage advertisements, the verses inside greeting cards. Many people read constantly without ever opening a volume of literature, or even of narrative fiction. There are people who read only history books, biographies, travelogues, volumes of philosophy, recipe books, or academic articles. Some people are mesmerized by true crime. And I'm one of them. I'm always dragging reluctant friends to the sites of famous murders, even when there's not so much as a worn stain left to mark the spot. For a while, I lived just down the street from where Jack the Ripper killed one of his victims, in London's East End; I went all the way to Plainfield, Wisconsin, to get a look at the home of the grave robber Ed Gein. At the Lizzie Borden Bed and Breakfast in Fall River, Massachusetts, the understanding proprietress left my boyfriend and me alone in the house all night (even though they were officially closed) in the upstairs murder room, where the furniture is reproduced exactly as it was back then, as you can see from the framed photographs of Mr. and Mrs. Borden lying bludgeoned RIGHT WHERE YOU'RE STANDING NOW . . .

When I was a kid at the fairground, I was most excited by the scary rides, the ghost train, and the haunted house. I'd do anything for that horrible feeling you get in the pit of your stomach when the front of the train smashes through the double doors into the darkness and your heart turns over in delicious fright when you realize it's too late to change your mind, you can't go back, and now you're REALLY in for it.

At the age of eight or nine, I remember being spellbound by the Chamber of Horrors at Madame Tussaud's in London. At first, too scared to go in, I hung around the entrance, waiting for my brothers to catch up. The Chamber of Horrors was a dark cellar, with walls painted black, and an odd, damp smell that brought to mind the rats we dissected in school, yellow with formaldehyde. In those days, about thirty years ago, the Chamber of Horrors featured waxwork tableaux of Victorian criminals, grotesque vignettes that made such a strong impression on me that I can remember them to this day.

There, in the center of the room, stood Jack the Ripper, leering over a woman's body lying in a pool of blood. To the left was a bathtub in which another woman's body lay half disintegrated, and behind her stood the "Brides in the Bath" murderer, John George Haigh. Next was Dr. Crippen, wearing a top hat like the Ripper, followed by John Reginald Halliday Christie, of 10 Rillington Place, in front of the brick wall behind which, the scene implied, he'd just finished burying the body of his latest victim. Finally came the famous poisoner Neill Cream, gleefully measuring out a dose of Prussic acid to drop in some nice old lady's tea.

People often think our fascination with violent crime is a recent phenomenon, a sign of cultural decline. TV pundits talk as though we were living in a uniquely voyeuristic and amoral society galvanized by a morbid interest in human suffering, but this isn't the case at all. There's always been a huge public appetite for details of real criminal cases, from ancient Rome, when spectators would clamor for the best view of gladiatorial combat, to the fascina-

tion in early modern England with public executions. These days, I'm told, the Chamber of Horrors has been turned into a "live event," where actors dressed as Hannibal Lecter from *The Silence of the Lambs* and Jack Torrence from *The Shining* chase screaming tourists through a maze, herding them toward the new "Spirit of London" animatronic ride. As George Orwell famously pointed out in 1946, the English murder has declined since its classical phase, and the cheapening of the Chamber of Horrors proves his point. Still, there's definitely something extra creepy about Victorian murder cases, of which none is more compelling, more conducive to research and speculation, than that of Jack the Ripper, a figure who remains in shadow despite regular claims by forensic experts, crime writers, and historians to have solved the mystery through fingerprinting, Masonic symbolism, DNA evidence, or past-life regression. For anybody who wants to sink their teeth into this fascinating case, by far the best book on Jack the Ripper is Alan Moore and Eddie Campbell's graphic novel *From Hell*, which is also, for my money, the most thorough and engaging study of late nineteenth-century London.

I can't quite put my finger on what makes Victorian murders seem so  nasty. I think it has something to do with the hypocrisy of those middle-class male-factors—the reputedly mild-tempered Dr. Crippen; John Christie, with his collection of female pubic hair kept in a tobacco tin; Burke and Hare, the Edinburgh body snatchers; John Haigh, the well-mannered choirboy who did away with his victims in a bath of acid. Secrecy and deceit, it seems, are elements as vital to Victorian murders as bloodstained wallpaper, unclaimed trunks at railway stations, quicklime, and a dose of strychnine in the teapot. Perhaps the special horror of these crimes has to do with their unexpectedness—all that bludgeoning, poisoning, and garroting going on in chintzy country houses and seaside hotels, in English parlors and strait-laced tea rooms, in the shadow of the gallows. Then, of course, a murder in those days was really rare and horrible, an event that called for boldface headlines, exclamation points, details "too shocking to be printed." Where I live now, in Baltimore, there are five or six murders every week, crimes so commonplace they barely make the newspaper.

Some "serious" readers, I've discovered, will turn up their noses at true crime; they see it as trashy, tabloid pulp, with no appeal for the healthy-minded intellectual. It may be the case that most true crime paperbacks don't have the intricate form and style of literary fiction, but form and style aren't everything. For me, the deep pull is in the thrilling notion that—how delicious—these awful things really happened.

Each afternoon of my final undergraduate year at Oxford, with every intention of studying for my exams, I'd sit surrounded by literary classics, volumes of Chaucer and Malory, persuaded that I was, in fact, hard at work, when what I was really doing was killing time while I waited for the hippie librarian to bring my special books from the stacks, books like *The Night Stalker*, *Burned Alive*, *With an Axe*, and *The Trunk Tragedy*, which he'd leave on my desk with (I always thought) an expression of sympathetic concern. And next thing I knew, the sun was going down, there were long shadows on the wall, and the closing bell had just sounded.

Cycling back for dinner, I'd always feel a bit ashamed of myself for spending my afternoon in one of the world's greatest repositories of literature reading about the Butcher of Düsseldorf and the Rostov Ripper, but never ashamed enough to break the habit; in fact, my interest only got sharper and more discriminating. I'd sometimes take the bus to London on the weekend to visit Murder One on the Charing Cross Road, a bookshop specializing in true crime (this was long before Amazon.com), that stocked a huge selection of American paperbacks with vivid color pictures in the middle. For a while I was spending as much time in the back corner of Murder One as I was in the Bodleian. You name it, I read about it, and the bloodier the better, from the Icepick Murders to the Torso in the Toolbox, from the Mann Street Massacre to the Cock Lane Killings. I subscribed to *True Detective*, *Master Detective*, and *Murder Most Foul*, and I even struck up a correspondence with a bona fide killer who'd placed an ad for pen pals in the paper. My housemates, when I told them my new friend was in prison for killing his pregnant girlfriend, started referring to him as "Slayer" (as in "it's Slayer on the phone for you"). We did more than talk on the phone—I went to visit my new pal four or five times in different prisons (for some reason I could never fathom, they always seemed to be moving him around). He seemed shy, polite, and gentle to the point of frailty; it was hard to imagine him carving a turkey, let alone stabbing someone to death with a kitchen knife. I'd write him letters asking questions about the murder, which, he told me, he'd answer if I sent him some "bikini shots" in return. I was flattered and embarrassed, though I never sent him any. True, I wanted to learn more about his crime, though it wasn't vicious or sensational, like the murders I read about. There were no axes or icepicks, just a sad domestic squabble that got out of hand, and an ordinary kitchen knife.

And to tell the truth, I was a bit too fat for a bikini.

crime and punishment

In his book *Illuminations*, Walter Benjamin claims that "what draws the reader to the novel is the hope of warming his shivering life with a death he reads about," an observation that seems to be even more applicable to true crime, a kind of writing that, at its best, suggests that our "shivering life" may, at any moment, be invaded and transformed by bad magic. Even more than fiction, true crime performs alchemy on the base metal of the everyday, spinning it into tales of deranged madmen, tormented villains who behave like characters in mystery novels. I know this is an idealized, even a sentimental view; I realize that murder is, in general, as banal and unexciting as any other daily tragedy. The best true crime, though, isn't set in the world I know, but in one very like it—my own world reflected through a funhouse mirror, with everything turned upside-down and inside-out: terrifying, exciting, but still recognizable. Even more than the most provocative fiction, true crime has the power to re-enchant the ordinary, to unearth hidden currents of life running parallel to ours, layers of tangents, secret coincidences, and questions so perplexing they make you start to suspect that, unlike dreams, nightmares really can come true. In this chapter, I'm going to guide you through the territory, showing you the kinds of things you can learn from this much-maligned but highly popular genre.

For a start, one of the things I like best about true crime is that it pays attention to the sort of detail that other kinds of writing often overlook. For example, in praising Diana Trilling's *Mrs. Harris*, a carefully discerning account of a trial that made a celebrity of a woman who murdered her lover (Herman Tarnower, the Scarsdale Diet doctor), *New York Times* critic Anatole Broyard wrote how impressed he was by the author's curiosity, "by her quality of close and sustained attention in our abstracted and inattentive age." It's precisely this quality that fans of true crime really love about it. If the bug bites you, it can be utterly fatal, and once you're in the grip of a book like this, it's almost impossible to put it down. For me, the more unsettling the material, the more riveting I find it. I love detailed books about thoughtful criminals. Two of my earliest favorites were Ludovic Kennedy's *10 Rillington Place*, about the murderer John Reginald Christie, and Joe McGinnis's *Fatal Vision*, about the Jeffrey MacDonald case. Christie and MacDonald were unusual characters who combined intellectual power with that painfully naked ambition, envy, and philandering that seem so often to be the "other side" of cleverness and a good upbringing. Personally, I find crimes so much more interesting to read about when they're committed by smart and successful people; it can be thrilling to track the furtive logic and demonic secrecy by which talented people can ruin their lives.

Fictionalized accounts of true crime, however well written—even the classics of the genre, like Truman Capote's *In Cold Blood* or Norman Mailer's *The Executioner's Song*—don't have quite the same appeal, for me, and neither does crime fiction; I suppose the frisson I'm looking for comes only with the knowledge that what I'm reading about "actually happened." More powerful than either Capote or Mailer, I think, are the two best accounts of the Manson murders, *The Family*, by Ed Sanders, and Vincent Bugliosi and Curt Gentry's *Helter Skelter*, both of which gave me a real sense of how ordinary people, like the girls recruited into Manson's "family," can cross the imaginary line that, we like to think, divides "us" from murderers. Both books bring out the cult's eerie pride, and the utter pointlessness of its crimes, in a way that I think would be quite impossible to do in fiction. Similarly, Ron Soble and John Johnson's *Blood Brothers*, about the Menendez murders, gets nicely specific about odd little details overlooked by news coverage of the case and made-for-TV "based on a true story"-type movies—details like Kitty Menendez's former life as a beauty queen, problems in the parents' marriage, the brothers' inordinate fascination with celebrity, Lyle's shrink, and Erik's toupee.

A lot of true crime writers are both skillful and prolific. Michael Newton, for example, has a talent for wrapping up the bloodier parts of a case in a formula that's both comfortable and predictable—the shock of the crimes, the search for evidence, the hunt, the arrest, the confession, the trial. Ann Rule, another prolific true crime writer, has a knack for describing the ripple effect of the crime on the victim's family and community, especially in *The Stranger Beside Me*, her book about Ted Bundy, whom she actually dated, briefly, when they were both young.

Books like *The Stranger Beside Me*, written by someone with a personal acquaintance with the subject, have an extra twist, especially when they're really honest. The best example is probably *A Father's Story*, by Lionel Dahmer, Jeffrey's father, whose sympathetic and intelligent attempt to make sense of his son counters the popular truism that all serial killers are the product of abusive parents. I found Mr. Dahmer's description of his son's inertia especially fascinating—the way Jeffrey would sit around drinking beer out of a brown paper bag, responding to his father's questions in monosyllabic grunts, just like many other inarticulate, directionless young men. Yet at the same time, in secret, he was building a shrine from human bones, drilling holes in people's heads, tenderizing human flesh for consumption—behavior that to his horrified father seems to have come out of nowhere, impossible to explain or account for.

If I had to make a list of the true crime books that have made the strongest impression on me, it would have to include *The Corpse Garden*, Colin Wilson's 1998 study of mass murderer Fred West and his wife Rose; *Beyond Belief*, Emlyn Williams's 1968 account of the "Moors Murders," and *Killing for Company*, Brian Masters's 1986 book about serial killer Dennis Nilsen. I've never believed my interest in true crime to have any national allegiance, but it occurs to me now that these are all British authors writing about British cases, and I see this is no coincidence. I spent the first thirty years of my life in England, and I think we tend to be particularly affected by murder cases, especially local ones, that we hear about when we're young.

Plus—and this is more idiosyncratic, perhaps—there seems to be a sort of damp sordidness about English crimes that appeals to me, in an odd way. As I mentioned earlier in relation to Victorian murders, there's something I find especially horrible about the juxtaposition of ordinary, straitlaced British life, with all the knots and tangles that can accumulate underneath it—dark family matters, perverse sexuality, occult rituals, strange beliefs. Without glamorizing or mystifying their subjects, and without neglecting the importance of mood, the best true crime writers combine meticulous research with enough nervy speculation to allow them to understand some of the moral complexities of the murderer's mind.

the history of a crime

Of all the true crime books I've read, one in particular is especially memorable. It was in the Murder One bookshop that I first came across a copy of *Somebody's Husband, Somebody's Son,* by Gordon Burn, a book widely agreed to be the definitive account of the life and crimes of Peter Sutcliffe, better known as the Yorkshire Ripper.

In May 1981, when I was a young teenager, Peter Sutcliffe, a truck driver, was tried at the Old Bailey and found guilty of thirteen counts of murder. His insanity defense fell flat, but after a few years behind bars, Sutcliffe was diagnosed as a paranoid schizophrenic and transferred to Broadmoor, the best-known British high-security psychiatric hospital (where he remains TO THIS VERY DAY . . .).

As with similar high-profile criminals (the Boston Strangler, the Manson family, Son of Sam), the Sutcliffe case strongly evokes the spirit of a particular time and place. It has always intrigued me, mostly because of its close associations with the time and place of my own childhood, and partly because—unlike major criminal trials in the U.S., which are always covered in great detail by the media—Britain has never allowed cameras in the courtroom, and there are strict laws governing television coverage of legal matters. Sutcliffe remained a mystery. All you ever saw of him were the same two or three family snapshots that were published in the papers, and a handful of courtroom sketches. He was never shown on television, you never heard his voice; he never had a full identity as a real human being, and since the heart of the case remains a blank, it has a kind of cold, nostalgic eeriness about it, even today.

Like the women killed by Jack, the original Ripper, Sutcliffe's victims were mainly prostitutes—or, in the ludicrous euphemism of the tabloid press at the time, "good-time girls"—but not all, and there was a lot of mud stirred up by the way the papers referred to these "others" as Sutcliffe's "innocent" victims. A few women survived his attacks, including an early victim who never came forward, and whom Sutcliffe, in his confession, recalled bludgeoning over the head with a stone tied inside a sock. When the police were unable to find this woman, they christened her with the grisly name of Stone-in-Sock, a name that brings to mind other semimythical apparitions—Typhoid Mary, Springheeled Jack.

And another Jack—Wearside Jack. Everybody who lived in Yorkshire at the time can remember the audiotape, supposedly from the Ripper, sent to the West Yorkshire Chief Constable, George Oldfield. They played it over and over again: on the radio, on television, at school, and through special speakers set up in bus shelters. There was even a Dial-the-Ripper phone line you could call to hear the tape. "I'm Jack," it began. "I see you are having no luck catching me." The crackly recording seemed to emphasize the mockery of the voice, with its pronounced lisp and the Newcastle accent that led the papers and police to come up with the nickname "Wearside Jack." The tape, in the end, turned out to be sent by a hoaxer, but that didn't make it any less horrible. Nobody ever found out who Wearside Jack really was, or what his reasons were for perpetrating the hoax. Like the mocking letter sent to the police in 1888, return-addressed "From Hell," believed to have been written by the original Ripper, Wearside Jack came out of the night and returned just as obscurely, alone and unknowable, like the tragic Stone-in-Sock.

When I was a child, growing up in Sheffield, I remember adults lowering their voices whenever the Ripper came up. Nobody ever spoke about what he did when he got hold of you. They didn't give details in the newspapers, either, which made it all the more terrifying. There were no photographs, except of the latest victim on a happier occasion, and the occasional blurred image of a heap covered by a raincoat on the grass.

I recently ordered a copy of *Somebody's Husband, Somebody's Son* to reread, to see if it had the same impact on me now as it did when I first read it twenty years ago. Unlike other books I've reread after a long stretch of time, it wasn't disappointing; in fact, it turned out to be just as gripping as I remembered. Even better, the used copy I ordered turned out to be a hardback, with a beat-up cover and pages that were a bit brown round the edges. The first thing I noticed when I opened it was its smell—not quite the musty, moldy smell of a book that's been kept somewhere damp, but something else, something a bit sharper. Was it my imagination, or did it contain a slight cast of formaldehyde?

A waxwork museum, interestingly enough—less famous than Madame Tussaud's, but more grotesque—played a notable role in the Sutcliffe case. At the end of the pier at Morecombe, a bleak little seaside town in the north of England, once stood a small wax museum whose upstairs floor

contained a pair of dark, sordid rooms called "The Museum of Anatomy." The first of these rooms contained nine life-size female torsos, with cross-sections cut from their lower abdomens, whose original function was to illustrate "The Nine Stages of Pregnancy" to the Victorian public. The second contained a macabre display of diseased genitals, ostensibly designed to reveal "The Awful Results of Men Leading Immoral Lives Before Marriage."

According to Gordon Burn, Peter Sutcliffe was fascinated by the Museum of Anatomy, and would visit often, lingering in the odd, dilapidated medical exhibit, which is described at some length in *Somebody's Husband*. Unlike many authors on the Sutcliffe case, and unlike a great deal of crime fiction, Burn resists the tendency to overreach and exaggerate, to make monstrous. He has no illusions about the tedium of Sutcliffe's life, or the fact that, by all accounts, he was a very ordinary man, no different from thousands of similar men who work in factories or mills, drive trucks or buses—married men who sometimes pick up prostitutes. After work, he'd go for a drink with his mates, then he'd go home for his tea and, most nights, spend the evening watching TV with his wife.

Most nights.

Working-class life in the north of England—as, no doubt, everywhere—can be grim and bitter, the stultifying monotony of one day barely distinguishable from the next. In *Somebody's Husband*, Burn evokes this cheerless tedium in suffocating detail, describing "Pete" and his mates sitting around in the pub after work and on weekends, nothing to talk about, nothing to do but drink, their barren routines broken up only by football games, cricket matches, and family functions—birthdays, funerals, weddings, and anniversaries. Wives and mothers were crucial—you had to get married if you wanted any kind of family life—but that doesn't mean they were inviolable. Women still needed to be put in their place every now and then, shown who was boss. Most men gave the missus a regular "back-hander" (also known as a "clip round the ear") whenever she stepped out of line. This was just what you did if you were a man, something as taken for granted as making jokes about your mother-in-law, or putting down the "prozzers" you picked up on the sly.

The point is never made explicitly in *Somebody's Husband* (it doesn't need to be), but Sutcliffe's crimes weren't an aberration. They were part of the misogyny endemic to British working-class life, with its boredom and its odd puritanism. The late 1970s were particularly redolent of this hypocrisy. It was a time of dirty postcards, smutty jokes, *Carry On* films, a leering Benny Hill being chased around by half-dressed women on TV. It was a time of blue comedians in smoke-filled workingmen's clubs doing routines about wogs and pakis, tits and cunts. In his character, as in his crimes, Sutcliffe was entirely representative of his class, gender, and generation, with its simultaneous fixation and disgust with female sexuality. But this unfriendly truth couldn't be spoken; it had to be twisted into something further from home. This, Burn implies, is how we came up with that terrible demon, the Yorkshire Ripper—a bloodthirsty fiend who prowled the streets and alleyways, a depraved monster who did "unspeakable things" to helpless young girls like me.

Woken in the night by strange noises in the street outside, I'd be rendered motionless with terror. Terrified to move a muscle, I'd lie there in bed telling myself that it wasn't really a muted scream I'd heard, just the yowl of a cat on the rooftops.

I believed in the Ripper. We all did. We couldn't help it. We'd been infected by the superstitious frenzy cooked up by press and police, by the shadowy haze of rumor and magic that settles around all unsolved crimes.

As for those "unspeakable things," the truth is that although Sutcliffe was one of the most prolific and violent murderers in British history, his method was actually quite brisk. It had to be, because unlike most murders, Sutcliffe's were committed in public places. Apparently, according to what he told the police, he'd feel the urge to violence gradually building up in him. When this urge became impossible to repress, he'd drive through the red-light district of a nearby town late at night, looking for a woman walking alone. When he noticed one, he'd slow down and speak to her, and, if she offered him sex, he'd pick her up and take her to a dark, quiet place. He'd get out of the car, start to get undressed and ask her to do the same, and as soon as she turned her back, he'd knock her out with a powerful hammer blow on the back of her head. If she didn't offer him sex, he'd park, get out of his car and follow her until they were in a quiet place, then just come up behind her . . .

What happened next, he told the police, would vary according to where they were, and how much time he had. In most cases, he'd pull up the unconscious woman's clothes and stab her a number of times in the breasts and stomach with a knife or sharpened screwdriver. On two occasions, he cut the torso right open. He rarely had sex with the women. In general, the earlier murders were more brutal and drawn out than the later ones. Autopsies showed that all the victims were unconscious while they were being stabbed, and died before regaining consciousness.

After each murder, Sutcliffe confessed, he felt an overwhelming sense of well-being, and usually drove home and slept peacefully in bed with his wife, Sonia. He attacked at least twenty-two women over six years, thirteen of whom did not survive. Gordon Burn, in *Somebody's Husband*, explains that the murders were a private, secret part of Sutcliffe's life, a dirty urge that sometimes popped up its ugly head, an urge that wouldn't ever entirely leave him alone, though he sometimes believed it had gone for good. His immediate motives remain unclear, but it's been widely reported that, as a young man, he was humiliated by a prostitute in a pub, and picked up an infection from another. Around the same time, he found out that Sonia, then his fiancée, was involved with another man, and that his mother was cheating on his dad. During his trial, naturally enough, these episodes were used as the foundation for an insanity defense, but the jury, who felt that Sutcliffe must have known what he was doing, decided (very wisely) that if a person was schizophrenic, he'd surely show signs of it more often than three or four nights a year.

And Peter Sutcliffe didn't. According to Burn's book, he was just another man with a nasty secret, a man who sometimes did things at night that were too awful to think about in the morning. Imagine him waking up in bed with his wife, believing at first that it had been a bad dream, then gradually realizing that it had really happened AGAIN, going downstairs in a cold sweat, wondering if they'd found the body yet, wondering if there'd be anything in the morning papers.

Still, let's face it: People murder each other everywhere, everyday. Even in England, husbands kill their wives in the kitchen, mothers drown their kids in the bathtub. Without minimizing the facts, Burn implies that what Sutcliffe did goes on all the time—in the form of domestic violence, as well as on television, in movies, or just in private fantasy—and the difference between us and Peter Sutcliffe is a difference of degree, not of kind. There's no need for any magic or madness.

At least, there wasn't at first. But if Sutcliffe wasn't the Ripper to start with, he soon turned into the Ripper, and this, I imagine, is what began to induce his psychosis. If he wasn't insane at the time of his crimes (and I think the jury was right to decide that he wasn't), his eventual break with reality may well have been occasioned by his dawning realization that never again would anyone see him as the mild, attractive, shy young man he'd always assumed himself to be. He was now Peter Sutcliffe, the Yorkshire Ripper. Once he'd confessed, he had to wear the mask, play the part, carry the full burden of public hate that had been festering in tabloid vitriol for the last six years. This is what radical psychiatrist R. D. Laing meant in *The Divided Self* when he said it's society that produces schizophrenia.

And here's something else I learned from *Somebody's Husband*. If you get deep enough into the banal, things start to look interesting. If you focus intensely enough on the commonplace, you can go all the way in and come out the other side; you can go through the mirror and discover something terrifying, amazing, miraculous. Strange as it may seem, there can be horror in the everyday, magic and wonder lurking in the ordinary details of familiar, domestic lives, like the dusty Museum of Anatomy in the bleak seaside town. And here's another example of something unexpected, something oddly out of place. The night his mother dies, Peter Sutcliffe goes round to his brother Mick's house, to tell him the news:

> Mick was eating the dinner that Susan had been keeping warm for him for hours when Peter arrived. The dinner was on a low table in front of the settee, and, as he leaned forward to load his fork during an uneasy silence, the plate appeared to move: all three present in the room that night would later swear that it rose of its own volition, and hovered five or six inches in the air.

This incident must have also struck Alan Moore, since he includes it in an illustrated panel in the afterword to *From Hell*, although the dinner plate has transformed into an ashtray (and the source cited by

Moore is not Gordon Burn but Roger Cross, from his 1981 book, *The Yorkshire Ripper*).

Books like *From Hell* and *Somebody's Husband* first taught me that true crime, unlike the "great books" I read at Oxford, could really shake up my life. This is why I love it. When I'm absorbed in it, I can believe, at least for a while, that although things might seem dull on the surface, in the hidden gaps and corners of this life strange, terrible things are happening—levitating plates, suicide cults, modern-day cannibals, hacksaw murders, a torso hidden under the floorboards, a severed finger in a jar of jam.

acquainted with the night

If the nineteenth century was the classic period of English murder, then the decade of the 1980s was the golden age of the serial killer. Go to the true crime section of any bookstore, and you'll find shelf upon shelf of books about serial killers. Best sellers include Michael Newton's *Encyclopedia of Serial Killers*, Harold Schechter's *Serial Killer Files* and *The A–Z Encyclopedia of Serial Killers*, Peter Vronsky's *Serial Killers: The Method and Madness of Monsters*, and David Lester and Charles Press's *Serial Killers: The Insatiable Passion*, which, though not intended to be, is an apt description of the public fascination with these crimes. Take a closer look, however, and you'll notice most serial killer books focus on certain "classic" cases that have been canonized by the true crime industry: Charles Manson, Ed Gein, David Berkowitz (Son of Sam), Albert DeSalvo (The Boston Strangler), Ted Bundy, Richard Ramirez (The Night Stalker), Henry Lee Lucas, John Wayne Gacy, and Jeffrey Dahmer. Ask anyone to name a serial killer, and chances are they'll name one of these. Let's face it, how many people can think of a serial killer since Jeffrey Dahmer?

The idea of the "serial killer" is a classic example of a moral panic, and a perfect paradigm for understanding the popularity of true crime, and how it relates to the way we see the world. In his book *Using Murder: The Social Construction of Serial Homicide*, sociologist Philip Jenkins explains how the political climate of the 1980s was especially ripe for the creation of a moral panic—a type of collective behavior characterized by "suddenly increased concern and hostility, in a significant segment of society, in reaction to widespread beliefs about a newly perceived threat from moral deviants." According to Jenkins, moral panics generally give rise to social movements aimed at eliminating such threats, and may generate moral crusades and political struggles over the use of the law to suppress them.

More than twenty years have passed since the serial killer "epidemic" of the 1980s, yet the myth of the serial killer seems to be as important to the way we perceive the world as it ever was—perhaps even more so, considering our incessant fixation on spectacular crimes. In fact, it's almost as if these "classic" serial killers of the 1980s are still with us, existing in a kind of perpetual present, out of time, removed from history altogether. To use an analogy with the humanities, Bundy, Gacy, Berkowitz, et al are the institutional texts, the dead white males of serial murder. Since Dahmer, very few mass murderers have fit the true crime industry's role requirements for the successful serial killer. The "true" in "true crime" is descriptive, not all-embracing; in other words, not everything that "really happened" makes good "true crime." It's a complex and fascinating genre, though part of the complexity, at least for me, lies in its boundaries and restrictions, which are rigorous, if implicit; as authors working in this field know very well, cases must be chosen wisely. The best true crime writers realize that the kinds of crimes people want to read about are crimes they're already familiar with (or think they are).

You might imagine, for example, that a serial killer would make the perfect subject for a true crime book, but in fact, this isn't the case. There haven't been many true crime books written about "foreign" serial killers. There isn't much true crime writing of any kind that deals with criminals in the developing world; fans of the genre aren't really interested in killers who prey on poor people in far-flung areas of the globe, however gory and sensational their crimes might be. I think this is partly because many of us imagine the developing world to be a hotbed of violence and corruption anyway—the kind of place where people disappear inexplicably all the time (unlike America, of course, where everybody is always accounted for). Implicitly, then, the notion of a "third-world serial killer" seems faintly ridiculous—tautological, even—and perhaps a kind of grandiose farce, like those photographs of malnourished children in African villages wearing Nikes.

Another thing to remember about true crime writing is that books only sell if their protagonist has a familiar face and name. We've all heard of Jeffrey Dahmer, John Wayne Gacy, and Ted Bundy, but how many people have heard of Japanese mass murderer Toshihiko Hasegawa, or cannibal killer Issei Sagawa? This might seem like a trivial point, but it's not: The fact that we all know the names of the "classic" serial killers is one of the ways in which they've become institutionalized. This is a common theme in narratives; folklorist Bill Ellis, in his book *Raising the Devil*, makes the point that "the recurrent motif in which a mortal gains power over a supernatural entity by guessing its name" expresses "a need to control the uncanny by capturing its essence in words."

When you get right down to it, in crime as in everything else, America has always considered itself more advanced than the rest of the world. At first, it might seem absurd that a country would want to see itself as "number one" even in its style of social dysfunction, but it's really not so surprising. After all, the notion of a socially dysfunctional individual suggests the rest of society must be working successfully, all the more so since the problem has been brought to our attention. In the kinds of communities we often imagine exist elsewhere, especially in the developing world, an aberrant individual would, we assume, never be noticed, since the entire culture is in chaos anyway. We tend to see serial killing as a very rare and advanced kind of social dysfunction, so we assume it only happens in the context of a smoothly functioning society, just as anorexia only becomes a problem in a culture with excess food.

This explains the popular superstition that serial killing is a side effect of capitalism. Random, motiveless violence is often considered to be the last resort of pathological personalities who can't be satisfied by the things that the rest of us find fulfilling—commodity acquisition and display, erotic attachments, success in the workplace, strong family structures, and so on. According to popular wisdom, people who kill at random do so because they've had enough of the anonymous, predictable tedium of their daily routine, a reaction nicely summed up by the expression "going postal." Gaudy, random crimes are typically believed to be the acts of unstable personalities driven to extremes by their meaningless lives, desperate for the notoriety such crimes will bring them. To many Westerners, then, it seems presumptuous that someone should "go postal" in a country that doesn't even have a proper mail service.

Another popular theme of true crime writing is that murderers, though evil "underneath," on the surface look just like everybody else. At the time of his crimes, for example, Peter Sutcliffe was a presentable, married, white man in his middle thirties. In other words, he was "one of us," which is, in part, what made his case so very compelling to press and public. Like

Sutcliffe, Dahmer, and Bundy, the most marketable serial killers are the kind of people we can identify with, the kind who might be played by John C. Reilly or William H. Macy in the made-for-TV movies of their lives. If true crime writing is anything to go by, we're not interested in the shabby crimes of homeless drunks or toothless drifters; we want our serial killers smart, clean, and articulate, preferably with a good job, a nice house (in the suburbs, natch), and a baffled family who "never suspected a thing."

In his book (written with Thomas Schachtman) *Whoever Fights Monsters: My Twenty Years Tracking Serial Killers for the FBI*, former FBI chief Robert Ressler describes the classic serial killer as a white male in his mid-to-late-thirties with a stable home and steady job. Usually of average or above average intelligence, he's often attractive and may be happily married. He might be a "monster" at heart, as Ressler suggests, but there's no visible evidence of his monstrosity. He's the man who lives next door; he goes to your church, lends you his lawn mower, drops your kids at the pool. He's just like you or me, a truism already implicit in titles like *The Stranger Beside Me*, *The Killer Next Door*, and *The Evil That Walks Among Us*.

As a result, in true crime, no one notices anything unusual about the serial killer until he's actually been caught—and if he's not caught, his crimes soon fade from memory. True crime writing is, essentially, a deeply conservative genre; its fans don't want to read about the failures and inadequacies of law enforcement, since it would disturb too many of our comfortable assumptions. In fact, some critics of the genre have claimed that one of the main social functions of true crime is to glorify the struggles of an understaffed police service, reinforcing public support for law enforcement.

Another imperative of true crime writing is that a killer is only considered to be as interesting as his victims, which explains the inordinate amount of attention given to "gay serial killer" Andrew Cunanan, whose crimes were widely ignored until he shot the famous fashion designer Gianni Versace. It also explains why so few books are written about so-called "Golden Age Killers"—usually nurses, or nurses' aides, who prey on their elderly, bedridden patients. Alongside the young, healthy victims of more spectacular crimes, these people aren't considered to be victims so much as grave dodgers, their lives all but over anyway. Their quiet deaths seem more like euthanasia than mass murder.

Even the Yorkshire Ripper didn't get much press until he started murdering "innocent" women, as well as the prostitutes of whom, he told police, he'd been commanded to "clean the streets" (and it's interesting that Sutcliffe only discovered his "mistakes" when he read about them in the papers the next day, like everybody else). Prostitutes, especially if drug addicted, alcoholic, or aging, are less socially "valuable" than other victims. There's an unspoken assumption that they're already criminals in their own right, for whom the threat of violence is always a possibility, the price to be paid for their "high-risk" lifestyles. Like junkies, pedophiles, terrorists, and other unfashionable pariahs, prostitutes are believed to live somewhere outside the law, a dark netherworld on the edge of ordinary life into which, if you wander alone late at night, you could easily find yourself being bundled into a white van, pushed down a well, or knocked unconscious by a man with a hammer.

Murders that captivate the wider public, by contrast—and consequently end up as the subject of true crime best sellers—tend to be those that feed our belief in "random violence," a belief that disguises the complex social and economic problems underlying every murder. Unsurprisingly, 99 percent of true crime writing is devoted to crimes whose victims are, in social and cultural terms, the most valuable and highly prized: attractive young white girls, especially blondes, from middle-class families. (Consider the inordinate media attention given to high-profile victims like beauty queen JonBenét Ramsey, college student Natalee Holloway, pregnant mom-to-be Laci Peterson, pretty intern Chandra Levy, church-going Elizabeth Smart.)

the altar of the dead

In fact, contrary to popular opinion, I sometimes think the victims play as important a role in true crime writing as the perpetrators of violence. Our fascination with the lives and deaths of murdered victims (usually young women) provides many of these books with their narrative drive, allowing us to linger in loving, anticipatory detail on the last days of these murdered girls, who then become a special kind of celebrity, sacrificed for our sins. As with other holy martyrs, every moment of their lives has been recorded and described. We're told what they had for breakfast, how much they loved to dance; we know the name of their dog, the size of their shoes. In fact, there's a whole category of true crime devoted solely to victims. Notable texts in the genre include Gary Kinder's *Victim: The Other Side of*

Murder, Sharon Tate and the Manson Murders by Greg King, *Laci* by Michael Fleeman, *Rachel Smiles: The Spiritual Legacy of Columbine Martyr Rachel Scott* by Darrell Scott, and an early classic on a fascinating subject, *Thirty-Eight Witnesses: The Kitty Genovese Case* by A. M. Rosenthal. Part of the appeal of these books lies in their concrete descriptions of everyday life; their authors pile detail upon detail as irrefutable evidence of the victim's "ordinariness," leading voyeurs everywhere to murmur under their breath that sacred axiom of *schadenfreude*, "There but for the grace of God go I . . . "

According to the art critic Robert Hughes in his 1993 book *Culture of Complaint*, where the fifteenth century was eager for saints and the nineteenth century looked for heroes, today we subscribe to the cult of the victim. As Hughes explains, to be vulnerable is to be invincible, and every month brings new trends in suffering: "Complaint gives you power—even when it's only the power of emotional bribery, of creating previously unnoticed levels of social guilt." So much attention is given to victims, in fact, it's hardly surprising we all want to be one. No role these days has more power, or greater appeal. "Almost everybody can claim victim status today, and they're busy doing it. It's what keeping up with the Joneses was in the 1950s," wrote critic James Bowman in *The New Criterion* in September 2004:

> In this culture, people lay claim to moral authority, to a state of moral grace, by saying, "I have suffered." That's what drives confessionalism. But it's not the suffering that really matters, it's the overcoming. Traditionally, what a culture claims on behalf of its heroes is that they've overcome something. What we're seeing now is that people expect that status simply from having suffered.

To achieve this status in true crime writing, however, the victim must be utterly blameless. The violence against her must come "out of the blue"; it must be sudden, senseless, and undeserved. Random violence has a very broad appeal, and has always been the central theme of true crime writing. In "real life," however (as opposed to "true crime"), most murders are the result of everyday issues like poverty, drug addiction, culturally sanctioned misogyny, and the repressive constraints of marriage, religion, and family life. In other words, most murders aren't random at all, but clearly patterned, with very obvious motives; but then, most murders don't make the headlines. If they did, we'd be forced to confront the disturbing truth that we're all responsible, at least in some part, for any act of violence committed against us.

Unconcerned with such mundane facts, true crime writing showcases only the spectacular, the extraordinary, the shocking and outrageous, lavishing attention on celebrity criminals in books that are avidly devoured, often by the very people who complain about the public's fascination with these "monsters." This, I think, is because true crime writing has a special appeal for people whose values are most seriously threatened, whose ideals are in grave danger of collapse. It displaces and disguises perils much closer to home, perils that are neither haphazard nor dramatic but banal and commonplace, like the thousands of unremarkable murders that are committed every year within the family, crimes whose causes are deep-rooted and impossible to resolve.

If this is the case, then true crime will continue to sell as long as it perpetuates the illusion that murder is caused by random evil, not by the failure of social policies and cultural institutions. But then, most people have never been much interested in dispelling illusion, as Gustave Le Bon pointed out in *The Crowd*, his famous 1886 study of the popular mind:

From the dawn of civilization onwards, crowds have always undergone the influence of illusions . . . The masses have never thirsted after truth. They turn aside from evidence that is not to their taste, preferring to deify error, if error seduce them. Whoever can supply them with illusions is easily their master; whoever attempts to destroy illusions is always their victim.

I really want to believe in subway stalkers and random slashers, axe murderers and family annihilators. I love reading about deranged madmen and sex-crazed psychopaths, even though, on another level, I know they're just an illusion. My pal "Slayer," for instance, was as dull as dishwater. The last time I heard from him, he was making the most of his time in prison, studying for an associate degree in philosophy, writing his under-graduate thesis on the nature of time and space. ("Good choice," said a prison warden. "You've got plenty of time, and not much space.")

The truth, however unpleasant to face, is that people who kill are just like everybody else; they're ordinary people, though their sense of self may be less stable, their tempers less controlled. They stand in line at the grocery store; they sit next to you on the bus. They're just people with problems, people like you and me, though we love pretending they're completely different "underneath"; we love believing they're just like us, AND YET . . .

It's this AND YET, this combination of repulsion and identification that makes true crime riveting enough to re-enchant our dull, everyday world.

Nonetheless, watch out. You're far less likely to be murdered by a random stranger than by the person sitting closest to you, right now, as you read this book.

In fighting to persuade us that reading literature is the only genuine path to internal self-development—an argument grounded, perhaps, in nostalgia for their own school days—the advocates of reading are overlooking some of our culture's richest, most imaginative productions.

In the last chapter, I showed how true crime can help you anatomize and explore the inner lives of people very different from you, people who—on the face of it, at least—are immoral, venal, vicious, and nasty. In this chapter, I'm going to take a look at another nonfictional form that, I believe, can also help you to understand the world around you in significant ways that other kinds of writing can't: the analytic case study. Reading case studies, as I'm going to explain, can help you to be less self-centered, help you to see the world through other people's eyes—even the kinds of people you might normally find frightening, and might want to avoid. The appeal of case studies, like that of the other nonfiction forms I've been discussing, is in their detail. "Caress the detail, the divine detail," Nabokov advised other would-be writers. What's fascinating about these particular kinds of details is their slice-of-life quality, their plausibility, as Nabokov well knew. Their mysteriously vivid, sensual quality seems proof of their authenticity. In the analytic case study, details suggest the intimacy of private knowledge, a personal recollection of lived experience. It's through the accumulation of such details that human consciousness is constructed—it's how you make sense of yourself, your life, who you've been, and who you've become.

Indeed, it's by discovering order and design in other people's affairs that we learn that most difficult of lessons: how to make sense of ourselves. In some ways, in fact, we actually need to know the personal and intimate details of other people's lives in order to help understand and control our own. When interviewing men about their sex lives, for example, the well-known sex researcher Alfred Kinsey discovered that most people he spoke to considered themselves abnormal; according to his findings, most people thought that others never did the kinds of things THEY liked to do. Many of the men interviewed by Kinsey admitted living in constant fear that their own "perversions," which were often as common as masturbation or an interest in pornography, would be exposed for everyone to see. Reading about other people's sexual tendencies would have helped reassure men like these that other people weren't so different from themselves, and that, at least where human sexuality is concerned, there's no such thing as "normal."

The classic of the case study form is Freud and Breuer's *Studies in Hysteria*, which I first stumbled upon by accident, browsing in my college library. I was instantly seduced by the book's graceful vignettes, which seemed to be strange combinations of the medical memoir and the sideshow exhibit. The second time I read them, however, they seemed to have been magically transformed into fairy tales about sad girls whose histories gave a brief glimpse into the peculiarities of memory and mental processing, dark mysteries hidden in an impenetrable past.

Studies in Hysteria appealed to me irresistibly, the way medical oddities and curios appeal to me; I've always been fascinated by pickled creatures in specimen jars, three-headed sheep, children raised by wolves. As a book of analytic case histories, *Hysteria* is a classic; each chapter is a story in itself, with a nice, clean narrative arc, and a mood of intellectual adventure. I loved the way the authors delve unflinchingly into private secrets and hidden desires; I loved their imaginative reconstructions of unrecoverable events. At the same time, for scientific studies, they seemed surprisingly gossipy, with their hints of lurid goings-on behind closed doors in wealthy, turn-of-the-century Viennese households, dark worlds haunted by catatonic girls, lecherous fathers, English nannies, and the ghostly smell of burnt pudding. In an article published in the *New York Review of Books* in 1971, Vladimir Nabokov dismissed the Freudian unconscious as "the garbage can of a Viennese tenement," which is a very interesting way of putting it. As scavengers and detectives (as well as psychoanalysts) have often proved, rubbish can be very revealing.

After 1918, Freud gave up writing full-blown case studies, and his work, though interesting in other ways, never resumed the intriguing tone of *Hysteria*, where his (and Breuer's) style and technique made me picture them as alchemists or magicians, rather than a pair of respectable physicians. This is one of the things I find so appealing about Freud—that, for a while at least, he was the opposite of respectable; more mesmerist than medic. According to researcher Peter Swales, Freud was known as "der Zauberer" ("the magician") by the children of Anna von Lieben, a rich patient whom he treated at home in the 1880s. Not quite a "proper doctor," he was, claims Swales, generally received at the back door of his patients' homes, rather than the front. Significantly, in their work on the history of psychoanalysis, Leon Chertok and Raymond de Saussure trace a line from the "universal fluid" theory of eighteenth-century magnetism, through mesmerism and hypnotism, to the Freudian concept of transference.

Studies in Hysteria was heavily influenced by Freud's apprenticeship with Charcot, the famous "mad doctor of Charenton"—the patients were mad, not Charcot—and it's well known that in the early days of psychoanalysis, Freud's analytic technique relied heavily on Charcot's own version of mesmerism. In his later essay, "On the History of the Psychoanalytic Movement," Freud describes these early years as his time of "splendid isolation," when, following the advice of his first master, he learned "to look at the same things again and again until they themselves begin to speak," to go over the same material endlessly, until, as he remarks in *Hysteria*, "the symptom would join in the conversation."

Hysteria is full of intriguing little glimpses into the potentially transgressive nature of Freud's work, such as his claim that, according to the evidence of psychoanalysis, "almost every intimate emotional relation between two people which lasts for some time—marriage, friendship, the relations between parents and children—contains a sediment of feelings of aversion and hostility, which only escapes perception as a result of repression."

It's hard for me to avoid the conclusion that the potential of Freud's work diminished as he gradually refined his thinking, downplaying the less popular implications of psychoanalysis in the attempt to mold it into a coherent and discrete "scientific system." We're introduced to some remarkable characters—the Wolf Man, the Rat Man, Little Hans—but compared to the women of *Hysteria*, their stories are much less vivid, their personalities less compelling. None of them evoke the haunted Victorian world of *Hysteria*, whose ending I've always found exquisite in its discreet understatement—that demure pronouncement that the end result of psychoanalysis is no more (and no less) than the transformation of "hysterical misery" into "common unhappiness."

One of the things I find most interesting about these case studies is not what's present, but what's absent—that is, the words of the women themselves. It's always the analyst, never the patient, who has the privilege of telling the story. None of Freud's "hysterics" are permitted to shape their own narratives; in psychoanalysis, shaping a story would involve resistance and denial; naturally, coherent narrative is the opposite of free association.

These days, the collection of case studies is a well-established form in its own right, and many volumes are published every year, although, since psychoanalysis itself is swiftly becoming a curiosity from the past, the authors of these books are usually therapists or counselors of various bents, rather than couch-happy old codgers. In today's case studies, not only do the patients have a voice, but the therapist might also talk about his or her own personal entanglement in the situation. One of my favorites is *The Fifty-Minute Hour*, by Robert Lindner, a modern classic from 1952, when psychoanalysis was still sexy. I have the original paperback, which looks like soft-core porn, with a sketch of a naked woman on the front, and the following warning on the back:

> I am a psychoanalyst. I meet and work with murderers, sadists, sex perverts—people at the edge of violence—and some who have passed that edge. These are their stories as they told them to me—searching, revealing, perhaps shocking.

Of course, I love to read well-written case studies in other fields, like forensic pathology and self-destructive behavior, but I rarely find them as addictive as the analytic narrative, which, at its best, has the eerie appeal of the crime scene photograph. Not without reason did the archivist Otto Bettmann call close-up photography "Freudian": By giving us special access to the subject out of context, both photography and psychoanalysis encourage a powerful sense of false intimacy. Both, too, are art forms new to the twentieth century. Despite Freud's original proclamation (and the claims of many practitioners), psychoanalysis has never been a science. Its results (through free association, for example) can never be replicated, and there's no such thing in psychoanalysis as an "exemplary case," only private narratives and peculiar curiosities. The analytic art of interpreting the unique nature of each patient's story, the

mysteries and accidents that make up singular lives, is exemplified today
in the best collections of modern case studies, which include, as well as
The Fifty-Minute Hour, Schopenhauer's Porcupines by Deborah Luepnitz, and
Love's Executioner by Irvin Yalom.

In *Studies in Hysteria*, Freud and Breuer make the startling claim that the responsible analyst should "put aside all his feelings, even his human sympathy," that he should be "opaque to his patients and, like a mirror, should show them nothing but what is shown to him." In other words, the analyst's interest in details of the patient's life should take the form of a benevolent, abstracted curiosity, not an involved and prurient voyeurism. At least, that's the theory. In practice, however, to believe you can draw a firm line between professional interest and private curiosity is at best bad faith, at worst hypocrisy, or even delusion. Let's face it: The psychoanalyst is no more (and no less) than a sanctioned voyeur.

Most obviously, both the psychoanalyst and the voyeur are both concerned with the intimate details of other peoples' lives. Unlike the common voyeur, however, the analyst generally sees these details as symptomatic of some deeper pathology, not as curiosities that are engaging in their own right. More critically, while the ordinary voyeur is drawn to cases that appear uniquely puzzling or lurid, the analyst endeavors to reassure his or her patients that they're not, in fact, conclusively different from other people, often by placing them in a broad diagnostic category.

People confess things to their analysts in the hope that their confessions will cleanse them and make them feel purified, but, on paper at least, these confessions can seem very dirty, which gives them the same magnetic appeal as intimate scandal. Even the way names are disguised—Anna O., Dora, Elizabeth von R.—recalls the hush-hush allure of the gossip column, with its transparent, revealing details. Detail is the treasure buried within the personal story, the hidden key that makes the case study, like the snippet of personal gossip, plausible, memorable, and worth passing on.

Intriguingly, Freud himself knew that his case studies provoked questions of uncertainty about the kinds of stories he was telling. In his discussion of the case of Fräulein Elisabeth von R. in *Studies in Hysteria*, he comments:

> It still strikes me as strange that the case histories I write should read like short stories and that, as one might say, they lack the serious stamp of science. I must console myself with the reflection that the nature of the subject is evidently responsible for this, rather than any preference of my own. The fact is that local diagnosis and electrical reactions lead nowhere in the study of hysteria, whereas

a detailed description of mental processes such as we are accustomed to find in the works of imaginative writers enables me, with the use of a few psychological formulas, to obtain at least some kind of insight into the course of that affection.

It seems curious that Freud would want to claim he's not responsible for the mysterious and exciting nature of these case histories, that he'd rather they were less entertaining and more "scientific," as though there were something dangerous in the forbidden pleasures of make-believe (in fact, in his 1907 essay "Creative Writers and Day-Dreaming," he claims that the love of making up stories suggests a retreat to childhood fantasy: The fully developed adult, he argues, has no interest in fantasy—including religion). His defensive tone is understandable: Freud positioned his unconventional work within the field of empirical science, whose practitioners are traditionally dismissive of the unique, the accidental, the specific, and the unrepeatable.

I suggested earlier that one of the things the analyst does is try to reassure his or her patients that they're not, in fact, crucially different from other people. This means that in the best case studies, we get the impression that all impulses, fantasies, and desires, however florid or frightening they might first seem, are part of our shared humanity. "The thing that's between us," wrote French author Marguerite Duras in her book *Practicalities*, "is fascination, and the fascination resides in finding out that we're alike." In other words, we're most engaged by things that are so familiar they're no longer recognizable, which is precisely Freud's definition of what he calls "The Uncanny"—in German, the "Unheimlich," or "unhomely" ("un" according to Freud, is the index of repression). Those of us engrossed by case studies, then, are driven to get to the heart—to solve the puzzle—of what motivates other people, people like celebrities and psychopaths, who in some respects appear to be indistinguishable from the rest of us, but in other ways—the things they do, the way they live—seem about as different as it's possible to imagine.

We assume that what makes us unique and original are the intimate details of our lives, but the case study shows us that this isn't always the case. In fact, intimacies can be related and connected in many conventional ways, importing the public into the private and showing how similar and alike we all are, which can be in turns comforting and disturbing, and sometimes both at the same time. Reading case studies can help us become experts in who we are, can make us aware of all our quirks and peculiarities, those things that make us different from others (which doesn't necessarily mean we want to be "cured" of them).

So what can case studies give us that literature can't? Well, I can only speak for myself, and for me, they have a twofold appeal. First, there's the thrill of learning about things that are horrible, shocking, and forbidden; next, there's the frisson that comes when I realize that these strange things—in that they're part of the shared continuum of human acts, emotions, and beliefs—are also, in fact, a part of ME. The case history, then, is both curiosity and exemplar, both a defiance of categories and a formulation of new ones that emerge from the struggle between analyst and patient, against one another and together, to separate the particular casualties of individual circumstance from the general misfortune of being human.

the doctor's dilemma

While advocates like Oprah have done a great deal to reduce the stigma of therapy by merging the private world of the therapist's office with the public realm of national television, a lot of us are still suspicious of strangers who want to poke their noses into our private lives. Some dismiss therapy as trivial and self-indulgent; others, however, have a genuine aversion to psychiatrists, analysts, therapists, and other headshrinkers, a superstition in the same category as the distaste for being stared at, the primitive fear of photography, the desire to harbor secrets, and the dislike of gossip. There's something nasty and invasive about having other people discuss (and, implicitly, judge) our desires and fantasies, although, of course, they do this all the time, as do we all. Children, in particular, don't like being stared at, but love to play games like hide-and-seek and peek-a-boo, and none of us ever really outgrows this ambivalent childhood voyeurism—the headshrinker, perhaps, even less than others. In this sense, the analyst is no different from anyone else with an avid interest in being an insider, in having the latest scoop—the name-dropper, the gossip columnist, the eavesdropper, the celebrity hanger-on, the reader—the only difference being that analysts keep this inside knowledge to themselves. Or, at least, that's the idea.

The veneer of secrecy and disguise in the case study is necessary because therapists are bound by a promise of confidentiality unless there's been a serious infraction of the law, in which case they may feel a duty to notify the police. The first Michael Jackson prosecution began this way, when secrets revealed by a young boy in therapy led his shrink to call the cops. But secrets spilled on the couch can creep out in other ways, too. The Menendez case was brought to trial when the analyst's girlfriend, sitting in the waiting room, "overheard" Erik and Lyle arguing about the murder of their parents (though some claim the whole thing was set up by the shrink, who apparently feared for his life). Dr. Ralph Greenson, one-time "psychoanalyst to the stars," let slip a smorgasbord of tantalizing tidbits from the lives of his celebrity patients, including Frank Sinatra and Marilyn Monroe, shortly after their deaths. And, like the rest of us, analysts naturally gossip about each other, both in their professional publications and in the wider public realm—consider the long battle between Janet Malcolm, author of two exposés of psychoanalysis (*The Impossible Profession* and *In the Freud Archives*) and Jeffrey Moussaieff Masson, former director of the Freud archives and author of *The Assault on Truth: Freud's Suppression of the Seduction Theory* and *Final Analysis: The Making and Unmaking of a Psychoanalyst*.

It wouldn't be going too far to say that psychoanalysis was founded in and through gossip, if we define gossip not as lies, but as the sort of inferences we draw when someone does something interesting and uncharacteristic. *Studies in Hysteria* is essentially a compendium of turn-of-the-century Viennese scuttlebutt, legitimized in the name of science, true enough, but compounded, like all gossip, from fables, fabrications, and theoretical make-believe. Today, these concoctions of myths have dissolved into a series of metaphors, many of which surface daily in the wit and wisdom of sages like Dr. Phil, the charismatic, balding tele-therapist whose trademark exhortation is to "get real!" This same impulse to expose private details also informs the current popularity in literary culture of confessional nonfiction, the personal essay, life writing, biography, and autobiography, not to mention various forms of group therapy, psychoanalysis, and twelve-step programs. Part of the reason for this "confession obsession" relates to the way our moral vocabulary (of good and evil) has been replaced by a therapeutic vocabulary (of repression and neurosis). The popular, contemporary version of Freudian psychoanalysis, channeled through the self-help ethos of Oprah and Dr. Phil, has led to the assumption that self-realization depends upon peeling off our various layers of "artifice" to get to the "core" at the "heart" of our "true selves."

According to current fashions in pop psychology, the more private people are, the more repressed they are; coming forward and telling one's secrets—even if those secrets embarrass and compromise others—is believed, rather like reading, to be a self-evident force of good. Exposure, we like to feel, is cleansing, honest, and healthy for all involved. According to popular opinion, individuals who are psychologically stable have nothing in their lives they need to keep to themselves. What popular opinion fails to realize, however, is that, while it's logical for us to feel that if we poke about in something for long enough, we'll eventually understand it—our childhood, our relationships, whatever it may be—experience shows this is rarely the case. Nonetheless, we keep on probing and prying, unable to shake off the ancient superstition that once we know all there is to know, everything will suddenly make sense.

In the last fifteen years, there's been huge growth in the publication not only of case studies, but also of personal memoirs that describe how it feels to experience different psychological states and conditions. Some of the most powerful of these include *The Noonday Demon*, Andrew Solomon's account of battling clinical depression; *An Unquiet Mind*, psychologist Kay Jamison's description of living with bipolar disorder; *Wasted*, Marya Horn-bacher's story of her anorexia and bulimia; and *Drinking: A Love Story*, a memoir of alcoholism by author and journalist Caroline Knapp. These are distinct from the subcategory of semifictionalized autobiographies by former psychiatric inpatients, the best of which are written by women: *Faces in the Water* by Janet Frame; *The Bell Jar* by Sylvia Plath; *Girl, Interrupted* by Suzanna Kaysen; and *I Never Promised You a Rose Garden* by Joanne Greenberg. Although subjective, these memoirs are no more or less "true" than the "clinical material" presented in college textbooks, or, for that matter, the stories any of us tell (or believe) about ourselves. In a similar way, documentary films can vividly limn the inner landscape of a person suffering from a psychological illness; fascinating examples include *Sick*, Kirby Dick's gut-wrenching portrait of a terminally ill masochist, *Jupiter's Wife*, Michael Negroponte's chronicle of a homeless schizophrenic, and *Grey Gardens*, Albert and David Maysles's sojourn in the isolated home of a codependent mother and daughter. I suggest a selection of these, or similar personal testimonies, to replace the many stiff, dull, outdated clinical articles that are still mandatory reading for psychoanalytic trainees (yes, it's true, some people still do train in psychoanalysis).

While "real life" case studies can be a lot more compelling than fictional accounts, the two forms are not completely different. Well-written case studies have to involve a certain amount of fiction if they are to present psychopathic personalities as endlessly, grotesquely fascinating, and not—as, in fact, is very often the case—dull, tedious, unpleasant, and annoying to be around, repeating their gripes endlessly to anyone prepared to listen. Despite what most trained professionals would have you believe, the majority of troubled people will gladly share their stories and talk about their problems with anyone who shows the slightest flicker of interest, regardless of the personality and behavior of the listener, as you'll no doubt know if you've ever found yourself trapped in conversation with a dotty neighbor or a rambling oddball at the bar. In other words, when it comes down to it, psychoanalysts and "good listeners" are pretty much interchangeable, as are the "dysfunctional personality" and the boring old man on the bus.

The reason why the "deviants" of case studies seem so much more interesting than anyone we've ever come across is because they've been made into semi-fictional characters, and, as a result, are drawn more vividly than people in "real life." In the same way, the *Diagnostic and Statistical Manual of Mental Disorders (DSM)*—the book of numerical codes necessary for insurance reimbursements—is more a handbook of Platonic ideals than of descriptions of real human experience. Vague, amorphous ailments like "Adjustment Disorder" and "Stage of Life Disorder" become distinct categories, as though they designated something as easily identified as tuberculosis or a case of the mumps. "Real people" are more complicated, more unpredictable, and often more difficult to pin down than characters in case studies because they're more changeable, and their behavior is more nuanced and subtle, more individuated and idiosyncratic (which doesn't necessarily mean it's more interesting). The "medicalization" of the range of ordinary human behavior in the *DSM* is appealing, however, because it offers us an escape from the real world of ambiguity, obscurity, doubt, compromise, and accommodation. It also implies that private difficulties are "medical problems," which makes them seem something more than ordinary elements of personality that we can all recognize: moodiness, belligerence, constant worrying, nerves.

Is it for this reason—to engage and maintain our attention—that analysts who write about their patients turn them into complex, absorbing figures that seem completely removed from the rest of us? By the same token, do we go into therapy for the same reason we tell stories—to hold on to someone else's attention? Do we all share the secret fear that, if we can't keep the interest of others, we'll cease to exist? Like Scheherazade in the *Thousand and One Nights*, are we dependent on sustaining the curiosity of others for our life's blood?

confessions

Most psychoanalytic training, even today, is deeply grounded in the Freudian method, and students are encouraged to consider Freud's works in the way a trainee for the priesthood might study the Bible. That might be a more onerous task if Freud weren't such a consummate stylist. In fact, to me, it's partly his literary style that makes Freud's work so compelling. Like many other scholars in the humanities, I came to Freud through psychoanalytic literary theory, not through science. The Freud I'm familiar with isn't a scientist but a philosopher of the mind, whose insights have helped us consider human beings and their endeavors from a radical new perspective—as, indeed, have the writings of other seminal thinkers, including Marx, Darwin, and Hegel. Freud offers metaphors to understand social and cultural formations, particularly power, and provides a fruitful way of addressing the complex relationship between the dominant and the repressed, the mainstream and the marginalized, the licensed and the taboo.

I'm also attracted to the enormous importance Freud gives to language—metaphors, puns, word games, and stories—as a key to those parts of ourselves of which we ordinarily remain unaware. In other words, what appeals to me about Freud is his art, not his "science." Indeed, Freud himself realized clearly and early on that psychoanalysis had little to do with nineteenth-century definitions of scientific empiricism. On the other hand, he had an extensive cultural education, and his theoretical writings are rich in allusions to artists and writers like Shakespeare, Michelangelo, E. T. A. Hoffmann, Botticelli, Wilhelm Jensen, Heinrich Heine, and others.

Most psychoanalysts, however, regard Freud as a "scientist" rather than a philosopher or man of letters, as though his works were supported by empirical evidence. Debatable Freudian assumptions are taken for granted—for example, that child-rearing practices have a lasting impact on personality, that our thoughts and deeds are driven by repressed sexual and aggressive urges, that children harbor erotic feelings toward the parent of the opposite sex, and that religion developed as an outlet for neurotic personalities. Moreover, Freud's writing is often treated as though the themes he writes about weren't present in psychology before him, or hadn't arisen elsewhere, outside Europe, independent of his influence.

Beyond the psychoanalytic community, of course, most mental-health professionals regard Freud as little more than a dead weight. Modern psychology dismisses his theories as shaky science, and regards his case histories as contaminated by misogyny and manipulation. It's taken for granted that a number of his theories, such as his early pathologizing of homosexuality and masturbation, are no longer tenable. Most psychologists consider Freud's theories of the human mind in the same way that modern biochemists think of alchemy—interesting historically, perhaps, but totally irrelevant to modern science. The Freudian method is now practiced by only a very small group of analysts even within the domain of psychoanalytic psychotherapy, which tends to focus on the kinds of short-term counseling more likely to be covered by "managed care."

That doesn't mean there's no place for Freud anymore, even within psychoanalysis, as long as his work is considered as a kind of rhetorical storytelling, as it is in the work of Adam Phillips, who began his academic career studying literature at Oxford and was, until 1995, principal child psychotherapist at the Charing Cross Hospital in London. The editor of volumes on Charles Lamb, Walter Pater, John Clare, and other literary figures, and author of books on psychoanalytic themes, Phillips was recently appointed series editor of the new Penguin Freud, in which each volume has a different translator, and there are no indexes or scholarly footnotes. In other words, Freud is being treated like other great imaginative authors.

Phillips is interested in the ways Freudian psychoanalysis can help us understand ourselves, our history, and our culture. He believes that the implications of Freud's writings reach far beyond the consulting room; in his book *Promises, Promises: Essays on Poetry and Psychoanalysis*, he defines psychoanalysis as "applied literature." At the same time, however, he's a practicing analyst deeply versed in Freudian theory, who appreciates the possibilities of the Freudian method. In books like *Monogamy* and *Houdini's Box*, Phillips provides a richly illuminating perspective on Freud as a writer, a theorist, and a philosopher, without clinging to the iconic version of Freud as medical doctor and scientist of the mind. Phillips believes in psychoanalysis, but with significant and necessary reservations. As he slyly points out, "When psychoanalysis is being wholeheartedly endorsed it is not being taken seriously, because the understanding of psychoanalysis involves a continuing resistance to it. To accept psychoanalysis, to believe in psychoanalysis, is to miss the point."

As the work of Adam Phillips testifies, psychoanalysis and the act of reading have a lot in common. Consider, for example, the process of reading—deep, immersive reading, where you're completely absorbed. Here, the exchange between author and reader takes place, like the analytic transaction, in the no-man's-land between public and private, between conscious and unconscious worlds. Ideally this should be a safe, protected space, away from the ordinary concerns of daily life, a place without social rules or bodily needs.

Many influential authors have recognized the narrative appeal of Freud and Breuer's *Studies in Hysteria*. Cultural critic Philip Rieff, for example, has drawn attention to the literary nature of the case study, and compares the history of Dora (Freud's "Fragment of an Analysis"), with its puzzling and complex structure, to a work of modernist fiction. In his essay on the same subject, literary historian Steven Marcus points out that although the characters in case studies may be "real" people, they are "real" people in disguise, just like the characters in a work of fiction, who also normally have real-world blueprints or prototypes. Marcus also characterizes the Dora case as "a great work of literature" that involves such distinctive features as "innovations in formal structure," a "Nabokovian frame," and an "unreliable narrator."

From the psychoanalytic perspective, case studies have a powerful unconscious dimension, which, according to the reader's critical perspective, may be a reflection of the mind of their author, of the culture that produced them, or of language itself. By looking at the case study as a sort of dream, by attending to symbolism, word choice, affect, and imagery, psychoanalysis grants us a glimpse into the process of creation, at its conscious and unconscious levels, and foregrounds the importance of narrative thought in all human endeavor.

For the analyst, reading case studies can provide a rich source of material, in both their conscious effects and unconscious residues. There's no doubt that the thoughtful reader experiences various kinds of transference during the process of reading, not only vis-à-vis characters in the case, but also vis-à-vis the author. In this sense, reading case studies can expand consciousness by helping us to understand how we relate to characters in a narrative. This kind of self-discovery should not be confused with pointless self-absorption; in fact, if successful, it takes us in the opposite direction from introspection, toward the diminution of the ego, which can, in turn, enhance our understanding of other people, and strengthen our connection with them. For everyone who reads them (and not only analysts), case studies can be an important way of enhancing empathy and enlarging vicarious experience. They can be a guide in the search for values; they can foster honest communication. Like the very best fiction, they can let us know what it feels like to be someone else.

conclusion

At the art college where I teach, students in their freshman year take a course called Critical Inquiry. In this class, they're required to read a series of texts—usually short stories or personal essays—and to produce a visual response. The class enables us to investigate different aspects of the creative process, especially the relationship between form and meaning, and the distinction between visual and language-based ways of thinking. A lot of the students are multiskilled, talented as both artists and writers. Others are highly visual thinkers, who find reading difficult and sometimes have trouble expressing themselves in words.

I teach Critical Inquiry twice a year, and it's really helped me to distinguish these different styles of thinking. The visual responses I'm presented with, whether performance pieces, paintings, or digital videos, are often provocative, and always revealing. Sometimes they'll illustrate a character, place, scene, or moment in the text; sometimes they'll reproduce the mood, tone, or atmosphere of the story. Sometimes they'll be based on an idea or issue raised by the text, often in the form of analogy—for example, one student responded to an essay about an endangered species of lizard by pouring cow's blood over himself, then emptying a box of popcorn over his head (leaving quite a cleanup job). Sometimes the connection will be oblique or obscure—a hamster running around the room inside a ball was, I recall, a response to John Updike's short story, "A&P".

At other times, the visuals will focus on a particular line, word, phrase or image. The first time I taught this course, one of the texts we used was "Gimpel the Fool" by Isaac Bashevis Singer, a folk tale (translated from the Yiddish by Saul Bellow) that reveals newer and deeper layers of resonance every time I read it. As his visual response, one of my students, Dylan, produced a beautifully textured, semi-abstract painting of what appeared to be four rabbis vomiting up a greenish-yellow river, which merged into a dirty stream made up of loaves of bread. It was a strange, evocative picture, with both traditional and contemporary elements, full of dark energy, though in the class discussion we found it hard to find specific connections with the story. After we'd groped around for a while and failed to see the link, we turned to Dylan, who explained that his painting was inspired by an episode in which Gimpel is visited at a bakery by the Devil, who encourages him to piss in the dough, proclaiming: "Let the Sages of Frampol eat filth!"

As often as I'd read the story, I'd never noticed that line—or, if I had, I'd never given it a second thought. But for Dylan, the line had jumped out straight away, instantly conjuring up this powerfully sinister image. In class, Dylan was reserved and laconic; like many visual thinkers, he wasn't especially good at articulating his ideas. Yet through the art they produce, these students have shown me again and again what a firm grasp they have of complex theoretical issues—an understanding they're often quite incapable of putting into words.

Sometimes, when working with art students, I start to worry about all the time I've spent reading. I start to think of literature as less "pure" in form than, say, music, or certain kinds of visual arts, because I can't help recognizing that words must have referents in the material world, even abstract ones, like love and beauty. While everyone's idea and experience of beauty or love may be different, we all share an understanding of what the words have come to mean—we have to, in order that language communicate anything at all. Words point to a shared world that exists "out there," and very rarely can they attain the same power as music, except sometimes through the use of rhythm, or incantation. To someone like me, who (still) looks to literature for an escape from the material world, the unique possibilities offered by language—metaphors and similes, unexpected comparisons and juxtapositions—can provide a way out, certainly, but they can also serve as restraints. Words can't function without "real world" referents, but musical notes, colors, and abstract forms can represent things that don't exist in the world beyond the work, so the work becomes a correlative of new possibilities, new states of mind, new avenues of thought and emotion. Music, like abstract art, can evoke things as they are, but it can also suggest things as they ought to be, or as they might be in an ideal world—things that words can only hint at, and then rarely. Abstract forms can suggest events that have never happened, ideas yet to be thought, feelings still unfelt. They can bring things together in a new way, things that have never been brought together before. Their effect is instant. You don't need to analyze them in order to feel their impact, though further study and interpretation may help you understand their power. They can suggest a world without organic forms, without decay, a world of unlimited shapes and colors, with the order and regularity whose absence can make the world we live in so limited and disheartening. In the first chapter of this book, I mentioned how, in his memoirs, the philosopher Jean-Paul Sartre expressed his disappointment on visiting the Luxembourg gardens, and seeing how impoverished *real* plants and animals were in comparison with those depicted in his Encyclopedia Larousse. It wasn't the words in the encyclopedia, however, but the ILLUSTRATIONS that led "real apes" to appear "less ape," "real people" to seem "less people."

Working with artists came as a real revelation to me, an introduction to the world of visual thought. Students like Dylan are by no means illiterate, but they're not primarily language-based thinkers, and are unaccustomed to expressing their ideas in words. Clearly, this is a disadvantage in our language-based, word-centered culture, and something that Critical Inquiry—and courses like it—attempt to address, if only to give students a sense of the different kinds of writing out there, to teach them what there is in language to like, so they can discover what they like and why they like it.

things fall apart

Throughout this book, I've been discussing some of the things literature—and literary fiction in particular—can't do, that other forms of writing can. Now I want to say a brief word about what literature alone can do, and why the focus of all those reading campaigns seems to be misguided.

In order to explain, let me describe a couple of other classes I've taught. The first was an undergrad course called Understanding Suicide, which I taught in Fall 2002. Through an unfortunate accident of scheduling, the class was held from seven till ten in the evening, in an airless basement classroom with no windows. The setting seemed to create an appropriate mood for the course. Over the semester, I guided eighteen students (eventually, only twelve) through a series of difficult, often cheerless texts that describe and analyze the disturbing phenomenon of suicide. Along with a number of case studies, we read about attitudes toward suicide in different times and cultures, from ancient Rome to modern Japan. We read Durkheim's *Suicide* and Camus's *The Myth of Sisyphus*; we listened to a recording of Sylvia Plath reading her last poems; we discussed the pros and cons of euthanasia and read stories like Willa Cather's *Paul's Case*, Dorothy Parker's *Big Blonde*, and Franz Kafka's *A Hunger Artist*.

Those who enrolled in the class, I soon discovered, had a variety of reasons for doing so. One girl told me she wanted help understanding the death of her best friend, who'd shot himself the previous summer. Some had experienced a suicide in their immediate family. One student disappeared halfway through the semester. It turned out that he suffered from manic depression, and had been hospitalized after experiencing a psychotic episode (he came back to class with his head shaved from the electroshock treatment). I wanted the course to be challenging and rigorous, but I hoped it would also be enlightening for the gifted, creative artists I teach. As a result, when reading my course evaluations at the end of the year, I was slightly disturbed to discover that one of them, Rachid, had described it as "great fun."

Perhaps, I thought, this was Rachid's somewhat inarticulate way of explaining that he'd found the course exhilarating and eye-opening, or perhaps he'd appreciated the opportunity to talk about American pop culture (I remember that he was especially animated during a discussion of the death of Kurt Cobain). Maybe the (dubious) expectation that good courses will also be "entertaining" is so widespread that students can think of no other way to frame their positive learning experiences. Or maybe Rachid did, in fact, find the course "fun," in a ghoulish, cemetery-tour sort of way. If so, then I see myself as having failed, at least as far as Rachid was concerned. My main objective in the course was to help the students begin to think about some of the most fundamental—although perhaps the most bleak—questions confronting human consciousness, such as why some of us elect not to go on with our lives.

Ideas that are important are not always pleasurable to think about, and this is just as true of our private reading as of books we read in school. Although a well-written book can give pleasure through its structure and style of expression, it strikes me that there are certain subjects and stories, which, if they're examined carefully, should be anything but "fun."

Tragedy shouldn't be fun, nor should books about the Holocaust. Nietzsche and Schopenhauer aren't exactly fun to read, and neither are many of the great Russian novelists. But these books, and others like them, can motivate us to think about some very profound and important questions—about evil, consciousness, inhumanity—which, while in many ways rewarding, should lead to the kind of enlightenment that's sobering, even depressing, rather than pleasurable. Reading such books helps us to understand the role played by these questions in human existence, and this understanding may, eventually, lead to a kind of satisfaction. But these books don't provide the immediate gratification or pride that can be boasted about on a slogan, button, or bumper sticker. Disillusionment is a more likely outcome, in the short term at least.

For many years, I've also taught an undergraduate course called Apocalypse Culture—another class that, if it goes well, should be anything but "fun." We begin by studying the biblical books of Daniel and Revelation, and go on to consider some of the many ways in which the end of the world has been depicted in literature and the other arts. My main aim in this class is to try to get the students to make sense of the eschatological impulse in American culture, from Pentecostal evangelism to Hollywood's multiple versions of Armageddon. Of course, there are always some light moments—it's hard to keep a straight face before some of the more bizarre contemporary narratives of the Rapture, in which the righteous are suddenly whisked skyward, leaving neat piles of clothes scattered around suburban lawns. On the whole, however, it's a pretty serious course, developed not only to introduce students to the apocalyptic imperative in Western life, but also to familiarize them with some of history's more destructive and violent episodes. We read some very dark and disturbing books in this course, including Joseph Conrad's *Heart of Darkness*, and *The Painted Bird*, Jerzy Kosinki's horrifying account of human brutality during the Second World War.

Outside the humanities, it's commonly accepted that there are areas of learning that shouldn't be "fun." Medical residents, for example, are subjected to notoriously exhausting shifts, partly—at least in theory—to help inoculate them against their patients' individual suffering. Although it's become increasingly controversial in recent years, the boot camp–like experience of being on call for thirty-six hours straight is supposed to toughen the young physician. Without it, many argue, the doctor's ability to cope with the anxiety, frustration, and seeming chaos of the hospital ward would be undermined. Somewhat similarly, students of mortuary science are generally required to take courses in topics like thanatology and grief counseling, which prepare them to deal with handling human corpses and to face the anguish of bereaved relatives.

Clearly, there's a great deal of sense to this: An overly emotional doctor would be as impractical as a squeamish mortician. But outside of such vocational courses of study, where there's nothing "practical" at stake beyond pure intellectual inquiry and curiosity, there's very little that compels people to read narratives that deal with the more dismal aspects of the human condition. After all, most of the time we pick up a book because we hope it's going to give us pleasure, and we usually look to fiction for entertainment and escapism. It's a lot easier for publishers to market and sell books that are fun to read, and are considered enjoyable and uplifting. Perhaps some people are afraid that, by reading depressing narratives, they may themselves turn into depressed, dislikable people. Authors who write stories that people find painful or difficult to face risk having their readers "blame the messenger" for the feelings of anguish that result.

Literature has given me a great deal of pleasure, and there are certain books I've returned to again and again. In retrospect, however, I realize that the books that have meant the most to me throughout my life have been those that, on first reading, I found very disturbing or very painful to read—including *Heart of Darkness* and *The Painted Bird*. In an essay published in *The Journal of Educational Sociology* in 1941, Mortimer J. Adler argued that "the practice of educators, even if they are well-intentioned, who try to make learning less painful than it is, not only make it less exhilarating, but also weaken the will and minds of those upon whom this fraud is perpetrated." Adler, founder of the Great Books program, believed that all genuine learning involves some degree of suffering. "Unless we acknowledge that every invitation to learning can promise pleasure only as the result of pain," he argued, ". . . all of our invitations to learning . . . will be as much buncombe as the worst patent medicine advertising."

I agree with this. There's plenty of disturbing fiction that is deeply satisfying to read, though in the most powerful books of this kind, the idea of "fun" is surely out of place, if only because the most sobering aspects of the human condition aren't easy to come to terms with. Personally, it's difficult for me to ask my students to read books that, if fully appreciated, should upset many of their preconceptions about the world, making them feel worse rather than better. This is why I think it's necessary for the teacher, like Freud's ideal psychoanalyst, to be sympathetic but a bit remote, in order to foster the insight that comes with a lack of emotional involvement. In this sense, teachers and psychoanalysts should consider themselves analogous to priests, whose distance from the flock is an important condition of their role. Lively sermons may be acceptable from time to time, but most of the congregation would look with suspicion on a priest whose services have a reputation for always being "fun." My favorite role model is that of the psychopomp—the shamanic leader who acts as a mediator between the spirit and the realm of the dead. The psychopomp orients his charges so they can safely embark to the next level of existence. These spirits may eventually come to appreciate their guide and thank him for his expertise—but the journey they have to take is unlikely to be a great deal of fun.

Irvin Yalom, the existential psychoanalyst, makes the case that human beings are, by nature, meaning-making creatures, and that a great deal of free-floating anxiety is generated by our conscious and unconscious endeavors to confront the meaningless truths of our existence, including the inevitability of death, our ultimate aloneness, and the absence of any obvious sense to life. It's this absence of meaning, Yalom explains, that makes us free to be anything but unfree. We are, as Jean-Paul Sartre puts it elsewhere, "condemned to freedom." Reading literature, according to Yalom, is one way of confronting (though not necessarily overcoming) this existential angst, in that it allows us to indulge our drive to explore the chaos surrounding us, and, to a degree, make sense of it, turn it into some kind of order, or at least comment on it, say what it's like for us. When the ideas in an author's mind become words on a page, and when those words on the page become ideas in your mind, or in mine, something important is happening, something that can't happen any other way.

To put it differently, one of the things literature can do, uniquely among all forms of writing, is show the hidden corners of life, secret moments of suffering, allowing us, just for a moment, to get a glimpse of what George Eliot in *Middlemarch* calls that "keen vision and feeling of all ordinary human life," which, if we possessed it at all times, "would be like hearing the grass grow and the squirrel's heart beat, and we should die of that roar which lies on the other side of silence." This is the unique capacity of literature, among all the art forms—it can lift the veil of illusion, just for a moment, and give us a glimpse into the ordinary human unhappiness of other people's lives, and also, by implication, illuminate the actual or potential unhappiness of our own. This conviction is powerfully expressed in the following passage by Franz Kafka, found not in a work of literature but in a private letter to his friend Max Brod, written in 1904:

> Altogether, I think we ought to read only books that bite and sting us. If the book we are reading doesn't shake us awake like a blow to the skull, why bother reading it in the first place? So that it can make us happy, as you put it? Good God, we'd be just as happy if we had no books at all; books that make us happy we could, in a pinch, write ourselves. What we need are books that hit us like a most painful misfortune, like the death of someone we loved more than we love ourselves, that make us feel as though we had been banished to the woods, far away from any human presence, like a suicide.
>
> A book must be the ax for the frozen sea within us. That is what I believe.

There are all kinds of books, and all kinds of readers, but in the end, I think, this is what literary fiction alone can do—it can "hit us" in a way that is neither safe, nor fun, nor spectacular. Literature of the kind Kafka describes is not the kind of literature that has many fans or enthusiasts. It's not the kind you'd necessarily want to identify with, or share with your friends, or chat about over coffee or at your book club. Its impact is private. It doesn't bring you pleasure, or make you want to hear the author interviewed on NPR, or inspire you to go to a book signing, or put the movie on your Netflix queue. Often, it doesn't sell. It certainly doesn't make you feel better, or even be "a better person," whatever that means, but it does help you to understand yourself more fully, your motives and wishes. It doesn't help you act on them, but it does help bring them to light, and expose them to a world shared with others. It does give you more of an understanding of what it means to be human, of the shared plight of consciousness.

In the novella *Dream Story* by the German writer Arthur Schnitzler—a friend and contemporary of Freud's—Fridolin, a young doctor, is walking at night through the streets of Vienna in a particularly desolate state of mind. Noticing a homeless man asleep on a bench, Fridolin wonders whether he should wake him up and give him money for a shelter for the night, but then realizes he'd have to give him shelter for the following night too, and the night after that, "otherwise there would really be no point." This line of thinking continues: "Why pick just this one? He asked himself. There are thousands of such poor devils in Vienna alone. What if one were to worry about all of them—about the fate of all the poor devils!" A moment later, the veil has dropped again, and Fridolin goes on his way, "glad that he was still alive, that in all probability he was still far from all these ugly things."

Over time, literary fiction can help us, gradually, to sustain our ability to think about the suffering of others, helping us to bear, for longer and longer moments, consciousness of "all the poor devils," of "ugly things," of "the roar on the other side of silence." At its deepest level, literature can work like that hammer imagined by Chekhov in his short story *Gooseberries*, continually reminding everyone who's happy and contented "that there are unhappy people; that however happy he may be, life will show him her laws sooner or later, trouble will come for him—disease, poverty, losses, and no one will see or hear, just as now he neither sees nor hears others."

Freud famously referred to psychoanalysis as "the talking cure." According to Adam Phillips, however, "Psychoanalysis . . . doesn't cure people so much as show them what it is about themselves that is incurable." When Phillips describes psychoanalysis as "applied literature," he means, I believe, that the practice of psychoanalysis calls for the same kind of critical discrimination needed to appreciate the inner workings of a novel, only the focus in analysis is on ourselves and our relationships (or those of the patient, depending on whether we're playing the role of analyst, analysand, or both). Phillips rejects the formulation "psychoanalysis and literature," in which the two are separated into discrete categories with a conjunction. Instead, he considers psychoanalysis to be a kind of literature, both in theory and in practice, as well as an oral tradition, in that they're both rhetorical forms whose aim is to persuade, and whose effect, if they're successful, is enhanced self-awareness and self-reflection. In today's culture, Phillips claims, psychoanalysis is no longer considered to be a supreme fiction, a privileged method of interpretation; it has a more modest and appropriate place, as simply one kind of fiction among many.

In psychoanalysis, as in the process of reading, there's an assumption that causes can be traced, that origins can be unearthed, and that this will help you make sense of your story, and, perhaps, may lead to the possibility of change. If you read the right kind of literature under the right circumstances, and if you read with enough attention and discrimination, you can

acknowledgments

Are lengthy and effusive acknowledgments a recent phenomenon? Every new book I read these days seems to start or end with references to an interminable roster of family members, friends, and colleagues to whom the author will remain forever indebted. I enjoy acknowledgments; I always read them, even if I don't get very far with the book itself. Actually, they fascinate me. Even the most meager acknowledgments seem to thank at least five thousand people, mentioning everybody from the author's partner and children to their friends, parents, agent, editor, therapist, stylist, nanny, assistant, dog walker, Web designer, and tatooist (and yes, these are all real examples).

A lot of books with long lists of acknowledgments are obviously "important" books—"important" in the sense that writing them must have taken years and years of research, investigation, interviews, travel, and personal soul-searching. Others owe their existence to time away from home or work, often purchased by a big advance, a sabbatical grant, or a quiet stretch at a writer's colony in the woods. But, since thousands of books are published everyday, this can be true for only a tiny minority. For all the others, including books like this one—mid-list or small press books written over three or four years, at the edges of a day job—I always wonder who these writers are, that have so many people to thank?

Is the world conjured up in a book's acknowledgments the same as the one I live in? It sounds like a dream to me, a utopia in which every author is supported through thick and thin by their loving and long-suffering family, their wonderful children and pets, their partner who reads every single draft of the manuscript at least five times. These lucky authors all seem to have loyal agents and devoted editors who are always taking them to lunch, publishers who lend them their summer house to get some quiet time, dozens of loving friends and colleagues, every one of them an ardent believer in the book from the very moment of its birth, when it was no more than a playful idea tossed around over too many martinis. Who are these people, all surrounded by allies and boosters who do everything they can to help the great work in progress, from proofreading and help with research to minding the kids, making the lunch, or walking the dog, just to give the author a few moments of extra time?

While I always find them fascinating, acknowledgments like these also make me feel a little pitiful, since I don't have an agent, a secretary, an intern, a research assistant, a therapist, or a dog walker, though if I did, you can be sure I'd be gracious and generous in my thanks. Still, I'm pleased to say that in this case, I really do have a number of people to acknowledge, including everyone who responded to my reading survey, both the anonymous respondents, as well as those friends and colleagues who took time to help me out, namely: Betsy Boyd, Yara Cheik, Firmin DeBrabander, Gadi Dechter, Amy Eisner, Laura Gaffney, David Gissen, Kerr Houston, Marcus Hoy, Mike Hoy, Alex Kafka, Judith Lidie, Bill Luhr, Harry Mattison, Bob Merrill, Saul Myers, D. Alan Orr, Rachel Schreiber, Ned Sparrow, and Jennifer Wallace. The project was supported in the first place by Karen Zarker and Sarah Zupko at PopMatters. Richard Nash at Soft Skull has been invaluable. The manuscript was carefully Ed. Nikki Tranter, Anne Horowitz, and Roxanna Aliaga, and the illustrations created by the students in José Villarrubia's Illustration Junior Thesis class at MICA: Ana Benaroya, Orpheus Collar, Nicolas Djandji, Eamonn Donnelly, Ryan Emge, Jeremy Enecio, Mark Grambau, Jingyao Guo, Bryce Homick, Marina Kharkover, Alessa Kreger, Alyse Poole, Megan Russell, and Ahu Sulker. Finally, David Sterritt gave me his laptop, meticulously corrected my spelling and grammar, and explained American style and punctuation to me over and over again, for which, as well as everything else, he has all my love.

works cited and sources

Adams, Richard, *Watership Down* (orig. 1972), New York: Scribner, 2005.

--------*The Plague Dogs* (orig. 1977), New York: Scribner, 2006.

Adler, Mortimer, "Invitation to the Pain of Learning," *The Journal of Educational Sociology* (14), Feb. 1941, 358–363.

Alberoni, Francesco, "The Powerless Elite: Theory and Sociological Research on the Phenomenon of the Stars," *Sociology of Mass Communications*, ed. Denis McQuail, London: Penguin, 1972.

Alcott, Louisa May, *Little Women* (orig. 1898), New York: Signet, 2004.

Ali, Monica, *Brick Lane*, New York: Scribner, 2004.

Allen, Brooke, *Artistic License: Three Centuries of Good Writing and Bad Behavior*, New York: Ivan R. Dee, 2004.

--------*Twentieth Century Attitudes: Literary Powers in Uncertain Times*, New York: Ivan R. Dee, 2004.

Amburn, Ellis, *The Most Beautiful Woman in the World: The Obsessions, Passions and Courage of Elizabeth Taylor*, New York: Harper-Entertainment, 2000.

American Psychiatric Association, *The Diagnostic and Statistical Manual of Mental Disorders*, 4th edition, New York: American Psychiatric Publishing, 2000.

Ames, Louise Bates, *Your Five-Year-Old*, New York: Dell, 1981.

Amis, Martin, *Experience: A Memoir*, New York: Vintage, 2001.

Andersen, Hans Christian, *The Little Mermaid* (orig. 1836), New York: Amber Lotus, 1996.

Anger, Kenneth, *Hollywood Babylon*, New York: Straight Arrow Books, 1975.

--------*Hollywood Babylon II*, New York: E. P. Dutton, 1984.

Anonymous, *The Anglo-Saxon Chronicle* (orig. AD 1–1144). Ed. Michael Swanton, London: Routledge, 1998.

Anonymous, *The Battle of Maldon* (orig. c. AD 991), trans. Bill Griffiths, Austin, TX: Harry Ransom Humanities Research Center, 2000.

Anonymous, *Beowulf* (orig. c. AD 700–1000), trans. Burton Raffel, New York: Signet, 1999.

Anonymous, *The Book of the Dead* (orig. c. 1600 BC), trans. E. A. Wallis Budge, New York: Gramercy, 1995.

Anonymous, *Go Ask Alice*, New York: Simon Pulse, 1998.

Anonymous, *Tales from the Thousand and One Nights*, trans. Richard F. Burton, London: Jaico, 2000.

Aristophanes, *The Complete Plays of Aristophanes* (orig. 448–388 BC), ed. Moses Hadas, trans. B. B. Rogers, New York: Bantam Books, 1999.

Arnold, William, *Frances Farmer: Shadowland*, New York: Jove Publications, 1979.

Asser, Bishop, *Life of King Alfred the Great* (orig. c. AD 895), trans. Alfred P. Smyth, Oxford: Oxford University Press, 1996.

Atlas, James, *Saul Bellow*, New York: Random House, 2000.

Auden, W. H., "At Last the Secret is Out" (orig. 1940), *As I Walked Out One Evening*, New York: Vintage, 1995.

Augustine, *Confessions* (orig. c. 397 AD), trans. Henry Chadwick, New York: Oxford World's Classics, 1998.

Austen, Jane, *Northanger Abbey* (org. 1817), New York: Modern Library, 2002.

--------*Pride and Prejudice* (orig. 1813), London: Penguin Classics, 2002.

Bach, Richard and Russell Munson, *Jonathan Livingston Seagull*, New York: Macmillan, 1970.

Barstow, Stan, *A Kind of Loving*, London: Penguin, 1962.

Basbanes, Nicholas, *A Gentle Madness: Bibliophiles, Bibliomanes, and the Eternal Passion for Books*, New York: Owl Books, 1999.

--------*Patience and Fortitude: A Roving Chronicle of Book People, Book Places, and Book Culture*, New York: Harper Perennial, 2001.

--------*Among the Gently Mad: Strategies and Perspectives for the Book-Hunter in the 21st Century*, New York: Henry Holt, 2002.

--------*A Splendor of Letters: The Permanence of Books in an Impermanent World*, New York: Harper Perennial, 2003.

--------*Every Book Its Reader: The Power of the Printed Word to Stir the World*, New York: Harper Perennial, 2006.

Baum, L. Frank, *The Wonderful Wizard of Oz* (orig. 1900), New York: Oxford World's Classics, 2000.

Baxter, Charles, *Burning Down the House: Essays on Fiction*, New York: Graywolf Press, 1998.

Beckett, Samuel, *Three Novels: Molloy, Malone Dies, and The Unnamable* (orig. 1951, 1953), New York: Grove Press, 1995.

Beerbohm, Max, *The Works of Max Beerbohm*, London: Bodley Head, 1923.

Belloc, Hilaire, *More Beasts for Worse Children* (orig. 1897), New York: Random House, 2000.

Benchley, Peter, *Jaws*, New York: Doubleday, 1974.

Benes, Barton Lidice, *Curiosa: Celebrity Relics, Historical Fossils, and Other Metamorphic Rubbish*, New York: Harry Abrams, 2002.

Benjamin, Walter, *Illuminations,* ed. Hannah Arendt, trans. Harry Zohn, New York: Schocken Books, 1969.

Bentley, Toni, *The Surrender: An Erotic Memoir*, New York: Regan Books, 2004.

Berman, Jeffrey, *Diaries to an English Professor: Pain and Growth in the Classroom*, Amherst: University of Massachusetts Press, 1994.

--------*Surviving Literary Suicide*, Amherst: University of Massachusetts Press, 1999.

Bettmann, Otto, *The Bettmann Collection: The Past Is Ever Present*, London: Corbis, 1997.

Bieber, Irving, *Homosexuality: A Psychoanalytic Survey of Male Homosexuals*, New York: Basic Books, 1962.

Bloom, Claire, *Leaving a Doll's House: A Memoir*, New York: Back Bay Books, 1998.

Bloom, Harold, *Where Shall Wisdom Be Found?*, New York: Riverhead Books, 2004.

--------*How to Read and Why*, New York: Scribner, 2001.

Blume, Judy, *Forever*, New York: Dell, 1975.

Bockting, Walter O. and Eli Coleman, *Masturbation as a Means of Achieving Sexual Health*, Binghampton, New York: Haworth Press, 2003.

Boorstein, Daniel, *The Image: A Guide to Pseudo-Events in America*, New York: Harper & Row, 1964.

Boxall, Peter, ed., *1001 Books You Must Read Before You Die*, London: Universe, 2006.

Brantlinger, Patrick, *The Reading Lesson: The Threat of Mass Literacy in Nineteenth Century British Fiction*, Bloomington, IN: Indiana University Press, 1998.

Breton, André, *Nadja* (orig. 1928), trans. Richard Howard, New York: Grove Press, 1960.

Brevig, K. L., *The Evil That Walks Among Us*, New York: Authorhouse, 2001.

Brontë, Charlotte, *Jane Eyre* (orig. 1846), London: Penguin Classics, 2003.

Brontë, Emily, *Wuthering Heights* (orig. 1847), London: Bantam Classics, 1983.

Brooks, Hugh Motram, *The Trunk Tragedy, A Complete History of the Murder of Preller and the Trial of Maxwell: Carefully Compiled from the Statements of the Officers and Testimony . . . With Interesting and Incidental Details*, St. Louis, Missouri: St. Louis News Company, 1886.

Brown, Dan, *The Da Vinci Code*, New York: Doubleday, 2003.

Broyard, Anatole, "Court of Love," *New York Times Book Review*, Nov. 8, 1981, 13–14.

Bugliosi, Vincent and Curt Gentry, *Helter Skelter: The True Story of the Manson Murders* (orig. 1975), New York: W. W. Norton, 2001.

Bunyan, John, *Grace Abounding to the Chief of Sinners* (orig. 1666), London: Whitaker House, 1993.

Burgess, Anthony, *A Clockwork Orange*, London: Heinemann, 1962.

Burn, Gordon, *Somebody's Husband, Somebody's Son: The Story of Peter Sutcliffe*, London: Heinemann Books, 1984.

Burnett, Frances Hodgson, *The Secret Garden* (orig. 1909), New York: HarperClassics, 1998.

Burroughs, Augusten, *Dry: A Memoir*, New York: Picador, 2004.

--------*Running with Scissors: A Memoir*, New York: Picador, 2003.

Bushell, Michaela, Paul Roddis and Helen Simpson, eds., *The Rough Guide to Cult Fiction*, London: Rough Guides, 2005.

Buzbee, Lewis, *The Yellow-Lighted Bookshop*, New York: Graywolf Press, 2006.

Campbell, Joseph, *Hero with a Thousand Faces*, Princeton, New Jersey: Princeton University Press, 1972.

Camus, Albert, *The Myth of Sisyphus and Other Essays* (orig. 1942), trans. Justin O'Brien, New York: Vintage, 1991.

Canetti, Elias, *Auto-da-Fé* (orig. 1935), trans. C. V. Wedgwood, New York: Farrar, Straus & Giroux, 1985.

Capote, Truman, *Breakfast at Tiffany's* (orig. 1958), New York: Vintage, 1993.

--------*In Cold Blood* (orig. 1965), New York: Vintage, 1994.

Carey, John, *The Intellectual and the Masses: Pride and Prejudice among the Literary Intelligentsia, 1880–1939* (orig. 1992), Chicago: Academy Chicago Publishers, 2002.

Carlo, Philip, *The Night Stalker: The Life and Crimes of Richard Ramirez*, New York: Pinnacle Books, 2004.

Carroll, Lewis, *Alice's Adventures in Wonderland and Through the Looking Glass* (orig. 1865, 1871), New York: Modern Library Classics, revised edition, 2002.

Carter, Angela, "The Courtship of Mr. Lyon," *The Bloody Chamber*, London: Victor Gollancz, 1979, 35–45.

Cather Willa, *Paul's Case and Other Stories* (orig. 1932), Mineola, NJ: Dover Publications, 1996.

Cervantes, Miguel, *Don Quixote* (orig. 1605, 1615), trans. Tobais Smollett, New York: Modern Library Classics, 2001.

Chaucer, Geoffrey, *The Canterbury Tales* (orig. 1390), trans. Nevill Coghill, London: Penguin Classics, 2003.

Chekhov, Anton, *The Essential Tales of Chekhov* (orig. 1919), trans. Constance Garnett, New York: Macmillan, 1998.

Chertok, Léon, MD and Raymond de Saussure, *The Therapeutic Revolution: From Mesmer to Freud*, Paris: Brunner Mazel, 1979.

Cleckley, Hervey, *The Mask of Sanity* (orig. 1941), New York: Textbook Publishers, 2003.

Coady, Roxanne J. and Joy Johannessen, *The Books That Changed My Life: 71 Remarkable Writers Celebrate the Books That Matter Most to Them*, New York: Gotham, 2006.

Coetzee, J. M., *Disgrace*, London: Secker and Warburg, 1999.

Conrad, Joseph, *Heart of Darkness* (orig. 1902), New York: Norton, 2005.

Corliss, Richard, *Talking Pictures*, New York: Overlook Press, 1985.

Corrigan, Maureen, *Leave Me Alone, I'm Reading: Losing and Finding Myself in Books*, New York: Vintage, 2006.

Crane, Stephen, *The Red Badge of Courage* (orig. 1895), New York: Monarch, 1986.

Crawford, Christina, *Mommie Dearest*, New York: William Morrow, 1978.

Cross, Roger, *The Yorkshire Ripper: An In-depth Study of a Mass Killer and His Methods*, Manchester, UK: Granada, 1981.

Crowley, Kieran, *Burned Alive: A Shocking True Story of Betrayal, Kidnapping, and Murder*, New York: St. Martin's True Crime Library, 1999.

Cruz, Nicky, *Run Baby Run*, New York: Logos Books, 1970.

Dahmer, Lionel, *A Father's Story*, New York: Avon Books, 1995.

Davis, Lennard J., "Huckleberry Who?," *Chronicle of Higher Education*, 53.29 B5, Mar. 23, 2007.

Defoe, Daniel, *Moll Flanders* (orig. 1722), New York: Modern Library Classics, 2002.

--------*Robinson Crusoe* (orig. 1715), New York: Signet Classics Paperback, 1998.

Delillo, Dan, *White Noise*, New York: Penguin, 1984.

Dickens, Charles, *A Christmas Carol* (orig. 1848), New York: Prestwick House, 2005.

--------*Great Expectations* (orig. 1860), New York: Washington Square Press, 1963.

Didion, Joan, *Slouching Toward Bethlehem: Essays*, New York: Farrar, Straus & Giroux, 1990.

Dirda, Michael, *Book by Book: Notes on Reading and Life*, New York: Henry Holt, 2006.

Dodson, Betty, *Sex for One: The Joy of Self-Loving*, New York: Three Rivers Press, 1996.

Dostoevsky, Fyodor, *The Brothers Karamazov* (orig. 1880), trans. Richard Pevear and Larissa Volokhonsky, New York: Farrar, Straus & Giroux, 2002.

Dumas, Alexandre, *The Three Musketeers* (orig. 1844), trans. Richard Pevear, New York: Viking, 2006.

Duras, Marguerite, *Practicalities: Marguerite Duras Speaks to Jerome Beaujour*, London: Flamingo, 1991.

Durkheim, Emile, *Suicide: A Study in Sociology* (orig. 1951), trans. John A. Spaulding and George Simpson, London: Free Press, 1997.

Eco, Umberto, *Foucault's Pendulum*, New York: Ballantine Books, 1990.

Edmondson, Mark, *Why Read?*, London and New York: Bloomsbury, 2004.

Eisenberg, Arlene, Sandee Hathaway and Heidi Murkoff, *What to Expect When You're Expecting*, New York: Workman Publishing Company, 2002.

Eliot, George, *Middlemarch* (orig. 1871), New York: Penguin Classics, 2003.

--------*The Mill on the Floss* (orig. 1860), New York: Penguin Classics, 2003.

Ellis, Bill, *Raising the Devil: Satanism, New Religions, and the Media*, Louisville, KY: University Press of Kentucky, 2000.

Elman, Richard, *Namedropping: Mostly Literary Memoirs*, Binghampton, NY: SUNY Press, 1997.

Epstein, Joseph, *Partial Payments: Essays on Writers and Their Lives*, New York: Norton, 1991.

Etcoff, Nancy, *Survival of the Prettiest: The Science of Beauty*, New York: Anchor, 2000.

Evans, Andrew and Glenn D. Wilson, *Fame: The Psychology of Stardom*, London: Vision, 2001.

Faulkner, William, *The Sound and the Fury* (orig. 1929), New York: Vintage, 1991.

--------*As I Lay Dying* (orig. 1930), New York: Vintage, 1991.

Fielding, Helen, *Bridget Jones's Diary*, London: Penguin, 1996.

Fielding, Henry, *The History of Tom Jones, A Foundling* (orig. 1749), Oxford: Oxford University Press, 1998.

Fitzgerald, F. Scott, *The Great Gatsby* (orig. 1925), New York: Scribner, 1999.

Flaubert, Gustave, *Madame Bovary* (orig. 1856), trans. Margaret Mauldon, New York: Oxford World's Classics, 2005.

Fleeman, Michael, *Laci: Inside the Laci Peterson Murder*, New York: St. Martin's True Crime Library, 2003.

Frame, Janet, *Faces in the Water*, London: George Braziller, 1961.

Franzen, Jonathan, *The Corrections*, New York: Picador, 2001.

Freud, Sigmund and Josef Breuer, *Studies in Hysteria* (orig. 1895), trans. Rachel Bowlby, London: Penguin Classics, 2004.

Freud, Sigmund, "Creative Writers and Daydreaming" (orig. 1907), *The Uncanny*, trans. David McLintock, London: Penguin Classics, 2003.

--------*The Ego and the Id* (orig. 1923), trans. James Strachey, Standard Edition, London: Hogarth Press, 1967.

--------*On the History of the Psychoanalytic Movement* (orig. 1917), trans. Ernest Jones, New York: Kessenger, 2004.

--------*The Uncanny* (orig. 1925), trans. David McLintock, London: Penguin Classics, 2003.

--------*The Wolfman and Other Cases* (orig. 1926), trans. Louise Adey Huish, London: Penguin Classics, 2003.

Frey, James, *A Million Little Pieces*, New York: Anchor, 2005.

Garfunkel, Art, *Still Water: Prose Poems*, New York: Dutton, 1989.

Glover, Edward, "Notes on Oral Character Formation," *International Journal of Psycho-Analysis* VI, 1925: 131–147.

Gissing, George, *New Grub Street* (orig. 1891), London: Penguin Classics, 1976.

Goethe, Johann Wolfgang, *The Sufferings of Young Werther* (orig. 1774), ed. and trans. Harry Steinhauer, New York: Bantam Books, 1962.

Gogol, Nikolai, *Diary of a Madman and Other Stories* (orig. 1835), trans. Ronald Wilks, New York: Vintage, 1973.

Gold, Joseph, *The Story Species: Our Life-Literature Connection*, New York: Fitzhenry and Whiteside, 2002.

Golding, William, *Lord of the Flies* (orig. 1954), New York: Penguin, 1999.

Grandin, Temple, *Thinking in Pictures: My Life with Autism*, New York: Vintage, 2006.

Grass, Günter, *Peeling the Onion*, trans. Michael Henry Heim, New York: Harcourt, 2007.

Graves, Robert, "Nobody," *Collected Poems 1965*, London: Cassell, 1965.

Greenberg, Joanne, *I Never Promised You a Rose Garden*, New York: Signet, 1989.

Greenburg, Dan, *How to Be a Jewish Mother*, New York: Price, Stern, Sloan, 1965.

Greenson, Ralph R., *The Technique and Practice of Psychoanalysis*, Miami, Florida: International University Press, 2000.

Grogan, John, *Marley and Me: My Life with the World's Worst Dog*, New York: HarperCollins, 2005.

Hammill, Pete, *A Drinking Life: A Memoir*, New York: Back Bay Books, 1995.

Hardy, Thomas, *Jude the Obscure*, New York: Penguin Classics, 1985.

Hawthorne, Nathaniel, *The House of the Seven Gables* (orig. 1851), New York: Norton, 2005.

--------*The Marble Faun* (orig. 1860), Oxford: Oxford World's Classics, 2002.

--------*The Scarlet Letter* (orig. 1850), New York: Penguin Classics, 2002.

Hayward, Brooke, *Haywire*, New York: Bantam Books, 1977.

Hazlitt, William, *Selected Writings* (orig. 1818–1830), Oxford: Oxford World's Classics, 1999.

Heller, Joseph, *Catch 22*, New York: Simon and Schuster, 1961.

Hemingway, Ernest, *The Sun Also Rises* (orig. 1929), New York: Scribner, 1995.

--------*For Whom the Bell Tolls* (orig. 1950), New York: Scribner, 1995.

Herbert, Frank, *Dune*, London: Chilton Books, 1965.

Hillman, James, "A Note on Story," *Children's Literature: The Great Excluded*, vol. 3, ed. Francelia Butler and Bennett Brockman, Philadelphia, PA: Temple University Press, 1974.

Hines, Barry, *A Kestrel for a Knave*, London: Gardner's Books, 1969.

Hinton, S. E., *That Was Then, This Is Now* (orig. 1971), London: Puffin, 1998.

Hornbacher, Marya, *Wasted: A Memoir of Anorexia and Bulimia*, New York: Harper Perennial, 1999.

Hornby, Nick, *Housekeeping vs. The Dirt*, New York: McSweeney's, 2006.

Houston, Kerr, "Out Damned Spot! Web Confessionals and the Allure of Admission," *Urbanite* #29 (Baltimore), Nov. 2006.

Hughes, Robert, *Culture of Complaint: The Fraying of America*, New York: Oxford University Press/New York Public Library, 1993.

Hunter, Tab, with Eddie Muller, *Tab Hunter Confidential: The Makings of a Movie Star*, New York: Algonquin Books, 2005.

Irving, John, *The World According to Garp* (orig. 1978), New York: Ballantine, 1990.

Jackson, Robert and Carol Zeman Rothkopf, eds., *Book Talk: Essays on Books, Booksellers, Collectors, and Special Collections*, Newcastle, DE: Oak Knoll Press, 2006.

James, Henry, *The Turn of the Screw* (orig. 1898), New York: Norton Critical Editions, 1999.

Jamison, Kay, *An Unquiet Mind: A Memoir of Moods and Madness*, New York: Vintage, 1997.

Janouch, Gustav, *Conversations with Kafka*, trans. Goronwy Rees, New York: Vintage, 1971.

Jeffers, H. P., *With an Axe, 16 Horrific Accounts of Real-Life Axe Murders*, London: Pinnacle Books, 2000.

Jenkins, Phillip, *Using Murder: The Social Construction of Serial Homicide*, New York: Aldine Transaction, 1994.

Johnson, Samuel, *Selected Essays*, London: Penguin Classics, 2003 (includes essays from *The Rambler*, orig. 1750–1752, and *The Idler*, orig. 1758–1760).

Johnson, Steven, *Everything Bad Is Good for You: How Today's Popular Culture Is Actually Making Us Smarter*, New York: Riverhead Books, 2005.

Joyce, James, *Finnegans Wake* (orig. 1939), New York: Penguin Twentieth Century Classics, 1999.

--------*Ulysses* (orig. 1922), New York: Vintage, 1990.

Kafka, Franz, *Letters to Friends, Family and Editors*, trans. Richard Winston and Clara Winston, New York: Schocken Books, 1977.

--------*A Hunger Artist* (orig. 1924), trans. Kevin Blahut, Prague: Twisted Spoon Press, 1996.

--------*The Metamorphosis* (orig. 1915), trans. Stanley Corngold, New York: Bantam, 1972.

Kamil, Michael L. and Diane Lane, "A Classroom Study of the Efficacy of Using Information Text for First Grade Reading Instruction," www.stanford.edu/~mkamil/Aera97.htm (1997).

Kaysen, Susanna, *Girl, Interrupted*, New York: Vintage, 1994.

Kelley, Kitty, *Elizabeth Taylor: The Last Star*, New York: Simon and Schuster, 1981.

--------*Jackie Oh!*, New York: Ballantine Books, 1984.

--------*His Way: An Unauthorized Biography of Frank Sinatra*, New York: Bantam, 1987.

--------*The Royals*, New York: Warner Books, 1998.

Kelly, Stuart, *The Book of Lost Books: An Incomplete History of All the Great Books You'll Never Read*, New York: Random House, 2006.

Kennedy, Ludovic, *Ten Rillington Place*, London: Avon Books, 1985.

Kernberg, Otto, *Borderline Conditions and Pathological Narcissism*, New York: Jason Aronson, 1975.

Kerouac, Jack, *On the Road* (orig. 1957), New York: Penguin, 1976.

Kinder, Gary, *Victim: The Other Side of Murder*, New York: Dell, 1983.

King, Clive, *Stig of the Dump*, London: Puffin, 1960.

King, Greg, *Sharon Tate and the Manson Murders*, New York: Mainstream Publishing, 2000.

Kipling, Rudyard, *The Jungle Book* (orig. 1894), New York: Signet Classics, 2005.

Knapp, Caroline, *Drinking: A Love Story*, New York: Dial Press, 1997.

Kosinski, Jerzy, *The Painted Bird* (orig.1965), New York: Grove Press, 1995.

Laing, Ronald David, *The Divided Self: An Existential Study in Sanity and Madness*, London: Penguin Psychology, 1960.

Larkin, Philip, "A Study of Reading Habits," *The Whitsun Weddings* (orig. 1964), London: Faber and Faber, 1986.

Lawrence, David Herbert, *Sons and Lovers* (orig. 1913), London: Penguin Modern Classics, 2000.

--------*Women in Love* (orig. 1920), London: Modern Library Classics, 2002.

LeBon, Gustave, *The Crowd* (orig. 1886), London: Transaction, 1995.

Lee, Chang-Rae, *Aloft*, New York: Riverhead, 2004.

Lester, David and Charles Press, *Serial Killers: The Insatiable Passion*, New York: Charles Press Publications, 1995.

Levy, Sean, *King of Comedy: The Life and Art of Jerry Lewis*, New York: St. Martin's Press, 1997.

Lewis, Matthew Gregory, *The Monk* (orig. 1796), London: Penguin Classics, 1999.

Lindner, Robert Mitchell, *The Fifty-Minute Hour*, New York: Bantam, 1955.

Lodge, David, *Changing Places*, London: Penguin, 1979.

Lopate, Phillip, *Getting Personal: Selected Writings*, New York: Basic Books, 2004.

Lorenc, Z. Paul and Trish Hall, *A Little Work: The Truth Behind Plastic Surgery's Park Avenue Facade*, New York: St. Martin's Griffin, 2005.

Lothian, Judith and Charlotte DeVries, *The Official Lamaze Guide: Giving Birth with Confidence*, NewYork: Meadowbrook, 2005.

Lovecraft, H. P. and Robert Bloch, *The Best of H. P. Lovecraft: Bloodcurdling Tales of Horror and the Macabre*, New York: Del Rey, 1987.

Luepnitz, Deborah Anna, *Schopenhauer's Porcupines: Intimacy and Its Dilemmas*, New York: Basic Books, 2003.

Mailer, Norman, *The Executioner's Song*, London: Warner Books, 1982.

Malcolm, Janet, *Psychoanalysis: The Impossible Profession*, New York: Vintage, 1982.

--------*In the Freud Archives*, New York: New York Review Books Classics, 2002.

--------*The Purloined Clinic: Selected Writings*, New York: Vintage, 2003.

Malory, Sir Thomas, *Le Morte d'Arthur* (orig. 1485), New York: Norton Critical Editions, 2003.

Manguel, Alberto, *A History of Reading*, London: Penguin, 1997.

Marcus, Steven, "Freud and Dora: Story, History, Case History," *Dora's Case*, ed. Claire Kahane and C. Bernheimer, New York: University of Columbia Press, 1990.

Marshall, James Vance, *Walkabout*, London: Penguin, 1959.

Martineau, Harriet, *Autobiography*, vol. 1 (orig. 1879), ed. Maria Weston Chapman, Boston: Houghton, Osgood and Company, 2000.

Masson, Jeffrey Moussaieff, *The Assault on Truth: Freud's Suppression of the Seduction Theory*, New York: Ballantine Books, 2003.

--------*Final Analysis: The Making and Unmaking of a Psychoanalyst*, New York: Farrar, Straus & Giroux, 1984.

Masters, Brian, *Killing for Company: The Case of Dennis Nilsen*, London: Stein and Day, 1986.

Masters, William H., Virginia E. Johnson and Robert C. Kolodny, *Masters and Johnson on Sex and Human Loving*, Boston: Little, Brown and Company, 1986.

Maturin, Charles Robert, *Melmoth the Wanderer* (orig. 1820), Oxford: Oxford World's Classics, 1998.

McCarthy, Cormac, *Blood Meridian* (orig. 1985), New York: Vintage, 1992.

McGinnis, Joe, *Fatal Vision*, New York: Signet Books, 1999.

Melville, Herman, *Bartleby and Benito Cereno* (orig. 1853, 1855), New York: Dover, 1990.

--------*Moby-Dick, or The Whale* (orig. 1851), New York: Modern Library, 1992.

Mendelson, Edward, *The Things That Matter: What Seven Classic Novels Have to Say about the Stages of Life*, New York: Pantheon, 2006.

Merkin, Daphne, "Acting the Victim: Claire Bloom vs. Philip Roth," *New Yorker*, Nov. 4, 1996, reprinted in *Dreaming of Hitler: Passions and Provocations*, New York: Harcourt, Brace & Co., 195–205.

Miller, Laura J., *Reluctant Capitalists: Booksellers and the Culture of Consumption*, Chicago: University of Chicago Press, 2006.

Millet, Catherine, *The Sexual Life of Catherine M.*, trans. Adriana Hunter, New York: Grove Press, 2003.

Milton, John, *The Complete Poetry*, ed. John T. Shawcross, London: Anchor, 1971.

Moore, Alan and Eddie Campbell, *From Hell* (orig. 1993), London: Top Shelf Productions, 2004.

Moore, Robert I., *The Birth of Popular Heresy*, Toronto: University of Toronto Press, 1975.

Morin, Edgar, *The Stars*, trans. Richard Howard, New York: Grove Press, 1961.

Morley, Sheridan and Ruth Leon, *Judy Garland: Beyond the Rainbow*, New York: Arcade Publishing, 1999.

Morris, William, *News from Nowhere* (orig. 1890), Oxford: Oxford World's Classics, 2003.

Morrison, Toni, *Beloved*, New York: Plume, 1987.

Morton, Andrew, *Diana: Her True Story in Her Own Words*, London: Pocket Books, 1992.

Nabokov, Vladimir, *Lolita* (orig. 1956), New York: Vintage, 1991.

-------- "Rowe's Symbols," *New York Review of Books*, Oct. 7, 1971.

Nafisi, Azar, *Reading Lolita in Tehran: A Memoir in Books*, New York: Random House, 2003.

National Endowment for the Arts, *Reading at Risk: A Survey of Literary Reading in America*, July 2004.

Nehring, Christina, "Books Make You a Boring Person," *New York Times Book Review*, June 27, 2004.

Newton, Michael, *Encylopedia of Serial Killers*, New York: Checkmark Books, 2000.

Nicholson, Vivian, *Spend Spend Spend*, London: Jonathan Cape, 1977.

Nietzsche, Friedrich, *The Philosophy of Nietszche*, trans. Walter Kaufmann, New York: Modern Library, 1954.

-------- *The Will to Power* (orig. 1901), trans. Walter Kaufmann and R. J. Hollingdale, New York: Vintage, 1968.

Oates, Joyce Carol, *The Faith of a Writer: Life, Craft, Art*, New York: Harper Perennial, 2004.

Orwell, George, "Decline of the English Murder" (orig. 1946), *Decline of the English Murder and Other Essays*, London: Penguin, 1991.

Ovid, Publius, *Metamorphoses* (orig. 8th century), trans. Denis Feeney and David Raeburn, London: Penguin Classics, 2004.

Painter, George D., *The Road to Sinodun: A Summer and Winter Melodrama*, London: Hart-Davis, 1951.

Parker, Dorothy, *Collected Poems: Not So Deep as a Well*, New York: The Viking Press, 1936.

-------- *Big Blonde and Other Stories* (orig. 1929), New York: Penguin, 1957.

Pawel, Ernst, *The Nightmare of Reason: A Life of Franz Kafka*, New York: Farrar, Straus & Giroux, 1984.

Pelzer, Dave, *A Child Called "It": One Child's Courage to Survive*, New York: Orion, 1995.

Phillips, Adam, *Houdini's Box*, London: Pantheon, 2001.

-------- *Monogamy*, London: Pantheon, 1996.

-------- *On Kissing, Tickling and Being Bored: Psychoanalytic Essays on the Unexamined Life*, Harvard, MA: Harvard University Press, 1998.

-------- *Promises, Promises: Essays on Poetry and Psychoanalysis*, New York: Basic Books, 2000.

Picasso, Pablo with Hiro Clark, *Picasso in His Own Words*, New York: Collins, 1993.

Pirenne, Henri, *Economic and Social History of Medieval Europe*, New York: Routledge, 2006.

Plath, Sylvia, *Ariel*, London: Faber and Faber, 1965.

--------*The Bell Jar*, New York: Bantam, 1963.

Plato, *The Collected Dialogues, Including the Letters,* ed. Edith Hamilton and Huntington Cairns, Princeton, NJ: Princeton University Press, 1961.

Plutarch, *Lives of the Noble Greeks and Romans*, (orig. AD 70–100), ed. Arthur Hugh Clough, trans. John Dryden, New York: Modern Library, 1992.

Poe, Edgar Allan, *Complete Tales and Poems*, New York: Vintage, 1975.

Priestley, J. B., *An Inspector Calls*, London: Penguin, 1945.

Prose, Francine, *Thinking Like a Writer: A Guide for People Who Love Books and for Those Who Want to Write Them*, New York: HarperCollins, 2006.

Proust, Marcel, *The Remembrance of Things Past* (orig. 1913–1922), trans. Scott Moncrieff, New York: Vintage, 1982.

Pynchon, Thomas, *Gravity's Rainbow* (orig. 1973), New York: Penguin, 1995.

Radcliffe, Ann, *The Mysteries of Udolpho* (orig. 1794), London: Oxford World's Classics, 1998.

Ressler, Robert K., Ann W. Burgess and John E. Douglas, *Sexual Homicide: Patterns and Motives*, New York: Free Press, 1988.

--------and Thomas Schachtman, *Whoever Fights Monsters: My Twenty Years Tracking Serial Killers for the FBI*, New York: St. Martin's True Crime Library, 1993.

Rice, Anne, *Interview with the Vampire*, New York: Knopf, 1976.

Rich, Motoko, "Potter Has Limited Effect on Reading Habits," *New York Times*, July 11, 2007.

Richardson, Samuel, *Clarissa, Or, The History of a Young Lady* (orig. 1748), London: Penguin Classics, 1986.

--------*Pamela, Or, Virtue Rewarded* (orig. 1740), London: Oxford World's Classics, 2001.

Rieff, Philip, *Freud: The Mind of the Moralist*, Chicago: University of Chicago Press, 1979.

Robinson, Edward Arlington, "Miniver Cheevy," *Selected Poems*, New York: Penguin Classics, 1997.

Rodriguez, Richard, *Hunger of Memory: The Education of Richard Rodriguez*, New York: Bantam, 1983.

--------*Days of Obligation: An Argument with My Mexican Father*, New York: Penguin, 1993.

Rosenthal, A. M., *Thirty-Eight Witnesses: The Kitty Genovese Case*, New York: McGraw-Hill, 1964.

Roth, Philip, *Portnoy's Complaint*, New York: Buccaneer Books, 1966.

--------*My Life as a Man*, New York: Vintage International, 1994.

--------*Operation Shylock: A Confession*, New York: Vintage International, 1994.

--------*The Ghost Writer*, New York: Vintage International, 1995.

--------*Deception*, New York: Vintage International, 1997.

--------*American Pastoral*, New York: Vintage International, 1998.

--------Letter, *New York Review of Books*, 46.4, Mar. 4, 1999.

--------*I Married a Communist*, New York, Vintage, 1999.

--------*The Human Stain: A Novel*, New York: Vintage International, 2001.

Rowan, Edward L., *The Joy of Self-Pleasuring: Why Feel Guilty about Feeling Good?*, Amherst, NY: Prometheus Books: 2000.

Rowe, Nicholas, *The Fair Penitent* (orig. 1703), Lincoln, NE: University of Nebraska Press, 1983.

Rowling, J. K., *Harry Potter and the Sorcerer's Stone*, New York: Scholastic, 1997.

--------*Harry Potter and the Chamber of Secrets*, New York: Scholastic, 1998.

--------*Harry Potter and the Prisoner of Azkaban*, New York: Scholastic, 1999.

--------*Harry Potter and the Goblet of Fire*, New York: Scholastic, 2000.

--------*Fantastic Beasts and Where to Find Them*, New York: Scholastic, 2001.

--------*Quidditch Through the Ages*, New York: Scholastic, 2001.

--------*Harry Potter and the Order of the Phoenix*, New York: Scholastic, 2003.

--------*Harry Potter and the Half-Blood Prince*, New York: Scholastic, 2005.

Rule, Ann, *The Stranger Beside Me*, New York: Signet Books, 1981.

Rushdie, Salman, *Midnight's Children*, London: Penguin, 1980.

Sacks, Oliver, *An Anthropologist in Mars*, London: Picador, 1996.

Salinger, J. D., *The Catcher in the Rye*, New York: Little, Brown, 1951.

Sanders, Ed, *The Family* (orig. 1971), New York: Thunder's Mouth Press, 2002.

Sartre, Jean-Paul, *The Words*, trans. Bernard Frechtman, New York: George Braziller, 1964.

Schechter, Harold, *A–Z Encyclopedia of Serial Killers*, New York: Pocket Books True Crime, 1997.

--------*The Serial Killer Files*, New York: Ballantine, 2003.

Schlink, Bernhard, *The Reader*, trans. Carol Brown Janeway, New York: Vintage, 1998.

Schnitzler, Arthur, *Dream Story* (orig. 1927), trans. J. M. Q. Davies, New York: Penguin, 2004.

Schorer, Mark, *Sinclair Lewis: An American Life*, Minneapolis, MN: University of Minnesota Press, 1963.

Schott, Ben, "Confessions of a Book Abuser," *The New York Times Book Review*, Mar. 4, 2007, 31, *Schott's Almanac*, London: Bloomsbury, 2006.

Scott, Darrell, *Rachel Smiles: The Spiritual Legacy of Columbine Matryr Rachel Scott*, New York: Nelson Books, 2002.

Selby, Hubert Jr. *Last Exit to Brooklyn* (orig. 1964), New York: Grove Press, 1988.

Sendak, Maurice, *Where the Wild Things Are*, New York: Harper & Row, 1963.

Shakespeare, William, *Macbeth* (orig. 1605), London: Arden Shakespeare, 1997.

--------*Much Ado About Nothing* (orig. 1600), London: Arden Shakespeare, 1981.

--------*Twelfth Night* (orig. 1602), London: Arden Shakespeare, 1975.

Shattuck, Roger, *Forbidden Knowledge*, New York: St. Martin's Press, 1996.

Shelley, Mary, *Frankenstein* (orig. 1818), New York: Bantam Classics, 1984.

Shepherd, Donald, *Bing Crosby, The Hollow Man*, New York: St. Martin's Press, 1981.

Singer, Isaac Bashevis, *Gimpel the Fool: Stories*, trans. Saul Bellow, New York: Farrar, Straus & Giroux, 1998.

Smiley, Jane, *Thirteen Ways of Looking at the Novel*, New York: Knopf, 2006.

Soble, Ron and John H. Johnson, *Blood Brothers: The Inside Story of the Menendez Murders*, New York: Onyx, 1994.

Solomon, Andrew, *The Noonday Demon: An Atlas of Depression*, New York: Scribner, 2002.

--------"The Closing of the American Books," *The New York Times*, editorial, p. 17, July 10, 2004.

Sophocles, *The Theban Plays*, trans. Peter Meineck and Paul Woodruff, New York: Hackett, 2003.

Spenser, Edmund, *The Faerie Queene* (orig. 1590–1596), London: Penguin Classics, 1979.

Spotnitz, Hyman, *Modern Psychoanalysis of the Schizophrenic Patient: Theory of the Technique*, (orig. 1969), New York: YBK Publishers, 1986.

Stahl, Jerry, *Permanent Midnight: A Memoir*, New York: Process, 2005.

Stein, Jess, ed., *Random House Dictionary of the English Language*, New York: Random House, 1967.

Steinbeck, John, *East of Eden* (orig. 1952), New York: Penguin, 2003.

Stevenson, Anne, *Bitter Fame: A Life of Sylvia Plath*, New York: Houghton Mifflin, 1989.

Stevenson, Robert Louis, *The Strange Case of Dr. Jekyll and Mr. Hyde* (orig. 1886), New York: Signet Classics, 2003.

--------*Treasure Island* (orig. 1883), New York: Signet Classics, 1998.

Stoker, Bram, *Dracula* (orig. 1897), New York: Norton Critical Editions, 1997.

Strachey, James, "Some Unconscious Factors in Reading," *International Journal of Psycho-Analysis*, 1930, 11: 322–331.

Strachey, Lytton, *Eminent Victorians* (orig. 1918), London: Penguin Classics, 1990.

Strunk, William and E. B. White, *Elements of Style*, New York, Macmillan, 1972.

Sumner, Robert Leslie, *Hollywood Cesspool: A Startling Survey of Movieland Lives and Morals, Pictures and Results*, Murfreesboro, TN: Sword of the Lord Press, 1955.

--------*Hell Is No Joke*, Grand Rapids, MI: Zondervan Publishing House, 1959.

--------*The Blight of Booze*, Murfreesboro, TN: Sword of the Lord Press, 1960.

--------*The Menace of Narcotics*, Grand Rapids, MI: Biblical Evangelism, 1971.

Sutherland, John, *How to Read a Novel: A User's Guide*, London: St. Martin's, 2006.

Swales, Peter, "Freud, His Teacher, and the Birth of Psychoanalysis," in *Freud: Appraisals and Reappraisals; Contributions to Freud Studies*, vol 1., Paul Stepansky, ed., Hillsdale, NJ: Analytic Press, 1986.

Szpilman, Wladyslaw, *The Pianist* (orig. 1945), trans. Andrea Bell, New York: Picador, 1999.

Tannen, Deborah, *You Just Don't Understand*, New York: William Morrow, 1989.

Tennyson, Alfred, Lord, "The Lady of Shallot," *Tennyson: Selected Poems*, London: Penguin, 1992.

Thompson, Hunter S., *Fear and Loathing in Las Vegas*, New York: Random House, 1971.

Thompson, Lawrence Roger, *Robert Frost: The Early Years, 1894–1915*, New York: Henry Holt & Co., 1966.

--------*Robert Frost: The Years of Triumph, 1915–1938*, New York: Henry Holt & Co., 1970.

Thomson, James, *City of Dreadful Night and Other Poems*, (orig. 1874), London: Rowan and Littlefield, 1974.

Tolkein, J. R. R., *The Hobbit*, London: Allen and Unwin, 1937.

--------*The Lord of the Rings*, London: Allen and Unwin, 1954, 1955.

--------*The Silmarillion*, London: Allen and Unwin, 1977.

Tolstoy, Leo, *Anna Karenina* (orig. 1873–1877), trans. Richard Pevear and Larissa Volokhonsky, New York: Penguin, 2004.

--------*The Brothers Karamazov* (orig. 1878–1880), trans. by Richard Pevear and Larissa Volokhonsky, New York: Farrar, Straus & Giroux, 2002.

--------*War and Peace* (orig. 1865–1869), trans. Constance Garnett, New York: Modern Library Classics, 2002.

Trilling, Diana, *Mrs. Harris: The Death of the Scarsdale Diet Doctor*, New York: Harcourt, 1981.

Turgenev, Ivan, *Fathers and Sons* (orig. 1862), trans. Constance Garnett, New York: Modern Library Classics, 2001.

Twain, Mark, *The Adventures of Huckleberry Finn* (orig. 1884), New York: Penguin Classics, 2002.

Updike, John, *A&P*, New York: Harcourt Brace College Publishers, 1997.

--------"One Cheer for Literary Biography," *New York Review of Books* 46.2, Feb. 4, 1999.

Virgil, Publius, *The Aeneid* (orig. c. 19 BC), trans. W. F. Jackson Knight, London: Penguin Classics, 1956.

Vonnegut, Kurt, *Breakfast of Champions* (orig. 1973), New York: Dial Press, 1999.

Vronsky, Peter, *Serial Killers: The Method and Madness of Monsters*, New York: Berkeley Trade, 2004.

Walpole, Horace, *The Castle of Otranto* (orig. 1794), Oxford: Oxford World's Classics, 1998.

Wells, Herbert George, *The Time Machine* (orig. 1895), New York: Penguin Classics, 2005.

Werris, Wendy, *An Alphabetical Life: Living It Up in the World of Books*, New York: Carroll & Graf, 2006.

West, Nathanael, *Day of the Locust* (orig. 1939), New York: Signet Classics, 1983.

White, E. B., *Charlotte's Web* (orig. 1952), New York: HarperTrophy, 2004.

White, T. H., *The Once and Future King* (orig. 1956), New York: Ace Books, 1987.

Wilde, Oscar, *The Picture of Dorian Gray* (orig. 1891), New York: Modern Library Paperbacks, 1998.

Williams, Emlyn, *Beyond Belief: A Chronicle of Murder and Its Detection*, New York: Random House, 1968.

Wilson, Colin, *The Corpse Garden*, London: Forum Press/True Crime Library, 1998.

Winn, Steve, *Ted Bundy: The Killer Next Door*, New York: Bantam, 1979.

Woolf, Virginia, *Mrs. Dalloway* (orig. 1925), New York: Harvest, 1990.

--------*To the Lighthouse* (orig. 1927), New York: Harvest, 1989.

Wurtzel, Elizabeth, *Bitch: In Praise of Difficult Women*, New York: Anchor, 1999.

--------*More, Now, Again: A Memoir of Addiction*, New York: Simon & Schuster, 2002.

--------*Prozac Nation: Young and Depressed in America*, New York: Riverhead Books, 1997.

Yalom, Irving, MD, *Love's Executioner and Other Tales of Psychotherapy*, New York: Basic Books, 1989.

Young, Toby, *How to Lose Friends and Alienate People*, New York: Da Capo Press, 2003.

comics, journals, and magazines

American Journal of Mental Retardation (1876–current).

The Fantastic Four, Stan Lee and Jack Kirby, Marvel Comics, Nov. 1961–Dec. 1996.

Journal of Negro Education (1932–current).

Master Detective, London: True Crime Library (1992–current).

Murder Most Foul, London: True Crime Library (1990–current).

Strange Tales #1–188 (June 1951–May 1968, Sept. 1973–Nov. 1976) New York: EC Comics.

Suicide and Life-Threatening Behavior (1976–current).

Tales from the Crypt #1–30 (Apr. 1950–Mar. 1955), New York: EC Comics.

True Crime, London: True Crime Library (1990–current).

True Detective, London: True Crime Library (1990–current).

Weird Tales #1–279 (Mar. 1923–Sept. 1954), #290–current, New York: DNA Publications.

online sources

Awful Plastic Surgery: www.awfulplasticsurgery.com

Babes with Books: www.babeswithbooks.blogspot.com

Beatrice: www.beatrice.com

Bookdwarf: www.bookdwarf.com

Book Fox: www.thejohnfox.com

BookSlut: www.bookslut.com

The Confessional: www.theconfessional.co.uk

Daily Confession: www.dailyconfession.com

Defamer: www.defamer.com

E-admit: www.e-admit.com

GalleyCat: www.mediabistro.com/galleycat

Garfunkel Library: www.artgarfunkel.com/library.html

Gawker: www.gawker.com

Group Hug: www.grouphug.us

Maud Newton: www.maudnewton.com

Near Death: www.neardeath.com

Not Proud: www.notproud.com

Post Secret: www.postsecret.blogspot.com

Slushpile: www.slushpile.net
The Smoking Gun: www.thesmokinggun.com
Tingle Alley: www.tinglealley.com
Wonkette: www.wonkette.com

dvd sources

Alice in Wonderland (Clyde Geronimi, 1951), Walt Disney Home Video, 2004.

Barry Lyndon (Stanley Kubrick, 1975), Warner Home Video, 2001.

Book Wars (Jason Rosette, 2000), Avatar Films, 2006.

Death Line (a.k.a *Raw Meat*) (Gary Sherman, 1973), MGM Video and DVD, 2006.

Dracula (Tod Browning, 1931), Universal Studios, 2006.

Dr. Jekyll and Mr. Hyde (Rouben Mamoulian, 1932), Warner Home Video, 2004.

Grey Gardens (Albert and David Maysles, 1976), Criterion Collection, 2001.

Hamlet (Franco Zefirelli, 1991), Warner Home Video, 2004.

Howard's End (James Ivory, 1992), Merchant Ivory Collection, 2005.

Jupiter's Wife (Michel Negroponte, 1995), New Video Group, 2004.

Limelight (Charles Chaplin, 1952), Image Entertainment, 2000.

The Little Mermaid (Ron Clements and John Musker, 1989), Walt Disney Home Video, 2000.

Macbeth (Roman Polanski, 1971), Sony Pictures, 2002.

The Merchant of Venice (Michael Radford, 2004), Sony Pictures, 2005.

Pride and Prejudice (Robert Z. Leonard, 1940), Warner Home Video, 2006.

The Shining (Stanley Kubrick, 1980), Warner Home Video, 1991.

Sick: The Life and Death of Bob Flanagan, Supermasochist (Kirby Dick, 1997), Lion's Gate, 2003.

Silence of the Lambs (Jonathan Demme, 1991), Criterion Collection, 1998.

Stone Reader (Mark Moskowitz, 2002), New Yorker Home Video, 2004.

A Tale of Two Cities (Jack Conway, 1935), Warner Home Video, 2006.

Titus (Julie Taymor, 2000), Twentieth Century Fox, 2000.

Troy (Wolfgang Petersen, 2004), Warner Home Video, 2005.